International indebtedness

MÜNSTER CONGRESS 1987
Latin America and Europe in Dialogue
Under the auspices of *rector magnificus*
Prof. Dr Hans-Uwe Erichsen

WORKSHOPS

1. THEOLOGY (Prof. Dr Dr Johann Baptist Metz)
2. PHILOSOPHY (Prof. Dr Fernando Inciarte)
3. LAW (Prof. Dr Dr Werner Krawietz)
4. ECONOMICS (Prof. Dr Manfred Borchert)
5. COOPERATIVES (Prof. Dr Rolf Eschenburg)
6. POLITICS (Prof. Dr Gerhard W. Wittkaemper)
7. ADMINISTRATION (Prof. Dr Rainer Frey)
8. MIGRATION (Prof. Dr Achim Schrader)
9. DIDACTICS OF GEOGRAPHY (Prof. Dr Juergen Buenstorf)

WESTFAELISCHE WILHELMS-UNIVERSITY
MÜNSTER (GERMANY)
27 SEPTEMBER–3 OCTOBER 1987

International indebtedness

Edited by

Manfred Borchert

and

Rolf Schinke

Contributions presented to the Workshop on Economics of the Münster Congress on *Latin America and Europe in Dialogue*

Routledge
London and New York

First published 1990 by Routledge
11 New Fetter Lane, London EC4P 4EE

Simultaneously published in the USA and Canada by Routledge
a division of Routledge, Chapman and Hall, Inc.
29 West 35th Street, New York, NY 10001

Typeset by Leaper & Gard Ltd, Bristol, England

Printed in Great Britain by
Billing & Sons Ltd, Worcester

British Library Cataloguing in Publication Data
Muenster Congress on Latin America and Europe in
Dialogue, *Workshop on Economics (1987)*
International indebtedness : contribuions presented
to the workshop on Economics of the Muenster congress
on Latin America and Europe in Dialogue.
1. Developing countries. External debts
I. Title
336.3′435′091724

ISBN 0 –415 – 04385 – 9

Library of Congress Cataloging-in-Publication Data
Workshop on Economics (1987 : Westfaelische Wilhelms-University, Muenster)
International indebtedness : contributions presented to the
Workshop on Economics of the Muenster Congress on Latin America and
Europe in Dialogue / edited by Manfred Borchert and Rolf Schinke.
p. cm.
"Westfaelische Wilhelms-University, Muenster (Germany), 27
September-2 October 1987"—Half title verso.
Includes bibliographical references.
ISBN 0-415-04385-9
1. Debts, External—Latin America—Congresses. I. Borchert,
Manfred. II. Schinke, Rolf. III. Title.
HJ8514.5.W67 1987 89-10983
336.3′435′098—dc20 CIP

Contents

Tables

Figures

Contributors

Abs, Ludger Dr, University of Münster

Angrick, Michael Dr, University of Münster

Auernheimer, Leonardo Prof. PhD., Department of Economics, Texas A & M University, Director of the Centro de Estudios Macroeconómicos de Argentina CEMA, College Station, Texas/USA

Bernard, Reimar Diplom-Volkswirt, Director of the Commerzbank AG, Frankfurt

Borchert, Manfred Prof. Dr, Department of Economics, University of Münster

Erlei, Mathias Diplom-Volkswirt, University of Münster

de Sousa **Ferreira**, Eduardo Prof. Dr, Instituto Superior de Economia de Universidade Técnica de Lisboa, Director of the Centro de Estudos da Dependéncia CEDEP, Lisbon, Portugal

Hemmer, Hans-Rimbert Prof. Dr, Department of Economics, University of Giessen, Trustee of the German Foundation for International Development, Berlin

Lizano, Eduardo Prof. Dr, Executive President of the Central Bank, Banco Central de Costa Rica

Massad, Carlos Prof. Dr, United Nations, Economic Commission for Latin America and the Caribbean, Universidad de Santiago de Chile

Meller, Patricio Prof. Dr, Corporación de Investigaciones Económicas para Latinoamerica CIEPLAN, Santiago de Chile

Nowak, Felicitas Diplom-Volkswirtin, University of Göttingen

Schinke, Rolf Dr, Ibero-American Institute for Economic Research, University of Göttingen

Schulte, Barbara Diplom-Volkswirtin, University of Münster

Trippen, Ludwig Dr, Deputy Chairman of the Managing Board of the Westdeutsche Landesbank WestLB, Münster and Düsseldorf

Valdés, Alberto Dr, Director of the International Food Policy Research Institute (IFPRI), Washington, DC, USA

Weiershäuser, Eberhard Dr, Member of the Managing Board of the Westdeutsche Landesbank WestLB, Düsseldorf and Münster

Wessling, Ewald Diplom-Volkswirt, University of Münster

Wionczek, Miguel S. Prof. Dr, the late Director of the Energy Research Programme, El Colegio de México, México

Münster Congress 1987 – Publications

General

1. Hans-Uwe Erichsen (editor)
Lateinamerika und Europa im Dialog. Menschenrechte – Wirtschaftliche Verflechtung – Menschenbild, Minderheiten, Medien – Politsche Beziehungen. (Latin America and Europe in Dialogue. Human Rights – Economic Linkages – Idea of Human Beings, Minorities, Media – Political Relations), Berlin 1989. *German*

Other workshops

2. Johann Baptist Metz/Peter Rottlaender (editors)
Lateinamerika und Europa – Dialog der Theologen (Latin America and Europe – Dialogue of the Theologians), Mainz/München 1988. *German*
3. Fernando Inciarte/Berthold Wald (editors)
Im Dialog mit Lateinamerika. Menschenrechte und Menschenbild (In Dialogue with Latin America. Human Rights and the Idea of Human Beings). *German*
4. Rolf Eschenburg (editor)
Formas de Cooperación en Europa y Latino America (Forms of Cooperations in Europe and Latin America), Münster 1989. *Spanish*
5. Rainer Frey/Gerhard W. Wittkaemper (editors)
Lateinamerika – Westeuropa: Annäherung oder Distanzierung (Latin America – West Europe: Approaching Towards Each Other or Becoming More Distant). Münster 1988. *German*
6. Achim Schrader/Karl-Heinrich Rengstorf (editors)
Europäische Juden in Lateinamerika (European Jews in Latin America), Stuttgart 1988. *German*

Preface

From 27 September 1987 to 2 October 1987 the University of Münster carried out a Congress on *Latin America and Europe in Dialogue, International Indebtedness* being a part of the Workshop on Economics.

Since the early stages in the preparation of the workshop it was our intention to concentrate the discussion on four closely-related topics: origins, significance, and development of the debt crisis; problems of managing the debt; deficiencies of the world monetary system; and the interrelations between indebtedness and growth. Therefore, we invited researchers from Latin America, Portugal, and the Federal Republic of Germany. The present publication contains the articles prepared for this workshop. Due to urgent duties in Washington Carlos Massad and Alberto Valdés could not present their papers personally. Nevertheless, their articles were included as valuable contributions to this volume.

Without financial help from various sources it would have been impossible to realize this meeting. Therefore we acknowledge gratefully the support given by BASF (Münster), Deutsche Bank (Frankfurt), Deutsche Bundesbank (Frankfurt), Deutsche Forschungsgemeinschaft (Bonn), Deutsche Ibero-Amerika Stiftung (Hamburg), Federal Ministry of Economic Cooperation (Bonn), the Government of the Federal State of North Rhine-Westphalia (Düsseldorf) and WestLB (Düsseldorf).

Dr Ludger Abs and also Dr Michael Angrick rendered great service in the preparation and organization of the workshop on international indebtedness. Ms Barbara Veltman translated all German manuscripts with great care. They, as well as Mr Mathias Erlei, Ms Barbara Schulte, Ms Christiane Vogell and Mr Ewald Wessling, did the proof-reading, and drew up the subject index. Mrs Angelika van Dillen made the manuscript readable with her usual circumspection and efficiency; the final make-up was done by my present secretary Ms Susanne Esselmann. Thanks to them all for their assistance.

Manfred Borchert
Rolf Schinke
Münster and Göttingen

Chapter one

Introduction

Rolf Schinke

Since late summer of 1982, when Mexico felt unable to service its foreign debt, a rather large number of books and articles have been published on the problems of the highly-indebted countries. This introduction does not intend to give a survey of the literature concerned. Instead, some of the key issues which regularly appeared will be taken up here. The objective is to relate them to the topics of this volume which contains the contributions prepared for a workshop on international indebtedness held in Münster, Germany.

The present situation

The current debt situation in Latin America can be characterized by the following stylized facts:

(a) Several major debtor countries succeeded to keep debts from growing, and some of them even experienced a decline in absolute indebtedness. According to estimates by the Economic Commission for Latin America (ECLA)[1] gross external indebtedness of all Latin American countries has declined by more than 2 per cent to 401.4 billion US dollars at the end of 1988.

(b) This reduction (1988), and overall increases (1983 to 1987) are smaller than debt service payments, resulting in a serious transfer of resources from the debtor to the creditor countries which has accumulated to 178.7 billion US dollars since 1982. In 1988 this transfer was as high as 28.9 billion US dollars.[2] Taking into account the negative change in the export prices[3] since 1980, the drain in 1988 amounts to 39.05 billion US dollars in real terms.

(c) With the exception of Chile, in 1987 investment measured in percentage of the GDP was still below the pre-crisis level.[4]

Consequently, the rate of growth of the GDP in 1988 has been depressed. As a whole, per capita incomes are below those prevailing at the beginning of the decade. It is generally expected that the same pattern will hold true in 1988, for which data are still unavailable. This points to the existence of a debt trap.[5] Despite policy reforms and high domestic saving rates, per capita incomes remain depressed because investment is constrained as a result of the net outflow of resources to creditor countries.

(d) While it is therefore correct to regard the 1980s as a lost decade for the debtor countries, the same does not hold true for the creditors. Loans to the debtor countries have stagnated and even declined since mid-1987.[6] The bargaining power of the banks has increased since massive loan loss reserves have been built up.[7] Today, the largest US money centre banks are far less vulnerable than at the beginning of the debt crisis.[8]

(e) Governments and banks of the creditor countries are furthermore reluctant to solve the debt crisis globally. Case-by-case treatment, with no overall corrections of the nominal value of the debt, is the preferred way of handling the difficulties of the indebted middle-income countries. Only low-income countries – mostly in Africa – and Bolivia received debt relief of a substantial size.[9]

(f) In solving, or at least managing, the debt problems three rather distinct means have lately received more attention than before:

- There are signs that governments of some debtor countries might co-operate more closely than they did before.[10]
- Market-orientated approaches[11] to the solution of the debt problem such as debt equity swaps are increasingly being used in several highly-indebted countries.
- Despite the acknowledgement that debt relief might create serious disincentives and moral hazard problems, proponents of this instrument are gaining in number even in scientific circles, pointing to the fact that their diagnosis of the debt problem is one of insolvency rather than illiquidity, the latter being the implicit diagnosis of the supporters of reschedulings on a case-by-case treatment.

The picture given by the debt scene so far reveals:

- there is no commonly-shared diagnosis of the debt crisis as being one of illiquidity, insolvency or as being none of both, and,

- policy measures to solve the debt crisis differ widely among the groups involved; growing out of the debt crisis remains as difficult as it has proved to be during the last years.

Key factors to the debt crisis

These divergent views and opinions are in contrast to the rather widespread consensus as to the origins and causes of the debt crisis. Four broad areas can be identified as being the key factors which led to the crisis.

(a) In the first place reference is made to the oil price increases of the 1970s which immediately led to current account deficits of the oil importing LDCs (less developed countries) and to parallel surpluses of the oil-exporting countries,[12] The latters' preferences for liquid assets in the Euro-currency markets provoked the banks to look for new customers within the group of newly-industrializing countries, thus fulfilling the objective of recycling the petro-dollars, which had been broadly advocated by governments of the industrialised countries, to finance the current account deficits of the LDCs. Adjustment to higher oil prices within LDCs took time, or was partially postponed, both leading to a higher indebtedness. The second oil price shock again led these countries to either finance adjustment or to postpone it, this time, however, at higher price and debt levels. But, different from the first oil price shock, there was no improvement in their terms of trade which, after the first oil price increase, had alleviated the real burden of some oil-importing LDCs in Latin America.

(b) The decade of the 1970s witnessed a world-wide inflation with rates higher and more persistent than ever since the 1950s.[13] In the industrialized countries there was a growing concern about its negative allocative and distributive consequences. Anti-inflationary measures, documented by the switch in monetary policy in the United States, led to a rise in nominal interest rates and to a reduction in inflationary expectations. Both resulted in unexpectedly high real interest rates. Stabilization policies pursued in several developed countries led to a further reduction of their already slow economic growth. The relative decline in their demand for the exports of the debtor countries led to a deterioration of the export prices of the oil-importing countries and, since 1982, of those of the oil exporters in Latin America. Worse still, there was a decline in the export volume by more than 7 per cent in 1982.[14] Rising nominal interest rates as well as declining export prices and quantities resulted in a sudden increase of the debt burden. Increasing protectionism in the developed countries further aggravated the situation of the debtor countries.[15]

(c) So far the description does not give an answer to the question why some countries ran into difficulties while others did not. The latter experienced equally high external shocks and were as highly indebted.[16] This evidence suggests that there were country-specific factors that have to be taken into account, too. This was especially the case in the southern-cone countries of Latin America,[17] where apparent inconsistencies in macroeconomic policies[18] led to a loss of credibility, suggesting that policies applied so far will not be pursued in the future. Corbo and de Melo (1987) point to the fact that external shocks cannot be blamed for the breakdown of the liberalization-cum-stabilization policies, although both – shocks and policy – contributed to higher external indebtedness.

A related issue concerns the question whether the debtor countries have used the resources productively. When distortions are prevalent, prices will give wrong signals, thus leading to inefficient use of resources.[19] The same applies when countries with high inflation rates aim at stabilizing their price level. Stabilization policy affects various prices in the economy to a different extent, which reduces the informational content of prices for resource allocation. Under such circumstances it must be expected that external resources are not always put to their most efficient use.[20] This, however, can lead to debt servicing difficulties, especially when appreciation of the real exchange rate led to a reduced profitability of the traded goods sector.

(d) However, there was not only imprudent borrowing by countries. Banks are said to have been imprudent in their lending activities as well. Indicators of their failures were their financing of capital flight from highly-indebted countries[21] and the banks' exposure in Latin American assets relative to their capital. In 1982 the nine major US banks' exposure in Latin American assets accounted for 176.5 per cent of their primary capital.[22] This concentration of lending activities occurred although profitability of loans to LDCs was, at least sometimes, relatively low. It is reported that the spread over LIBOR (London Interbank Offered Rate) was often as low as 50 to 100 basis points.[23] Magee and Brock[24] have shown that the market valuation of the banks' shares did not reflect future troubles with LDC debts. As sometimes has been argued, banks ultimately perceived the risks involved in international lending only as those of possible losses in debt reschedulings. A different picture has resulted since the beginning of the debt crisis. As Sachs and Huizinga[25] have demonstrated, market valuation of bank shares reflected the declining market value of loans to Argentina, Brazil, Mexico, and Venezuela in the period 1983 to 1987. This suggests that in the pre-crisis era risks had been underestimated by banks and their shareholders.

Several explanations have been given for the banks' failure to correctly estimate the risks. Guttentag and Herring[26] have hypothesized that banks:

- were subject to disaster myopia,
- miscalculated risks because of inadequate analysis and information, and
- were gambling.

Disaster myopia originated from the non-existence of an objective frequency distribution of country defaults. Under such circumstances, decision-makers will resort to heuristics which can lead to biased estimates of risks[27] with the high-loss-low-probability risk being totally excluded from the analysis. When banks recognized their mistakes they often increased lending. Psychologically this behaviour has been interpreted as cognitive dissonance. This explains why some countries could strongly increase their borrowing in the last years before the debt crisis broke out.

Inadequate risk analysis may also originate from fallacies of composition. During the 1970s lending at variable interest rates became more and more customary.[28] The rationale behind this behaviour was the banks' desire to minimize risks from adverse interest rate movements. However, by shifting the risk to the debtors, it has been mostly overlooked that an extraordinary increase in the real interest rate for all indebted countries jeopardized the financial system as a whole.[29] There was no longer a low covariance between the different Latin American assets of the most exposed money centre banks.[30]

A fallacy of composition can also be seen in the banks' belief that to get rid of troubled debtors in LDCs they could shorten the maturity of the loans. Should a single bank experience difficulties with a specific debtor, non-prolongation of loans would immediately lead to a liquidity crisis as other banks would behave in the same manner.[31]

Gambling may have resulted from the banks' conviction that governments, central banks, or the International Monetary Fund would act as a lender of last resort, especially if survival of the financial system was at stake. Possibly banks were aware of the public goods character of the safety of the national and international payments system.[32] The higher the threat to stability was, the more likely public help would be for banks and indebted countries. Risk-taking, therefore, seemed to be relatively harmless, especially when exposure and consequently threat to the financial system was high.[33]

Problems created by the debt crisis

Discussion of the problems that were created by the debt crisis centred around the questions of how the debt crisis could be solved or how indebtedness could at least be made manageable. It was always regarded as a necessary precondition that debtor countries had to undergo a process of adjustment to the new conditions prevailing after the debt crisis. Usually this process was carried out with the help and policy guidance of the Bretton Woods institutions. But since it took time to achieve positive results, and since new loans were difficult to obtain, import compression was usually the first measure resorted to. With idle capacity and devalued real exchange rates, the second step consisted in an expansion of the volume of exports. Due to declining prices for Latin American exports in 1986, foreign exchange receipts from export activities, however, were around 12 per cent less than those of the crisis year 1982 and about 14 per cent lower than in 1980.[34] Thus, despite higher export volumes, there was no overall improvement in the debt service to exports ratio of public and publicly-guaranteed debt until 1986.[35] In order to sustain a viable balance of payments position, imports of goods and non-factor services remained at a low level, although there was a small increase in import volumes since 1983 caused mainly by a decline in unit values of imports.[36]

Since much of the debt had been assumed by the state or was originally taken up by governments themselves, the rise in real interest rates caused serious problems for government finance. Since 1982 Latin American central government deficits were about 7 per cent of the GDP compared to 2 per cent in the pre-crisis era.[37] Therefore, fiscal adjustment, mostly by expenditure-cutting, usually ranked high in the list of the tools advocated in stabilization programmes of the International Monetary Fund. Adverse social and growth impacts of these programmes called for discussion of the problems of conditionality usually attached to these programmes. Often governments executing stabilization programmes were under strong internal pressure to ease the burden of the programmes.

Closely related is the issue of reversing the net flow of resources. If the debts are to be serviced, new foreign capital is thought to be indispensable. This is all the more so if the debtor countries are to grow. But with depressed incomes domestic savings are low, and as a consequence of high interest payments investment must remain at a still lower level if foreign capital is lacking. Thus, low investment is not only a consequence of the lack of foreign exchange. But even if the foreign exchange constraint is dominant, the prospects for increasing investments by earning more foreign exchange are bleak as it proves to be difficult to increase exports of agricultural and manufactured products from Latin America to the United States, Europe and Japan in view of the protectionism prevailing in the industrialized countries. Thus, many of the writings on debt problems are devoted to adjustment problems, to that of achieving internal stability, to the promotion of exports, and to the problem of protectionism.

A different line of publications centre around the financial as opposed to the 'real' aspects of the debt problem mentioned in the last paragraph. Prominent among them are those concentrating on the relationship between debtors and creditors. Problems of uncertainty and lack of information[38] usually encountered in credit markets[39] are further complicated in international transactions where, in the absence of a common legal framework, debtors can benefit at the expense of their creditors by repudiating. Therefore, borrowers can face a debt ceiling which assures that the benefits from repudiation, that is, debt service not paid, are less than the costs the debtor has to bear as a consequence of his default. Debtors failing to fulfil their obligations may be sanctioned by exclusion from the credit market. Therefore, borrowers who further rely on external loans are eager to demonstrate their creditworthiness.[40] This demonstrates the importance of careful debt management by the debtors.

Concluding remarks

The listing of the problems is far from exhaustive. Completeness, however, was not intended. Some, but not all, of the problems are taken up in the papers in Parts one to four of the present volume.

The reader who is interested in getting an overview of the contents of each paper is referred to the summary in Part five.

The papers in Part one are mostly concerned with the developments since the crisis broke out. In Part two emphasis is put on budgetary problems, debtor-creditor relations and debt management by debt equity swaps. Part three is devoted to the problems of a reduction of the debt overhang and/or of the debt burden in Latin America. Special attention is given to difficulties and costs arising from protectionism in industrialized countries. Finally, in Part four, questions on the adequacy of the international financial system and of the methods of solving the debt problems used so far are raised.

Notes and references

1. Comisión Económica para América Latina (CEPAL) (1988) *Balance Preliminar de la Economía Latinoamericana 1988. Notas sobre la Economía y el Desarrollo*, no. 470/471, December, p. 24.
2. Ibid., p. 17.
3. CEPAL (1988), p. 20.
4. Inter-American Development Bank (IDB) (1988) *Economic and Social Progress in Latin America, 1988 Report*, Washington, DC, p. 30.
5. Krueger, A.O. (1987) 'Debt, Capital Flows, and LDC Growth', *American Economic Review*, Papers and Proceedings, p. 163.
6. Bank für Internationalen Zahlungs-Ausgleich (BIS) (1988) *Die Fälligkeits- und Sektorenverteilung der internationalen Bankausleihungen, Erstes Halbjahr*, p. 3.
7. World Bank (1987–8) *World Debt Tables*, 1987–8 edn, I: xxix.
8. World Bank (1988), ibid., p. xxvi; *The Economist*, 10 September, 1988, p. 83.
9. World Bank (1988), ibid., p. xvii.
10. Neue Zürcher Zeitung, 31 December 1988; Latin American Regional Reports, Brazil, 5 January, 1989, p. 5.
11. Feldstein, M. (1987) 'Latin America's Debt. Muddling Through can be Just Fine', *The Economist*, July, pp. 21–5.
12. Grosse, R. (1988) 'Resolving Latin America's Transfer Problem', *The World Economy* 11: 424; Krueger, A.O., op. cit., p. 160.
13. International Monetary Fund (1988) *International Financial Statistics. Yearbook 1988*, p. 116f.
14. Calculated from data in International Monetary Fund (1988), op. cit., pp. 123, 135.
15. World Bank (1985) *World Development Report*, pp. 37ff.
16. Sachs, J.D. (1985) 'External Debt and Macroeconomic Performance in Latin America and East Asia', *Brookings Papers on Economic Activity* 2: 526.

17. Corbo, V. and de Melo, J. (1987) 'Lessons from Southern Cone Policy Reforms', *Research Observer* 2: 111–42.
18. Khan, M.S. and Zahler, R. (1985) 'Trade and Financial Liberalization Given External Shocks and Inconsistent Domestic Policies', *International Monetary Fund Staff Papers*, 32: 24.
19. World Bank (1983) *World Development Report*, p. 60.
20. Corbo, V. and de Melo, J., op. cit., p. 116.
21. Guttentag, J.M. and Herring, R. (1985) 'Commercial Bank Lending to Developing Countries: From Overlending to Underlending to Structural Reform', in G.W. Smith and J.T. Cuddington (eds) *International Debt and the Developing Countries*, World Bank, p. 129.
22. Sachs, J.D. and Huizinga, H. (1987) 'U.S. Commercial Banks and the Developing-Country Debt Crisis', *Brookings Papers on Economic Activity* 2: 555–601, p. 558.
23. Guttentag, J.M. and Herring, R., op. cit., p. 132.
24. Magee, S.P. and Brock, W.A. (1984) 'The Rise in the Third World's External Debt/Equity Ratio as a Redistributive Game and the Political Regressivity of Adverse States of Nature', Paper Prepared for a Conference on the World Debt Crisis, Middlebury College, Middlebury, p. 240.
25. Sachs, J.D. and Huizinga, H., op. cit., pp. 580ff.
26. Guttentag, J.M. and Herring, R., op. cit., pp. 130ff.
27. Ibid., pp. 132ff.
28. While in 1975 the proportion of the stock of public loans at variable rates to total public debt was less than 20 per cent for all the developing countries, in 1982 this ratio was nearly 40 per cent. The respective proportions for Latin America were 37.8 per cent and 62.4 per cent (World Bank (1988), pp. 3, 19).
29. Note, that ex post-real interest rates of 15 per cent had already been reached after the first oil price shock in 1978. However, they lasted only for a very short time. In 1979 rates were again negative as they were in 1976/77 (World Bank (1988), p. xv).
30. Eaton, J. and Taylor, L. (1986) 'Developing Country Finance and Debt', *Journal of Development Economics* 22: 241.
31. Ibid., pp. 240f. and Guttentag, J.M. and Herring, R., op. cit., p. 136.
32. Diaz-Alejandro, C. (1985) 'Good-bye Financial Repression, Hello Financial Crash', *Journal of Development Economics*, 19: 5.
33. Guttentag, J.M. and Herring, R., op. cit., pp. 13f.
34. World Bank (1988), op. cit., p. 21.
35. Ibid.
36. Inter-American Development Bank, op. cit., pp. 14 and 541.
37. International Monetary Fund, op. cit., p. 157.
38. Swoboda, A.K. (1985) 'Debt and the Efficiency and Stability of the International Financial System', in G.W. Smith and J.T. Cuddington (eds) (1985) op. cit., p. 154.
39. Stiglitz, J.E. and Weiss, A. (1981) 'Credit Rationing in Markets with Imperfect Information', *American Economic Review* 71: 393.
40. Eaton, J. and Taylor, L., op. cit., p. 223.

Part one

Development of the international debt crisis

Chapter two

The causes and the development of the current debt crisis in Latin America

Ludwig Trippen

Introduction

Since the Mexico shock more than five years ago, the debt problem has cast a shadow over the relations between the industrial and the developing countries. It is true, the debt management of the past years prevented the collapse of the international financial system. However, a final solution to the debt crisis and, as a result, normal financial relations, and normal relations in real terms between the industrial countries and the developing countries are not yet in sight.

On the contrary, the recent incidents seem to have made the situation even more complicated. The slump in the oil price, Brazil's, that is, the biggest debtor's, dishonour by non-payment, some debtor countries' adjustment problems, and the heightened provision for risks on the part of many international banks aroused once more the discussion about appropriate debt strategies. It is scarcely surprising that opinions differ widely according to the respective points of view. While some advocate a remission of debt, others take the view that the 'policy of small steps', which has been pursued up to now, proved worthwhile, and is therefore the only practicable solution for the future. Thus the question is the following – do we really need new and more rigorous approaches to a solution, or should we complete existing plans and carry them out more consistently than hitherto? By recalling the causes and the development of debt crisis we will obtain a clue to this question. In accordance with the topic of this conference I shall confine myself to the particularities of the situation in Latin America. That in so doing I shall look at my topic from the point of view of a European banker rather than a Franciscan friar will not surprise you.

The origin of the Latin American debt crisis

By the end of 1986 Latin America's external debt amounted to 380 billion US dollars, that is to say, more than a third of the developing countries' total debts concentrate on this region. For the most part, this enormous mountain of debt piled up between 1975 and 1982, and this was due to a variety of reasons. In 1945, Argentina, after the United States, was the richest country of the world. What made the situation change so drastically?

In the beginning there was the first oil price shock in 1973 and 1974. Practically overnight there was a high current account surplus, which flowed into the financial markets. On account of this sudden inflow of liquidity the commercial banks involved were faced with the problem of finding profitable investment opportunities for the oil-producing countries' bank deposits without delay. Thus the recycling of the oil billions set in, a step for which the banks in the industrial countries were praised at first – after all, they took the risks for the poor countries which the oil sheikhs themselves were not prepared to take. There was no serious credit risk involved though, with the economic area of Latin America dynamically expanding and being rich in raw materials. For at that time both theoreticians and practicians believed that the price of oil – the developing countries' most important export base – would tend strongly upwards. Let me remind you of the book, *The Limits of Growth*, by the Club of Rome, in which the authors predicted a shortage of raw materials within a very short time, and which caused a sensation. This belief turned out to be an error of serious consequence, not only for the creditors, but also for the Latin American countries.

For almost all those Latin American countries that were rich in raw materials seized the opportunity to supply their financial needs by relatively cheap loans obtained abroad. However, the strong demand for credits did not arise from the increased oil bill alone, but also from a more expansive general thrust of economic policy. Disequilibria, high public deficits in particular, and a faster and faster spinning inflationary spiral were either not fought at all, or only fought half-heartedly. Thus the countries that were rich in raw materials took to circumventing the necessary domestic economy adjustments by foreign borrowings. They wanted to finance the difficult situation at that time by means of the rise in the price of raw materials that had been predicted for the future. As the funds often flowed into prestigious, though not very profitable, capital investment and development programmes, the actual capacities of these countries were frequently overrated. Thus, in many cases, the growth of the export proceeds fell behind the rapid rise of the debt service.

In 1979, the debt service already consumed 40 per cent of the currency receipts, and the foreign debts were twice as high as the receipts from the export of goods and services. At that time, at the latest, Latin America should have taken economic correcting measures, all the more as a deterioration of the international economic condition as the result of the second oil price shock loomed on the horizon. At first, however, the second oil price rise at the end of the 1970s was only thought to support the belief that the price of raw materials would rise, whereas none realized that it might result in a world-wide recession with a dropping price of raw materials. The industrial countries' adjustment to the second oil price shock produced exactly this world-wide recession, in the course of which the world trade weakened and the price of raw materials – and therefore the developing countries' export proceeds – sagged. At the same time the industrial countries began to fight the high and still rising rates of inflation by a change of course in their monetary policy. The entailing rise in the interest rates reinforced the recession and weighed heavily on the developing countries' balance of trade in goods and services, for in the preceding years the developing countries had financed a growing part of their deficits by taking up credits on a floating-rate basis.

Despite the deterioration of the general situation, many Latin American countries held on to their expansionary economic policy. This put additional pressure on their balance of trade in goods and services. Evidence of this can clearly be seen in Mexico, where between 1979 and 1981 the current account deficit increased in spite of the rise in the price of oil. Thus it is not surprising that it was an oil-exporting country after all that set off the payment crisis.

However, the current account deficits alone do not account for the clearly-accelerated rise of the foreign indebtedness between 1980 and 1982. Rather, a marked capital flight had to be financed in this very period of time. This capital flight was a symptom of Latin America's grave economic, social, and political problems, and it was additionally encouraged by the overrated exchange rates and the partly negative domestic real rate of interest. It is estimated that, up to the outbreak of the debt crisis in Latin America, about 30 per cent of the then total debt of 333 billion US dollars went abroad again through capital drains – and most of the time this happened in an absolutely legal way. From 1977 to 1985, for instance, 60 billion US dollars from Mexico flowed into the United States, that is, more than 50 per cent of Mexico's external debt.

From Venezuela, 30 billion US dollars, that is all of its external debts, flowed into the United States.

However, at the beginning of the 1980s not only the domestic investors, that is, those that made a capital flight, but also the foreign lenders became more cautious, which resulted in a growing amount of short-term financing. Thus a variety of internal and external factors determined Latin America's cash pressures. The ratio between the debt service on the one hand and the currency receipts on the other hand worsened rapidly. As a result, some countries were no longer able to fulfil their obligations in the form of interest payments and redemption payments.

The development of Latin America's debt crisis

Although this development had been feared for a long time, there was no strategy for further action existing, unless faith in God and the hope that nothing would happen are considered a strategy. Thus in a first phase, when Mexico stopped its payments, all the parties involved were compelled to develop *ad hoc* solutions. First the Bank for International Settlements (BIS) helped out by means of bridging loans as a sort of first aid. Then the debtor countries took correcting measures regarding their economic policy, and the International Monetary Fund (IMF) supported this step financially, provided that they submitted to its conditions. At the same time, such an IMF programme was a prerequisite condition to a debt rescheduling agreement with the commercial banks and with the official lenders, who joined together in the Paris Club. This agreement was to include new credits too.

The debt management of the first years proved to be quite successful. By 1985 the debt reschedulings had reduced the debt service burden to the level of 1979, although the interest margins were raised at first. At the same time, Latin America's successful external economic adjustments diminished its need for new credits to a considerable extent. In 1984 and 1985 the accumulated balances of trade in goods and services of all the Latin American countries showed only minor deficits. However, the individual countries differed widely in their capability of adjustment. While Argentina, Chile, Ecuador, and Peru had to fight on against disequilibria, the oil-exporting countries, that is, Venezuela and Mexico, achieved a current account surplus. Owing to its wider range of export, Brazil was the only country to gain from the world economic upturn in 1984 and 1985 – thus its balance of trade in goods and services was even.

It is true the other countries tried to expand their export

volume, and they succeeded in doing so. However, owing to the continual terms of trade losses, that is, the falling export prices of raw materials and the rising import prices, these attempts did not result in rising export proceeds. This is why the debt service burden did not decrease to a greater extent and why the debt burden even continued to increase. By 1985, the level of debt was already three times as high as the export proceeds. In addition to that, there were further problems existing.

The adjustment policy entailed losses to the economic growth and the welfare of the rapidly growing population. These losses heightened the already existing social tension at a time when many Latin American countries had only just succeeded in taking the plunge into democracy. However, the reward they had hoped for, that is, the recovery of their creditworthiness, failed to materialize because in many cases the stabilization of the domestic economy had not been tackled resolutely enough. The very programmes of the IMF that concerned domestic disequilibria often could not be translated into action.

Some of these problems were taken up by the Baker initiative in the autumn of 1985. The purpose of this initiative was to restore the debtor countries' creditworthiness and to lead them back to their former path of dynamic economic growth. The target group were the fifteen most-highly-indebted countries with a medium-sized income, and eleven of them were Latin American countries. These countries were to introduce growth-orientated structural reforms, to give more leeway to private initiative, and to continue their internal stabilization. The World Bank, the local development banks, and the internationally active commercial banks were required to support this growth-orientated economic policy by stretching their credit extensions, and the industrial countries were to see to stable growth and to open markets.

What are the results of the Baker initiative after two years? Some Latin American countries have initiated free-market structural reforms.

In Chile, the liberalization of foreign trade and the privatization of public enterprises improved the climate for investments, and together with the relaxed regulations governing foreign investments these steps contributed substantially to the success of the Chilean debt equity programmes. At the present moment debt equity swaps are in vogue. The way they work is as follows: The Chilean government buys foreign currency claims against domestic currency, provided that the seller – a foreign bank or business firm – promises to invest the equivalent amount in Chile. So far more than 10 per cent of the medium-range foreign indebtedness have been repaid in this way. Through these measures, and through the export diversification, Chile's debt ratio improved.

Mexico, too, has begun to restrain the government's traditionally strong influence on the economy. Half of the government-owned enterprises were sold, merged, or closed down. Others, such as the government-owned railroad or the electricity companies were modernized. Price controls and public subsidies were reduced, and the liberalization of foreign trade was promoted. Measures concerning the exchange rate policy made a contribution to the still-lasting boom in the export of industrial goods. Today Mexico obtains more than half of its export proceeds by non-oil products.

Colombia, too, which was the only big Latin American country to avoid an official debt rescheduling, successfully reduced its dependency on coffee exports and is now endeavouring to maintain its competitiveness regarding the price of its export goods.

In most of the other countries, however, the very measures of structural policy that aim at an export promotion are still in their infancy. This goes for Argentina too, which promised a reform programme within the framework of its latest financial package. We, that is, the western industrial countries, do not make things easy for the Latin American countries though. The West German farmers will not like to hear the following, but are the European Communities really morally justified in expecting Argentina to keep its borders open for our industrial goods, while impeding the import of Argentinian beef, although the Argentinians produce beef in a more cost-effective way?

While there are some positive approaches discernible with regard to structural policy, the external economic adjustment suffered serious setbacks, especially during the past eighteen months. In 1986, Latin America registered a current account deficit of 13 billion US dollars again. In Brazil the deteriorated external situation was mainly due to wrong economic decisions, whereas in the other countries it was due to the slump in the price of oil and raw materials and to crop failures.

Since the beginning of this year (1989) the domestic disequilibria in almost all the Latin American countries have been increasing, too. For this reason Argentina had to negotiate on its IMF programme again in mid-July. Apparently the Latin American countries still lack determination when fighting inflation and reorganizing their budgets. However, this is easier to say from the point of view of western wealth than of Latin America's situation; for in Latin America it is difficult to determine whether its poverty is due to its lack of determination or whether the cause and effect relation works the other way round.

The second pillar of the Baker initiative was the financial support of economic reforms by commercial banks and multilateral institutions. In 1986 the World Bank increased its net cash investments in the fifteen countries that had been mentioned in the Baker plan by 1 billion US dollars measured against the previous year. The IMF, too, raised its stand-by arrangements slightly; however, owing to repayments due, 2 billion US dollars net flowed back into the Fund. In Latin America the banks contributed to new credits for Mexico and Argentina. Recently the US banks extended Venezuela's trade credit line too, and at present there are negotiations over a credit of 1 billion US dollars for Colombia. The fact that a higher capital inflow was not achieved is doubtlessly due to economic setbacks in the Latin American countries, but it is also connected with the fact that even today the Latin American countries order and finance frigates and submarines, and that, therefore, the trust in their investment policy is not exactly growing.

The third component of the Baker initiative, too, that is, the industrial countries' contribution, has fallen behind the expectations in various respects. Instead of opening their markets, the industrial countries increasingly take to protectionist measures, for example, against Argentinian beef. Besides, the economic growth fell behind the desired rate by 2 to 2½ per cent in 1987 and 1988. And in supplying frigates and submarines we surely help our shipyard industry, but we do not support South America's economic development.

Approaches to a solution in discussion

The somewhat disappointing experiences with the execution of the Baker initiative again nourished the old belief that in the end the problem of out-standing debts can only be solved by a waver of debts. Besides, some debtor countries think that, in the face of the heightened provisional expenses, the banks are well prepared for such a step. It is true the banks set up liability reserves which cover a quarter of the problem credits world-wide – they cover between a third and a half or even more in Germany. However, despite the fact that many US-American banks improved their provision for risks, the value adjustment approaches in the world of banking still differ widely, so that a standard solution is simply impossible.

There is another and more important reason though why such a solution would not work. The poor South American countries – just like the rich Federal Republic of Germany – will in future, too, be dependent on lenders. Every year Mr Stoltenberg pays off and services his long-standing debts, although the federal debt as such is still growing year by year. If he denied even some of his interest and redemption commitments, he would not get one more penny, and the rich Federal Republic of Germany would be at the end of its tether. The same would happen to the Latin American countries if they denied their financial obligations.

After such a general solution the banks would be even less willing and able than before to provide fresh money; neither could the banks answer for such a step, nor could it be expected of the owners and shareholders. It is more than doubtful whether private investors would throw themselves into the breach. A private investor cannot be convinced by a remission of debt, but only by free-market reforms. The same goes for those who made a capital flight; a remission of debt would not prompt them to repatriate their funds abroad. For they would rightly doubt whether the debtor countries' governments would return to a sound economic policy if they had good prospects of a possible remission of debt. Thus, the only remaining source of fresh money is the public sector, that is, the taxpayer, in the industrial countries, and surely this is not a realistic solution.

From the point of view of the debtor countries nothing would be gained by a remission of debt under these circumstances: In many Latin American countries, except Brazil, debt rescheduling agreements with longer redemption-free periods have already come into force. For the short term, a remission of debt would therefore reduce the debt service only slightly, namely through lower interest payments. This release must be weighed against the much higher risk that the capital inflows might dry up completely, and that the flight of capital might increase again. Peru's experiences are a good example of the negative effects of moratoria. For some time now Peru has limited its debt service to 10 per cent of its currency receipts and has taken an unyielding course with regard to the IMF and the World Bank. Today Peru is practically cut off from credits and handles part of its foreign trade by means of barter trading. However, for Latin America's threshold countries, which want to become industrial countries, this is not a reasonable strategy to overcome their debt problems and to develop their economy. Therefore the approach to a solution cannot be a remission of debt, but it has to be the Latin American countries' recovery of creditworthiness. Like the Federal Republic of Germany, Brazil will then increase rather than decrease the total amount of its debt; however, it will pay interest on and repay its sole debt.

Despite the debt problems, the industrial countries and Latin America should keep up and intensify their trade relations for their mutual benefit. This is only possible in an atmosphere of co-operation. Thus the debt problem requires co-operation instead of confrontation.

The big Latin American debtor countries can achieve a great deal by themselves. For, in contrast to the African countries, they all have considerable natural resources, a comparatively high level of education, well-developed patterns of production, and last but not least, extensive foreign assets. This economic strength could be developed by a sound and calculable economic policy and consolidated by appropriate reforms. There is no generally applicable strategy possible for this course of action because the conditions and problems in Bolivia, in Brazil, in Argentina, or in Mexico differ too widely. Each country has to find its own mixture of measures concerning its structural policy, its stabilization policy, and the establishment of a free-market system subordinated to the requirements of its own economic condition. If possible, they should do so by consulting the advice of the IMF and the World Bank.

I could make a number of propositions now about what in my opinion could be done better in Latin America. I shall not do so, but I would like to pick out one point.

Stabilization policy as a fundamental

Structural reforms, and a more fundamental orientation towards free-market principles, cannot produce a positive effect unless the stabilization policy is carried out more consistently than it has been so far. This year the budget problems in all the big debtor countries are increasing again, and the inflation mentality has by no means been overcome. On the contrary, Mexico, Argentina, and Brazil will record three-digit inflation rates again this year. In 1986 Argentina had an inflation rate of 140 per cent, Brazil one of 220 per cent, and Bolivia one of 400 per cent (in February 1986) and of 980 per cent in November 1985. Even in countries with a traditionally stable price climate, such as Venezuela or Ecuador, the inflationary spiral is spinning faster again. Interventions in the pricing mechanism could not solve the problem. They rather created an additional uncertainty on the part of local and foreign investors with regard to planning. Because of the elections facing these countries it is to be feared that they will not keep a tighter rein on their stabilization policy. You may remember the following remark from the time of the social liberal coalition in Germany: 'I prefer an inflation rate of 5 per cent rather than an unemployment rate of 5 per cent'. From a moral point of view I say now exactly what I used to reply then to that remark: Since the times of the Pharaohs there has never been an inflation that was not paid for by the ordinary citizen, and therefore inflations are thoroughly unsocial.

Economic reforms in Latin America will only bear fruit if the industrial countries for their part make up their failings more determinedly. There is still a gaping abyss between the declared belief in an increasing growth and in open markets on the one hand and the reality of the past years on the other hand.

Here I would like to go into the banks' contribution in more detail. First of all, the banks are prepared to go on with the traditional debt rescheduling procedures, provided that the debtor countries fulfil their loan commitments and carry out effective economic programmes controlled by the IMF and the World Bank. For some time now the banks have been prepared to accept long-term debt reschedulings while managing long-standing debts. This plan implies certain concessions regarding the interest margin too, that is, about the diminution of the interest load – provided these concessions stay within justifiable bounds. The developing countries find it hard to pay the extremely high inflation interest of western industrial countries; in this context I would like to mention the prime rate of more than 20 per cent in the United States at the beginning of the 1980s.

In the context of a co-operative strategy the banks, too, must, of course, supply fresh money, for the growth strategy of the Baker initiative requires capital inflows from the outside in the future too. The extension of new credits should be based on the following premises:

1. New credits can only be provided if the debtor country in question is willing and able to carry out appropriate structural reforms and to take suitable economic policy measures.
2. A dynamic development of the Latin American economies requires more imports and, in particular, imports of investment goods instead of frigates. However, this implies inevitably a rising demand of trade financings. In the face of these problems regarding long-standing debts, a stronger involvement can only be expected of the banks if the industrial countries' governments are prepared to hedge part of the risks by means of export credit guarantees and suretyships. Therefore it is necessary for the export credit insurances to rethink their restrictive coverage policy of the past years; at least they

should do so if the debtor countries 'behave well' in the sense described above.

Project financings and balance of payments financings

The banks are also interested in project financings, through which the developing countries' export strength is heightened, and especially in co-financings with the World Bank. From the creditors' point of view project financings are advantageous because the export proceeds from these projects are, so to speak, reserved for the respective country's debt service. However, the risks of such financings, which are often very high, must not be overlooked.

Despite the banks' heightened willingness to take risks, it is obvious that the problems facing us cannot be solved unless the state lenders and the supranational lenders contribute to new lendings to a greater extent. Compared with these requirements, the creditors' contribution has been disappointing for the past two years. In 1985 and 1986 they provided no more than 50 per cent of the gross new credits for debt rescheduling countries. On a net basis the figures are even more dissatisfying. From 1983 and 1984 to 1986 the net lendings to the Latin American continent were almost cut in half, that is, they went down from 11 billion to a good 6½ billion US dollars. Since 1986 the IMF has been receiving net returns on investment and, owing to the redemption structure, this trend will last for the next few years, unless the lending policy of the IMF is reconsidered. Despite a slight rise in the net lendings the contribution of the multinational development banks has fallen far behind the ideas of the Baker initiative. Moreover, the net contribution of the Paris Club has been declining for the past two years.

A deeper involvement of the official creditors depends also on the debtor countries' behaviour though. The IMF will not be able to play an active part unless the Latin American countries cooperate with it. The same goes for the World Bank, whose structural and sectoral adjustment credits are bound by certain conditions too. Besides, a more active part of the international institutions requires that the industrial countries provide these institutions with the necessary funds. For quite a long time the increase of funds for the World Bank was blocked because the United States refused to go along with it. Now the US Minister of Finance, Baker, has announced that the United States are willing to agree to a capital increase.

Final remarks

The slump in the oil price, the insignificant growth in the OECD (Organization for Economic Co-operation and Development) countries, the capital flight, and the adjustment problems in Latin America, were the main causes of the debt crisis. The development of the past years shows that both the Latin American countries and the creditor countries have made good progress in coping with Latin America's debt problem. Still, they have only insufficiently succeeded in realizing the ideas of the Baker initiative so far. It is clear to everybody that a solution to the debt problems is not a question of a few years. This, however, makes it all the more important to take the right steps now. For the key to a long-term solution to the problems of indebtedness in Latin America is not a cut in the debt mountain with a single stroke of the pen, but close co-operation between all the parties involved and a great deal of patience.

Chapter three

Recent developments in the debt crisis and ways to its solution

Eduardo de Sousa Ferreira

For a long time now Europe has tried to tackle certain problems concerning Latin America by means of a direct dialogue and independently of the aims of the superpowers. As a result, some of those that are on Latin America's side hold quite different views regarding the solution of these problems. Owing to the complex political, social, and economic situation in Latin America, the European ideas meet with a lot of resistance though. A few weeks ago an interparliamentary conference of the European Communities and Latin America took place in Lisbon, and at this conference problems of solidarity, co-operation, and communication were intensively discussed.

It was no coincidence that the conference was held in Lisbon, for Portugal and Spain joining the European Communities might be one of the first steps towards an improvement of the forum for discussion, and for a dialogue between Europe and Latin America; after all, there is a special historical and cultural relation between Portugal, Spain, and Latin America. With politics and economy being closely interrelated, it is not surprising that the problems of foreign indebtedness was very important at this politically-significant meeting, and that it became the foremost topic in the course of the discussion.

The agony of the international lendings

John Reed, the president of Citicorp, the most powerful bank in the world, recently surprised the financial community by announcing that, owing to the uncertain debts of the Third World, his bank had decided to set aside an additional amount of 3 billion US dollars for reserves. In June 1987 he declared that his bank was willing to invest a billion US dollars in private and public enterprises of the debtor countries. Since Mexico's moratorium in 1982 there have been many reactions, of course; however, this was the first concrete and original initiative. Since Mexico's declaration the situation has become more and more complex, and an increasing number of agreements have not been fulfilled.

With a foreign debt of over 100 billion US dollars, Brazil was at the lead of the debtor countries in 1987; however, not only Brazil is highly indebted, but almost all the main debtors are Latin American countries. In February 1987 Brazil practically announced a moratorium, unless the international commercial banks were prepared to refinance at least 50 per cent of the capital that had to be repaid. In June 1987 Brazil declared its willingness to repay half of its debt, though, and to develop a stabilization programme so that the external credits could be rescheduled.

The Ivory Coast followed Mexico's and Brazil's example by declaring, after a moratorium in 1984 and 1985, that it was unable to fulfil its obligations in 1987 and the two following years. In 1987 the debt service of the Ivory Coast amounted to 1.1 billion US dollars; its main export products are coffee and cocoa, the price of which has recently gone down by 20 per cent. This slump in prices diminished the Ivory Coast's export earnings by 600 million US dollars. Although the Ivory Coast is well known for always having fulfilled the programme of the International Monetary Fund (IMF), its payment problems had become so grave that it had to inform the IMF and the Paris Club.

It is perhaps the Ivory Coast's loyalty to the IMF that marks the country as candidate for the Baker plan. This decision means that, in debt negotiations, the creditors will on the whole accept the financial condition of the Ivory Coast, for which the country is not necessarily to blame. Thus a rescheduling operation will be carried out, which allows for longer time limits as well as for a method of repayment that takes into account the country's financial condition as regards foreign exchange.

Thus the above-mentioned statement by Citicorp can also be considered as a reaction to Brazil's behaviour. Citicorp is particularly involved in Latin America, especially in Brazil with 4.6 billion US dollars and in Mexico with 2.8 billion US dollars. At the same time Citicorp declared that 20 per cent of the debt would have to be regarded as lost. It was not clear, however, how the other banks would react to these statements. By now it is well known, though, that the Chase Manhatten Bank and the Security Pacific Bank have begun to pursue a similar policy.

Reasons for the 'new' policy of the international banks

Mexico's declaration in 1982 was perhaps not as important as Brazil's, for since then it has been feared that a kind of 'OPEC of the debtor countries' would come into existence. Such an organization would be a cartel of debtor countries which might collectively refuse to pay off their debts. It is, however, exaggerated to consider this fear to be the motive of the policy of Citicorp and the Chase Manhattan Bank, for the power of such a cartel, which would consist of very heterogeneous countries, can be estimated as relatively small.

The list of debtor countries ranges from South Africa, where repayments are practically guaranteed, Korea, which actually used its credits for productive investments, Colombia and Paraguay, which are not at all in the so-called debt trap, to Brazil, Chile, Mexico and others. Since its payment crisis in 1982, Chile has tried to improve its external payment condition, an attempt which involved unbearably high internal costs though. Since 1986 Mexico, and Argentina too, have had a debt agreement with their creditors. The Philippine Islands, that is, the most highly-indebted Asian country, are similar to most of the Latin American debtor countries. As regards their debt management, however, they would not easily join a cartel of non-paying debtor countries, not least because they would be afraid of losing the United States' sympathy for Corazon Aquino.

Therefore a cartel – if it really came into existence – would not be a noticeable power factor, for the national interests differ too widely. Thus the banks' new policy cannot be put down to fear of a confrontation with such a cartel, but it must have other reasons.

It is almost certain that the indebted countries will not be able to repay anything anyway. Thus a relief programme is needed, which gives these countries scope for development and enables them to repay their 'forgotten' debts later on. However, opinions concerning the choice of an appropriate programme are divided.

A moratorium without a time limit, however, goes against the principles of the Federal Reserve System of the United States because the rates of interest are fixed on the basis of a previously specified date of repayment. Now, if there is no fixed date of repayment, the object of this calculation and even the justification of the interest as such are questionable. On the other hand, there are certain methods of debt management which seem to be acceptable to both the private banks and American monetary institutions. The foremost among those methods is the conversion of enforceable legal documents into shares in enterprises of the debtor countries. Even if the point of view of Citicorp was initially astonishing and surprising, it is quite understandable if taken as the conversion of debts into direct investment capital of enterprises in the debtor countries. Such conversions practically amount to debt equity swaps.

Thus, by now Chile has paid off 20 per cent of its debt by selling some of its own enterprises. This means that Chile's economy is virtually being sold out. In Mexico, the same procedure has now been initiated. However, there are much more serious problems of national sovereignty involved as in the case of Chile. Problems of sovereignty represent the main difficulty in the attempt of paying off debts by a transfer of ownership of domestic assets to foreigners. Besides, there may be technical difficulties, for in many countries there are simply not enough enterprises which the creditors would consider to be possible as an offer for a conversion of debt.

In its latest report from 1986 the World Bank states that, in fulfilling their debt service, the developing countries paid 15 billion US dollars more than they received in the form of foreign loans. Unless the terms of repayment are improved, it is highly improbable that the investments that these countries financed by means of their foreign borrowings can set off economic growth to an extent which would suffice for their debt repayments. Therefore, the World Bank appeals to the banks and creditors, telling them that an insufficient provision with financial resources would make the macroeconomic restructuring and adjustment of these countries impossible and would aggravate the problem of repayment.

The 'blame' for indebtedness

The suggestion that the debt should not be repaid is justified in so far as the industrial countries themselves put their rather abundant liquidity at the developing countries' disposal in the form of lendings. In the 1970s petrodollars had to be invested so that credits were practically forced on third countries. On the one hand the terms of credit were very severe because they were fixed by private banks, which operate on the basis of free-market principles. On the other hand, the banks made their lendings easily accessible, thus increasing the temptation to accept these credit offers contrary to economic good sense. And it is often not easy to resist temptation.

This opinion does not justify a non-payment of debts though. The fact that the industrial countries extended loans in a selfish way, that is, without considering what such a wave of loans would mean to the future of the developing countries, does not justify the developing countries' present unwillingness to pay off their debts. At most, this fact can mean that industrial countries have to accept losses and to review their credit periods and interest terms. The result of the negotiations about loans should do justice to the economic, political, and social condition of the respective country.

Of course, one cannot declare the developing countries to be irresponsible minors by releasing them from the duty to pay off their debts. They knew exactly what they would have to pay, and even if the behaviour of the industrial countries was not unselfish, the debtor countries must not react by just as incorrect behaviour.

One of the arguments in favour of a debt service boycott is the fact that the debtor countries are strongly dependent on the international economic centres in the industrial countries, although they had intended to use the extended loans just in order to restructure and adjust their economy. However, the politicians in power did not use the money for the intended restructuring but for private and public consumption expenditure. Their purpose was often to win the approval of the population by means of financial contributions, that is, they bribed the population by loans obtained abroad, thus giving them the feeling that with this government – meaning with a strong spending power – they could improve their standard of living. This illusion has nothing at all to do with the industrial countries' blame. The politicians in the developing countries should explain to the population that things cannot go on like this any more. These politicians have misused the loans obtained abroad, and it cannot be accepted that they go on acting according to the motto 'We shall not pay our debts'.

The role of the World Bank and the International Monetary Fund

It is generally agreed that the debtor countries cannot budget much longer without additional financial resources because their savings do not suffice for the financing of big projects. Thus the parties involved must realize that both for the restructuring and adjustment of the economy, and as a guarantee for minimal growth, some other ways of bringing further capital into the country has to be found.

The World Bank should take a main part in the solution of this liquidity problem. However, it is doubtful whether the World Bank is really able to contribute to such a solution. The same goes for the IMF, which has recently announced that in its new programmes it would take into account the demand side more than the supply side.

The World Bank has one item in its programme, though, which might improve the situation: it accepted a stronger say of Third World countries in capital investment planning. Yet it remains to be seen whether the representatives of the Third World countries in the IMF are really those that make appropriate suggestions for their countries.

The three levels of the debt problem

There are three different levels on which the debt problem can be analyzed. First, the rules of the existing economic system in the west should be discussed. Second, the alleged orthodox economy of the neo-classical type should be questioned. Third, further attempts should be made to develop this system in future.

As regards the rules of the western economic system, some ideas have already been presented. Among them is the revival of Keynes's proposals in connection with the agreement of Bretton Woods, where he suggested to form an international clearing union, in which current account surpluses occurring world-wide would be put at the disposal of countries with a balance of payments in deficit. This step could be a way of stabilizing international economy in the long run.

On this first level, another successful strategy might be a modification of the international payments system. The special drawing rights, for instance, met a lot of resistance initially, especially on the part of the United States. It might be considered now whether the creation of special drawing rights should no longer be left to the IMF alone, and whether national governments and even private parties should be included in such decisions instead. By a redefinition of the special drawing rights, international indebtedness could be joined directly to new special drawing rights.

According to the logic of orthodox, that is, neo-classical economics, basic conditions for the solution of the debt problem have to be created on the second level. First, the debtor countries must be enabled to realize their development potential. This requires fresh money for new investments which guarantee a certain level of profit. Second, a structural adjustment process has to be carried out. Such a process requires a long-term policy, and therefore the present short-term terms of credit have to be rethought too. Third, the world trade must be stimulated and protectionism must be restricted so that it does not impair the debtor countries' economy.

The third level, that is, a further development of the present economic system, goes beyond these orthodox rules. However, the use of suggestions which extend the system does not imply that older methods on the other two levels should be discarded. In principle, the parties involved should proceed on all three levels simultaneously and always try to achieve an extension or an improvement. The problem of indebtedness is neither an exclusive problem of the financial community, nor an exclusive problem of the banks, it is a political problem too, and the past provides some clues about its solution.

The lesson from the past

Portugal closely experienced similar problems in the course of its decolonization. All its colonies were in debt to Portugal, as most colonies used to be to their home countries. The debts were due to credits which Portugal had extended to its former colonies for plans whose realization was to make the colonies operate as an annexe of Portuguese economy. Although this observation is not meant to equate colonialism and 'neo-colonialism', they do have some characteristics in common. Thus it was impossible to bring the negotiations about decolonization to a close as long as Portugal insisted on having its 'due to banks' paid off. The decolonization could only be solved politically.

It might be an advantage for all parties involved if a different way from the purely financial way is chosen for the solution of the debt problem. Approaches that include ideas about a future development of society as a whole might be superior to purely economic strategies. For if the present debt problem is not solved properly, other strategies will be tried out, and they might be even more difficult to handle. And if the necessary decisions are not prosecuted on all three levels at the same time, with the third level given precedence, more insoluble problems will arise. It should be kept in mind that in the course of history a shift of power from the Mediterranean to the Atlantic occurred by and by, and that a similar shift of power from the Atlantic to the Pacific is in the air.

Part two

Causes, consequences, and debt management

Chapter four

On the significance of foreign debt: some 'fundamentals'

Leonardo Auernheimer

Introduction

The international debt question has lately become, and rightly so, a favourite topic among theoreticians, world financial organizations, international economists, and even financial tycoons. At the applied policy level, the favourite exercise is to show that in many cases the international debt of some countries cannot possibly be paid, and to investigate the possibility that through some very complicated manipulations the debtor countries might see their situation being improved without the creditors being disturbed. At the theoretical level, important work is being developed in order to understand 'game theory' situations better in which the players (competing creditor banks and debtor countries) face a variety of possible strategies.

The purpose of this contribution is removed from that mainstream, in that it addresses a couple of more conventional, simpler 'fundamentals'. These fundamentals have to do with the origin of governments' debt in some important instances and, given the structure of such debt, the consequences of alternative policies implemented to pay for it. In other words, at least part of this contribution is concerned with the question of 'how to pay for the debt' rather than 'how not to pay for it'. It seems to be important to clarify, at this point, that when we refer to 'paying for the debt' we mean to pay for the interest in a manner which is bearable in the long run. Therefore, instead of discussing the problem of possible arrangements to 'pardon' or reduce part of the debt, we take its amount as given.

The second section deals with the question of the origin of the debt, from the point of view of both economic theory and empirical evidence – the latter specifically referring to the case of Argentina. The origin of the debt, in turn, determines its current 'structure', that is, the net wealth position of both the government and the private sector. We will argue that it is important to recognize the distinction between 'government' and 'country' debt, that the two can be very different, and that a correct analysis requires that such a distinction should be kept in mind. Still more specifically, the neglect of such a distinction seems to have helped to put an undue emphasis on 'balance of payments' policies rather than on 'budget' policies, so that the government budget constraint and the country constraint were confused at times.

In the third section we suggest a very simple model of a small open economy with perfect capital mobility, which places emphasis on the explicit distinction between the government's and the private sector's budget constraint.

In the fourth section within the context of the model, we discuss the effects of paying for the debt by changes in the inflation tax, conventional taxes and/or the level of government expenditures.

On the origin of the debt and its current structures 'government' and 'country' debt

In view of the massive, unprecedented levels of government foreign indebtedness, the obvious question is where those funds went. The common scenario is the idea of a 'country' (government and the private sector) having gone through a period of high levels of consumption and, perhaps, low return investment undertakings, in very much the same way as an irrational consumer goes through a credit card consumption spree for which he is not able to pay. Such a scenario is, in most cases, consistent with the figures: for the case of Argentina, for example, where foreign debt amounts to over 47 billion US dollars (after deducting central bank reserves), which is approximately 80 per cent of the annual gross national product (GNP) and seven times the level of the total exports during 1986.

A more careful analysis suggests a different interpretation. First, most figures on the foreign debt of countries are often misleading, as they fail to accurately reflect the net foreign asset position of private country residents. Second, simple economic theory would tend to suggest that, from the aggregate point of view (that is, with government and private asset positions consolidated), such a scenario is very unlikely to happen in a world of rational agents. Third, a deeper analysis of the data is not consistent with that scenario.

The first point essentially refers to a confusion of the government and the private sector budget constraint, on the one hand, and the difference between either of those two and the country constraint, that is, the balances of payments, on the other hand. The fact is that most of the debt is government debt, and the private sector is represented only as far as it has declared debt (probably most of it), while the private sector's accumulated foreign assets, most of them not officially declared, are therefore ignored.

The second point has been analysed by the author in a recent paper[1] in which the discussion centres on inconsistent stabilization programmes and their outcome. Of course, in some cases government debt accumulation has not been the result of stabilization programmes, but this seems to be the case for at least one country (Argentina), and the general analysis could be extended to other cases. The theoretical conclusion is that, with capital mobility, the final outcome of an inconsistent stabilization programme is that government ends up with higher negative foreign assets (debt), while the private sector accumulates assets by exactly the same magnitude. In other words, the aborted stabilization effort results in a redistribution of foreign assets from government to the private sector.

The mechanism by which the result is obtained can be sketched as follows – an 'inconsistent' stabilization programme is one in which the adopted paths of government expenditures, conventional taxes, and the inflation tax are not sustainable in the long run. In particular, as in the case of Argentina, the inflation rate is set at 'too low' a level, so that during the duration of the programme the government borrows in international markets, and rational individuals, who perceive the eventual demise of the programme and the forthcoming higher level of the inflation tax, accumulate foreign assets. Notice that this is very similar to the analysis of Sargent and Wallace.[2] In both cases, the level of the inflation tax, and therefore the inflation rate, is higher after the demise of the programme than it would have been without the programme: in addition to the current deficit an increase of interest payments on the debt accumulated during the programme must be financed.

The third point refers to the specific empirical evidence for the case of Argentina. In a recent study Rodriguez[3] carefully analyses the evolution of the Argentine debt since 1978 (the year in which the programme devised by the Minister of Trade and Commerce, Martinez de Hoz, went into effect). From 1978 to 1982 the declared foreign debt increased by almost 34 billion US dollars, and between 1983 and 1986, by about 11.7 billion US dollars (of which 3.4 billion US dollars were accumulated as central bank reserves). The only important trade account deficit, though, occurred in 1980, with 2.5 billion US dollars.

Rodriguez carefully estimates possible undeclared imports (smuggling), tourists' expenditures abroad and other items, and calculates, as a residual, the private sector accumulation of foreign assets, on the basis of those foreign assets yielding an interest rate of only 60 per cent of the rate paid by the government on its debt. The final estimation is that, by the end of 1986, the private sector will hold over 31 billion US dollars of foreign assets. Added to the 6.4 billion US dollars in central bank reserves, the true country foreign debt would then come to 17.5 billion US dollars (against an apparent debt of 55 billion US dollars). As the author points out, all his estimations are extremely conservative, so that even such a true country debt is probably still an overestimation.

What is the relevance of all of this for the situation faced by governments? In general terms, the consideration of alternative policies should put emphasis on the government budget constraint rather than on the overall country constraint (the balance of payments). The government budget constraint indicates that there are only three ways in which government debt (whether it is domestic or international) can be paid for – by increasing taxes, by increasing the revenue from the creation of money, or by reducing government expenditures. Projections of future balances of trade surpluses are of no value *per se*, unless those surpluses affect the variables mentioned above. For example, some 'capitalization of the debt' schemes assume that the purchaser of foreign debt who exchanges it for domestic money on the condition that they buy real capital assets in the country will automatically be willing to hold the additional domestic money, that is, the demand for money will rise, and with it the government revenue from money creation; the question is, of course, different, if those real capital assets belong to the government.

In the next section we will develop a simple framework for the analysis of alternative forms of repayment of government debt, which seems to be adequate for the analysis of these questions. We will show, for example, the manner in which taxation and/or a reduction in government expenditures can act as a mechanism to generate a reversed flow transfer of privately-held foreign assets for the payment of government's debt.

A simple stylized model of trade, debt, and payments

In this section we develop a very simple but rather complete model of a small open economy as a framework for the analysis of some of the issues. It is, of course, a very 'stylized' construction, but an adequate framework to give an idea of the fundamental forces at work. We assume rational expectations (which, in a non-random context, imply perfect foresight). As will become clear, the structure of such a model purposely highlights the connection between government and private ownership of foreign assets (or debt), which has so far been ignored in the discussion.

Consider the case of a small open economy producing flows of a non-tradable commodity (the 'home' or 'domestic' good) x_1, and a tradable commodity (the 'traded' good) x_2. Given a stock of fully employed resources, that is, along the conventional transformation curve, the quantities produced can be expressed by:

$$x_1 = x_1(\varepsilon) \text{ with } x_1' > 0 \text{, and} \tag{1}$$

$$x_2 = x_2(\varepsilon) \text{ with } x_2' < 0, \tag{1'}$$

where

$\varepsilon \equiv P_1/P_2$ is the 'real exchange rate', that is, the ratio of the domestic money price of the traded good, P_1, to that of the non-traded good, P_2. If arbitrage assures the continuous equality of domestic and world prices of the traded good, then by arbitrarily equating the world price (expressed in terms of foreign money) to unity, equation (2) can be expressed by

$$\varepsilon = E/P_2, \tag{2}$$

where E is the nominal exchange rate, represented by the price of foreign money in terms of the domestic monetary unit. The general price level, then, is an index of the form

$$P = \varepsilon^{\sigma} P_2^{(1-\sigma)} \text{ with } 0 \leq \sigma \leq 0. \tag{2'}$$

Calling M the nominal money stock, the real money stock then is $m \equiv M/P$, and using equation (3), the overall inflation rate II is

$$\text{II} = \sigma \text{II}_1 + (1 - \sigma)\,\text{II}_2, \tag{3}$$

where $\text{II}_1 = (dE\ dt)\,(1/E)$ and $\text{II}_2 = (dP_2/dt)\,(1/P_2)$ are the proportional rates of change of the nominal exchange rate (the 'rate of devaluation') and of the price of the non-traded good, respectively.

Residents hold domestic money and securities denominated in terms of the traded commodity (or, which is the same in this case, in terms of foreign currency) which earn a real rate of interest, r, in the world market; for the sake of simplicity, we take such securities to be 'call bonds' of zero maturity, so that capital gains and losses do not take place when unexpected changes in the interest rate occur. Notice that, naturally, those securities, which we denominate as k, can be negative.

The representative individual's budget constraint, expressed in terms of domestic goods, can then be expressed by

$$x_1\varepsilon + x_2 + kr\varepsilon - (dm/dt)\,\varepsilon^{\sigma} - m\varepsilon^{\sigma} \quad [\Pi - (d\varepsilon/dt)\,(1/\varepsilon)\,(1-\sigma)] = (dk/dt)\,\varepsilon + c_2 + c_1\,\varepsilon + T, \tag{4}$$

where c_1 and c_2 are the flows of consumption of the traded and the domestic good, and T is the level of 'head' taxes.

Government imposes taxes, prints fiat domestic money, spends and holds a stock of financial assets, a, identical in nature to those held by individuals, on which it receives the same real interest rate, r, as the private sector. Of course, it is perfectly possible for such a stock of government assets to be negative. For the sake of both simplicity and realism, we assume that all government expenditures, g, are in domestic goods. The government budget constraint then, expressed in terms of domestic goods, can be described by

$$\varepsilon ar + (dm/dt)\varepsilon^{\sigma} + m\varepsilon^{\sigma}\,[\Pi_1 - (d\varepsilon/dt)\,(1/\varepsilon)\,(1-\sigma)] + T = g + (da/dt)\,\varepsilon. \tag{5}$$

Define 'total non-monetary' wealth as $w \equiv k + a$. Then, recognizing that the aggregate clearing in the market for domestic goods requires $c_2 = x_2 - g$, from equations (4) and (5) we obtain the overall budget constraint

$$(dw/dt) = wr + x_1 - c_1. \tag{6}$$

Expression (6) is, of course, the balance of payments equation, with the term $(x_1 - c_1)$ being the balance of trade and its right hand side the current account.

Individuals have perfect foresight, and at each point in time, $t = 0$, they maximize the utility function

$$\int_0^{\infty} U(c_1, c_2, m)\, e^{-\rho t}\, dt \tag{7}$$

subject to the budget constraint in equation (4), $U(\ldots)$ being the instantaneous utility function (satisfying the usual requirements of continuity and differentiability), and p the constant rate of time preference. Of course, inflation rates and the real interest rate are given for each individual.

Maximization of equation (7) subject to equation (4) yields the Euler equations:

$$(dU_1/dt)/U_1 = [\sigma - r - (d\varepsilon/dt)]\,(1/\varepsilon) \tag{8}$$

$$(dU_2/dt)/U_2 = ((d\varepsilon/dt)/\varepsilon) + p + \Pi_1 - [U_m)/(U_2\varepsilon^{\sigma})] \tag{8'}$$

$$U_1 = U_2\,\varepsilon, \tag{8''}$$

where U_m, U_1 and U_2 are the marginal utilities of money and consumption of each of the two commodities. By differentiating equation (8″) with respect to time and inserting it into equation (8), and by equating equations (8) and (8′), we obtain

$$(dU_1/dt)\,(1/U_1) = p - r, \text{ and} \tag{9}$$

$$U_m = \varepsilon^{(p-1)}U_1\,(r + \Pi_1). \tag{9'}$$

We will assume, at this point, that the utility function is separable in money and consumption of either of the two commodities. Such an assumption, used previously in other articles (see, for example, Calvo[4] and Obstfeld and Rogoff[5]), is crucial for the simplicity of the results and needs some justification. One justification is that at least its introduction allows one to explore direct results which are presumably of a larger order of magnitude than cross, indirect effects, thus giving an initial indication of the direction of changes and of the fundamental forces at work. Another point is that such separability still allows to generate 'sensible' results, in particular concerning the demand for money equation.

Assuming separability, then, and again recognizing that the aggregate consumption of the domestic commodity is given by the difference between production and the level of government expenditures, we obtain

$$dc_1/dt = (U_1/U_{11})\,(p - r). \tag{10}$$

Assume now that r, the real interest rate which government and residents of the country in question face in the world market, depends on the level of aggregate non-monetary wealth, w, as defined above, so that

$$r = r(w) \text{ with } r'(\ ) < 0,\ r''(\ ) > 0. \tag{11}$$

This assumption serves two purposes. First, it facilitates a solution of the model – an alternative treatment would be to imply a fixed world real interest rate instead of assuming a variable rate of time preference as in Obstfeld and Rogoff[6]. Second, it incorporates the realistic idea of a 'country risk' element; the fact that both private and government assets or debts receive or pay the same interest rate as influenced by their sum (w) merely means that, for a given level of its expenditures and taxes (that is, the deficit), government policies can eventually be geared towards extracting or transferring resources from or to the private sector, and this fact is perceived by the market. Of course, the dependence of the world interest rate (which the country in question has to face) on its aggregate level of (non-monetary) wealth, w, is more defensible for negative values, which we will assume.

By a few transformations and substitutions, then, we can obtain the two simple differential equations for the variables w and c_1, for a given level of government expenditures, g:

$$dc_1/dt = (U_1/U_{11})(p - r(w)) \tag{12}$$

$$dw/dt = w\,r(w) + x_1(\varepsilon(c_1, g)) - c_1. \tag{12'}$$

Notice that the function $\varepsilon = \varepsilon(c_1, g)$ is derived from equation (8″), and that $(\delta\varepsilon/\delta c_1) < 0$, $(\delta\varepsilon/\delta g) < 0$. The solution of this system contains two real roots of different signs, guaranteeing the existence of a unique saddle-path.

Without any loss in generality, and for the sake of computational simplicity, we will assume that the separable utility function is of the form

$$U(c_1, c_2, m) = c_1^{\alpha} c_2^{\beta} + v(m) \text{ with } 1 > (\alpha + \beta) > 0,$$

that is, that the 'consumption of commodities' side of the function is of a Cobb-Douglas form. Then, after a few substitutions, the complete *aggregate* system becomes

$$dc_1/dt = (c_1/[1 - \alpha])(r(w) - p) \tag{13}$$

$$dw/dt = w\,r(w) + x_1(\varepsilon(c_1, g)) - c_1 \tag{13'}$$

$$c_1\varepsilon/(x_2(\varepsilon) - g) = (\alpha/\beta) \tag{13''}$$

$$m = l(c_1, \varepsilon, (r(w) + \Pi_1)) \text{ with } \delta m/\delta c_1, \delta m/\delta\varepsilon > 0, \tag{13'''}$$

where equation (13‴), the demand for money, is the general expression for

$$v_m(m) = \varepsilon^{\beta((\alpha+\beta-1)/(\alpha+\beta))}\alpha^{(1-\beta)}\alpha^{\beta}c_1{}^{(\alpha+\beta-1)}(r(w)+\Pi_1).$$

After all this tedious arithmetic, notice a few features of the model. First, the two expressions (13′) and (13″) describe the non-monetary 'block', for a given level of government expenditures, in terms of the variables w and c_1.

The real exchange rate, ε, and with it x_1, x_2 and c_2, are simultaneously determined by the behaviour of c_1 and w dictated by those two expressions. All of this – independently of monetary considerations, in particular the 'policy rule', that is, the choice of a constant devaluation rate or a constant rate of monetary expansion – is the manner in which the 'degree of freedom' is taken up by the monetary authority. Figure 4.1 shows the 'phase diagram' corresponding to the non-monetary sector, with the arrows showing the laws of motion of the system.

Figure 4.1 Phase diagram of the model's behaviour.

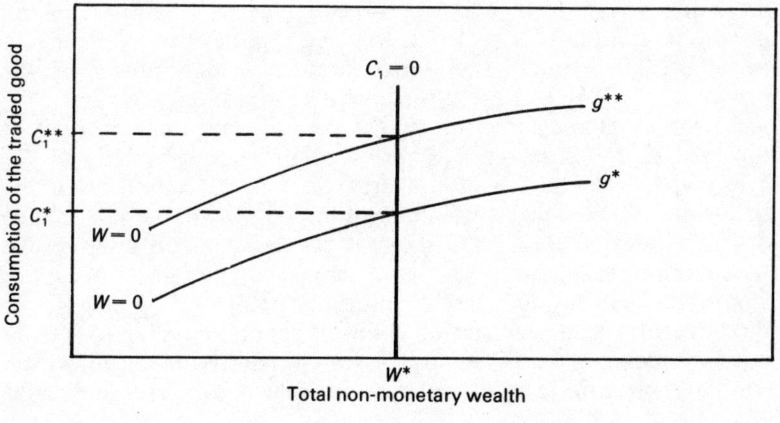

Notice that along the saddle-path the real exchange rate and the trade balance, $x_1 - c_1$, will fall when total non-monetary wealth is rising and vice versa, but there are efficient, non-saddle-paths which could be relevant under some circumstances and for which such standard correspondence does not hold.

Second, expression (13‴) is the demand for money, determined by the path of the real exchange rate, ε, the consumption of traded goods, c_1, and the real interest rate, $r(w)$, as well as the 'rate of devaluation', Π_1. Notice that, of course, $(r(w) + \Pi_1)$ is the prevailing nominal interest rate. It is, of course, the rate of devaluation reflects the 'monetary events'. If the policy-maker follows an 'exchange rate rule' (that is, announces and maintains the path of the nominal exchange rate, as in the case of the stabilization experiments of some Latin American countries during the 1970s and early 1980s), Π_1 is given by policy, and the path of the real money stock can be ascertained. If a 'monetary rule' is followed (that is, a constant rate of change of the money supply), the solution for the path of the real money stock will be found by using the identity

$$(dm/dt)(1/m) = m(dM/dt)(1/M) - m\,\Pi,$$

where M is the nominal money stock, and some transversality conditions will be given by the consistency of policies as discussed in Auernheimer.[7] Notice, however, that, in either case, along the saddle-path the real money stock will rise (or fall) together with both the total non-monetary wealth w, and the consumption of the traded good, c_1.

Finally notice that the variables a and k (the stocks of government and private foreign assets, respectively) do not appear in any of the equations (13)–(13‴) that determine the rest of the variables. The path of these two variables is determined by the private sector (4) and the government (5) budget constraints, for some initial values are given by the past history, and the path of the rest of the variables is determined by equations (13)–(13‴). The paths of a and k will converge on a finite value only if the behaviour of the policy variables g, T and Π_1 (or the rate of change of the money supply) is 'consistent' as defined and analyzed in Auernheimer[8] – although such a policy might not exist. Conversely, for a policy determining the paths of T, g and Π_1 (or the rate of monetary expansion), it is, in general possible to find an initial critical value of a and k for which both variables will converge on a finite value. Notice also that non-convergent paths of a and k are possible even if the system (13)–(13‴) is in its long-run equilibrium position, in which case $(dw/dt) = 0$ and $(da/dt) = -(dk/dt)$. This, in fact, is not unlike the debt position of some countries and the possibility that we analyse in the next section.

On the effects of paying for government debt

The foreign debt situation of some countries, as characterized in the second section, will be described in this section in terms of the framework developed in the third section. Consider the case of the non-monetary and the monetary sectors described by expressions (13)–(13‴) in their saddle-paths towards their long-run equilibria, but in which the initial values of government foreign assets, a, and private foreign assets, k, are such that both variables do not converge on a finite value. In particular, the case of interest for our analysis is when the former is 'too low' and the latter is 'too high'. Such levels, of course, can both either be positive or negative, but the specific case we wish to analyze is when the stock of government-owned foreign assets, a, is negative and 'too high' (in absolute terms).

It is convenient and means no loss of generality to take the particular case where the system (13)–(13‴) is resting in its long-run equilibrium position, perhaps with $w < 0$. Although one may doubt for this to be the case, the nature and the direction of the conclusions do not change in any important way, and the gain in simplicity is considerable. Also, in order to facilitate the analysis, suppose that an 'exchange rate rule' is followed, so that Π_1 is directly established by the monetary authority (thus rendering, of course, the rate of change of the money supply an endogenous variable).

For this long-run equilibrium, with $(dc_1/dt) = (dw/dt) = 0$, the equilibrium level of the variables is given by

$$r(w^*) = p \tag{15}$$

$$-w^* r(w^*) = x_1(\varepsilon(c_1^*, g^*)) - c_1^* \tag{15'}$$

$$c_1^* \varepsilon^* / (x_2^*(\varepsilon^*) - g^*) = (\alpha/\beta) \tag{15''}$$

$$m^* = l(c_1^*, \varepsilon^*, (r(w^*) + \Pi_1^*)), \tag{15'''}$$

where a star (*) indicates the initial equilibrium values of the policy variables g and Π_1 and of the rest of the endogenous variables.

Given those long-run equilibrium values, the expression we are now interested in is the government budget constraint (5), which becomes

$$da/dt = a\,r(w^*) + l\,(c_1{}^*, \varepsilon^*, (r(w^*) + \Pi_1{}^*))\,\varepsilon^{*(\sigma-1)}\,\Pi_1 + (T^*/\varepsilon) - (g^*/\varepsilon), \tag{5'}$$

and for which, given the long-run equilibrium values of the other variables, the initial value of a is negative and 'too low', so that $(da/dt) < 0$. In other words, we are in the typical situation in which government revenues from conventional taxes and the inflation tax do not suffice to pay for government expenditures and the interest on its debt, so that the government suffers an increase in debt while paying for the interest. Of course, if nothing changes, then debt accumulates at an increasing rate.

Within this framework, we are interested in the consequences of eliminating (or at least decreasing) the rate of government debt accumulation (da/dt) via the only three possible ways in which it can be done – (a) by increasing the inflation tax (that is, a rise in Π_1), (b) by increasing conventional taxes T, or (c) by reducing government expenditures g. More specifically, we investigate the net effects of changing those policy variables on (da/dt).

Increasing the inflation tax

In practical terms, an increase in the inflation tax seems to be one of the least promising possibilities in many countries, not only because of the inefficiencies involved and the increasingly adverse public opinion, but simply because inflation rates are already so high that the point of maximum revenue is either very close or, in a few cases, has already been surpassed; in fact, in view of the once-and-for-all asset effect,[9] a subcase could be considered for a fall in the inflation rate as a means of increasing revenues from money creation. We nevertheless show the result for the sake of completeness, assuming that a rise in the inflation rate will bring about a rise in those revenues.

As is clear from equations (15)–(15″), a change in the inflation rate does not change the real exchange rate, ε, and therefore leaves the levels of c_1, c_2, x_1, and x_2 unchanged. There is neither change in the total balance of trade, nor in its components, and no 'side effects' affect other terms in expression (5′). The change in the rate of debt accumulation, then, is

$$d\,(da/dt) = m\,\varepsilon^{(\sigma-1)}\,(1+\eta)\,d\,(\Pi_1), \tag{18}$$

where η is the elasticity of the demand for money with respect to the *nominal* interest rate, reflecting the fact that, in the case of the exchange rate rule, a rise in the inflation rate, with no discontinuity in the level of the exchange rate, will bring about an instantaneous fall in the level of government-held assets by the same amount as the fall in the real money stock.

Increasing conventional taxes (T) per capita

The analysis of the effects of a fall in the level of taxes per capita is also straightforward. Here, as in the previous case, there are no changes in any of the variables determined by equations (15)–(15‴) and no 'side effects', so that

$$d(da/dt) = m\,\varepsilon^{(\sigma-1)}\,(1+\eta)\,d(\Pi_1), \tag{18}$$

and every unit increase in taxes is exactly matched by a unit fall in the rate of debt accumulation.

Reducing the level of government expenditures (g)

A fall in the level of government expenditures, *g*, brings about a slightly more complicated outcome – since *g* is an argument in the determination of the real exchange rate, ε, changes in *g* do have an effect on the long-run equilibrium values of several of the variables determined by equations (15)–(15‴), the exception being the level of total non-monetary wealth, *w*, and therefore the real interest rate. The direction and magnitude of those changes is given by:

$$d\varepsilon^* = [-(\alpha/\beta/\{c_1^* + (\delta x_1/\delta\varepsilon)\,\varepsilon^* - (\alpha/\beta)\,(\delta x_2/\delta\varepsilon)\}]\,dg \tag{17}$$

$$dc_1^* = (\delta x_1/\delta\varepsilon)\,d\varepsilon \tag{17'}$$

$$dc_2^* = (\beta/\alpha)\,\{c_1^*\,d\varepsilon + \varepsilon^*\,dc_1\} \tag{17''}$$

$$dm = (\delta m/\delta c_1)\,dc_1 + (\delta m/\delta\varepsilon)\,d\varepsilon. \tag{17'''}$$

Given the signs of the partial derivatives $(\delta x_1/\delta\varepsilon) > 0$, $(\delta x_2/\delta\varepsilon) < 0$, $(\delta m/\delta c_1) > 0$ and $(\delta m/\delta\varepsilon) > 0$, it is clear that a fall in government expenditures raises the real exchange rate, increases the production of the traded commodity x_1, while lowering the production of the domestic good x_2, but raising the consumption of *both* commodities and the real money stock.

Figure 4.2 Impacts of the government's expenditure.

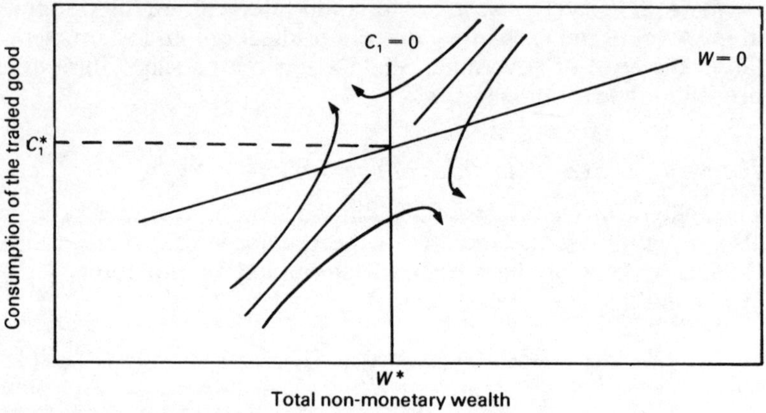

Notice that, in the balance of payments equation (15′), the left-hand side remains unchanged, so that the rise in the production of the traded good is matched by an identical rise in its consumption, which in turn leaves the balance of trade at its previous level. This can be visualized in Figure 4.2 – the fall in government expenditures brings about an upward shift of the $dw/dt = 0$ schedule, with an immediate rise in the consumption of the traded good.

The effect of a reduction of government expenditures on the rate of change of the government debt is then given by:

$$d\,(da/dt) = \tag{18}$$

$$(r^* + \Pi_1)\,\varepsilon^{(\sigma-1)}\,dm + \{(\sigma-1)\,m^*\,\Pi_1\varepsilon^{(\sigma-2)} - ((T^* - g^*)/\varepsilon^2)\}\,d\varepsilon - (1/\varepsilon)\,dg.$$

Besides its direct, one-to-one effect on the rate of debt accumulation, a change (reduction) of government expenditures has some other 'side effects' – (a) since both the real exchange rate and the consumption of the traded commodity rise, the real money stock rises, and as a result there is also an increase in the revenue from the inflation tax; (b) the rise in the real exchange rate, *per se*, has two additional effects: (i) depending on whether in the initial situation the level of taxes T^* is higher or lower than the level of government expenditures g^*, there will be a loss or a gain in government receipts; since in general $T^* < g^*$ is given, this is an additional gain; (ii) although revenues from money creation rise in terms of real money (that is, the nominal money stock will be deflated by the general price level), there is a detraction of such an increase in terms of foreign exchange. Without given particular values for the coefficients involved, it is uncertain which of these effects will dominate, but repeated computer simulations for 'reasonable' values of those coefficients indicate that the net indirect effect is positive, that is, that a reduction in government expenditures decreases the rate of increase in government debt by more than the amount of such a reduction.

Conclusions

The exercise we have just performed serves to clarify and formalize several propositions:

1. The problem of the debt is a problem of the government budget rather than a 'balance of payments' problem. Of course, in any macroeconomic set-up, all variables interact, and policy changes in the components of the government budget do have balance of payments implications, but as we have just shown, there are cases in which effective changes do not necessarily imply or result in an improvement of either the balance of trade or the current account, if the country's balance of payments is correctly defined.
2. In particular, policies aimed at only 'improving' the balance of payments do not necessarily imply an improvement in the debt situation, unless they affect one or more of the three variables that would allow government to solve its debt situation, namely conventional taxes, the 'inflation tax', or the level of expenditures.
3. There seems to be a distinctive advantage in stabilizing the governments' debt situation by a reduction in government expenditures. Not only is such a reduction a gain in itself and seems to win the increasing support of public opinion, but it also seems to have a stronger effect on the debt situation than have equal increases in the level of taxation.

Notes and references

1. Auernheimer, L. (1987) 'On the Outcome of Inconsistent Programs under Exchange Rate and Monetary Rules' *Journal of Monetary Economics* 19: 279–305.

2. Sargent, T.J. and Wallace, N. (1981) Some Unpleasant Monetarist Arithmetic, *Federal Bank of Minneapolis Quarterly Review* 1: 1–17.
3. Rodriguez, C. (1986) 'La Deuda Externa Argentina', *Centro de Estudios Macroeconomicos de Argentina (CEMA)*, Working Papers, p. 54.
4. Calvo, G.A. (1981) 'Devaluation: Levels versus Rates', *Journal of International Economics* 11: 165–72.
5. Obstfeld, M. and Rogoff, K. (1983) 'Speculative Hyperinflations in Maximizing Models: Can we Rule them Out?' *Journal of Political Economy* 91: 675–87.
6. Ibid.
7. See Auernheimer, L., op. cit.
8. Ibid.
9. Ibid.

Chapter five

Debt equity swaps, investment, and creditworthiness: the Chilean example[1]

Rolf Schinke

Introduction

Signs of increasing difficulties in the management of the debt crisis can hardly be overlooked. Opposition rises against the debt strategies pursued so far. New lending is impossible and the burden of indebtedness has tended to increase. Furthermore, the process of adjustment pursued seems to be no longer feasible in some of the highly-indebted countries of Latin America. Calls for debt forgiveness gain in numbers.

Against this background the recent enthusiasm for debt-equity swaps as a new instrument, which seems to enhance growth and to reduce indebtedness (or which at least seems to allow a less pronounced increase of indebtedness) at the same time and at very low cost, is quite understandable. Debt-equity swaps (DES), although not seen as a panacea against the debt crisis, are considered to be a welcome instrument in a market approach to the solution of the debt problems.

One of the main ideas behind DES can be resumed in two sentences from *The Wall Street Journal*.[2] 'When a debt is uncollectable, convert it into equity ownership. If you don't make the payments on your car loan, the bank gets the car'. But this is only one aspect of these transactions. The other is that LDC debts are traded on the secondary loan market with large discounts. Thus, to give an example, in October 1986 Mexican debts had been valued at 58 per cent of their face value. An investor who needed Mexican pesos could buy this currency at a discount if he bought Mexican debts on the secondary market and presented them to the Mexican authorities for redemption. Even if he did not manage to receive 100 per cent of the face value of the loan, the Mexican currency would be sold to him at a highly preferential rate.

Essentially this subsidization inherent in the preferential exchange rate is the cause of a controversy on the benefits of DES.

While some argue that DES will increase foreign investment as a result of the subsidy and, therefore, enhance growth, while at the same time debts are diminished and therefore creditworthiness is increased, others are rather critical of the benefits of DES. They argue that it is incorrect to compare a situation with and without foreign investments because foreign '. . . investment would have come in anyway'[3] or because they regard DES as a means of financing investments that has to be compared with other instruments serving the same objective.[4]

Therefore, the questions to be solved are whether DES will increase foreign investment beyond the level that would be realized anyway and whether DES will promote the debtor countries' creditworthiness. The present study aims at extending this discussion. It is argued that if DES are viewed as an alternative means of financing foreign investment, theoretical arguments for a promotion of foreign investment by DES and empirical evidence for an increase in creditworthiness can hardly be found.

This contribution is organized in the following way. The next section contains a brief summary of the essence of DES transactions, using the Chilean system as an example. It is followed by a summary of the pros and cons of DES. In the following section the question whether DES further foreign investment is discussed. The fourth section is devoted to an empirical investigation of the effects of DES on creditworthiness, taking Chile as a case study. The last section contains some final remarks.

Before the discussion of the main questions of this contribution some definitions have to be clarified. The first concerns the proper meaning of DES. The term is used only if there really is a conversion of debts into equity capital. This is what generally is meant by DES. In some cases, however, debt swaps take on the form of a conversion of debt denominated in foreign currency into a debt denominated in domestic currency. Hence, this will be called debt conversion (DC). Both, DES and DCs are debt swaps. Note that these distinctions are made according to the formal character of the transactions, that is whether the hard currency debts are exchanged into equity or into domestic (soft) currency denominated debts. This procedure must be distinguished from loan currency substitution, which takes place when the monetary authorities sell money market instruments to neutralize an increase in money supply as a result of debt-equity swaps.[5]

DES transactions: maintained advantages and disadvantages

DES were introduced in a number of Latin American countries and in the Philippines. The typical net benefit of DES used for investment in priority projects ranges from 36 per cent in Ecuador to 2.5 per cent plus a 30 per cent tax credit in Argentina.[6] Thus, gains from DES can be substantial if they are compared with an exchange of hard currency at the official exchange rate. The margin narrows down, however, if a black or parallel market is used for comparison, and if the investment is undertaken in sectors with no priority at all. This illustrates the importance of the proper choice of a reference system if one wishes to evaluate the net benefits of DES.

Although Chile was not the first country that introduced debt swaps, its system has become the most famous so far. With all kinds of swaps added up, it succeeded in converting loans of more than 1589 millions of US dollars between June 1985 and January 1987, which is more than 10 per cent of all Chilean external loans eligible for DES (excluding credits from multilateral and governmental sources).[7] Out of all the swaps, the swap transactions of chapters 18 and 19 of the Chilean Foreign Exchange Law account for nearly 1 billion US dollars. The main difference between both chapters of the Chilean system is that chapter 18 transactions involve a loan conversion from US dollar-denominated into peso-denominated debts, while chapter 19 transactions are those which are normally understood as debt-equity swaps – an exchange of debts for equity capital. Beside this difference there is another one which concerns the group of investors. While chapter 18 transactions were designed to give incentives for the repatriation of Chilean flight capital, chapter 19 transactions are more or less destined for foreign investors. In order to provide Chileans with the possibility of doing DES (in the strict sense), an addition to chapter 18 was introduced in 1986. Quantitatively the result of this change has been only of minor importance, however. While chapter 19 transactions have to get approval of the central bank on a case by case basis, chapter 18 transactions underlie an auction mechanism that allows the central bank to capture nearly the whole rent involved. Accordingly, data on yields reveal great differences between both chapters: 2.4 per cent in the chapter 18 auction-loan conversion scheme, and 25.9 per cent for chapter 19 DES.[8]

In view of these returns, proponents of DES generally argue that DES will increase foreign investment and reduce indebtedness at the same time. Thus, the debtor country will have '. . . access to modern technology, management skills and export markets'.[9] Apart from increasing foreign investment, debt swaps are said to give an incentive for the repatriation of flight capital.[10] Others consider DES-related developments as market approaches to the solution of the debt problem,[11] approaches that were prompted among other things by the fact that US banks have recently devaluated part of their Latin American assets. Finally, the debtors hope that, by introducing DES, they might be able to get better terms in the current round of reschedulings.[12] The maintenance of financial stability is considered to be the main problem of DES. Usually DES tend to increase money supply, thereby threatening the stability of the price level, whereas DCs, by issuing new domestic debt instruments at higher financial cost,[13] may lead to budgetary problems. However, as the Chilean system shows, these problems can be overcome by adequate regulations of the market.

In sum, with the help of DES the debtor countries hope to get not only more but also better resources, and at the same time a reduction of the debt service. Thus, growth and creditworthiness would be enhanced.

These arguments can be criticized because it is wrong to compare a situation with DES and one without DES and thereby to assume implicitly that investment increases by the same amount as DES do. DES are a means of financing a (given) investment. Therefore, the alternative to DES is a conventionally financed investment where the investor's hard currency is exchanged at the official rate and where he gets a subsidy equivalent to that implied in DES transactions.[14] On the basis of this assumption it is shown that the debtor country will gain only if the country and the investor gain because the financial cost of the subsidy has to be borne by the debtor country's government. Therefore, DES are beneficial only:[15]

- if they impose negative external effects on others, such as banks;
- if they improve efficiency in the capital market or elsewhere, thus benefiting the debtor country; or
- if the debtor country raises additional gains from DES either by increasing its ability to pay, its creditworthiness, and its sovereignty, or simply because of budget illusions.

Negative external effects can be generated because DES provide incentives for debtor country governments to use debt policy in order to reduce the price of loans in the secondary markets. Inasmuch as this happens, the government can pay a subsidy, which is costless, unless banks react with higher spreads or cancel credits. DES-induced improvements in efficiency are difficult to assess. The transaction costs of both ways of financing differ in several respects. DES may change creditworthiness because they lower or raise some or all of the determinants of creditworthiness as perceived by banks. But it must be kept in mind that conventional financing may equally change creditworthiness and thus leave the outcome insecure.

Therefore, the main distinction between the arguments of the advocates of DES and their opponents concerns the question whether DES do or do not:

- increase the gains from foreign investments beyond a level that would be realized anyway; and/or,
- enhance creditworthiness of the debtor countries that are actively engaged in DES transactions.

DES and net gains from foreign investment

The question to be discussed in this section can be stated in the following way – will DES increase net gains from foreign investment? This question can be subdivided into three further questions:

First, will DES increase net gains from a given amount of investment?

Second, will DES increase investment?

Third, are there any net benefits from additional investments?

As to the first question, namely whether DES will increase net gains from a given amount of investment, it is hard to see any advantage as regards direct profitability in the use of DES as such. A rather large increase in the direct productivity of the project financed by debt swaps is a necessary condition for achieving net gains, for transaction costs involved in swapping are likely to be higher than in conventional financing.[16] As DES are essentially nothing but a different method of financing the same investments, it is not clear where the gain in productivity of the project to be financed should come from.

Therefore, the problem is reduced to the second question, whether or not DES will increase investment and thereby lead to additional gains for the DES country.

If higher returns are necessary for attracting additional foreign investments, the improvement in profitability can be traced back to gains in direct returns or in indirect returns. The latter may be split into higher subsidies and reductions in risk, which may stem from increased legal protection of property, better use of macroeconomic policy especially in the field of foreign exchange and external debt, and so on. Generally, DES affect returns via the same channels as conventional methods of financing. An increase in indirect returns might be achieved by implying higher subsidies or a reduction in risk. As in the previous case, with conventional methods of financing foreign investments as a point of reference, it is difficult to see where additional direct returns should come from. By definition, there is no direct additional advantage for the investor in using DES because it is assumed that the funds are allocated to the same use irrespective of how the investment is financed. Hence, additional returns can only be explained by the non-equivalence of the subsidies or by a different impact of DES on risk reduction compared with conventional methods of finance.

Thus it is possible that the investor reaps additional returns from DES if one or several of the following conditions hold:

First, in the debtor country there might be political opposition to overt subsidization as compared with more hidden forms of subsidizing by DES. If so, DES can imply higher subsidies.

Second, the assumption of equal transaction costs may be wrong. Thus there might be a higher subsidy net of transaction costs in the DES case.

Third, there may be an improvement in creditworthiness if DES affect the determinants of creditworthiness more positively than conventional methods of financing foreign investments would do. In that case investors might fear future exchange restrictions less.

The discussion so far leads to the conclusion that reduced resistance to disguised forms of subsidies paid to foreigners, lower transaction costs, or an increase in creditworthiness may bring about an increase in returns and, therefore, more foreign investments, provided they are financed by DES rather than otherwise. The empirical relevance and the logical consistency of these arguments for DES, however, seem to be small. The first argument rests on the assumption that individuals have illusions about the true nature of DES and therefore react irrationally. Apart from the fact that a perceived irrationality points to errors in model building,[17] it is an empirical question whether individuals have illusions or not and if so, how long they will persist. Second, as already mentioned, it seems unlikely that transaction costs for investments financed by DES will be lower than those financed conventionally. Although spreads and commissions for DES transactions have been lowered substantially,[18] they are still considerably higher than in normal foreign exchange transactions. With regard to the third argument, it seems rather unlikely that an investor will associate increased creditworthiness with his investment. Besides, it is an empirical question whether DES will promote creditworthiness more than conventionally-financed foreign direct investments. This problem will be discussed at more length in the next section.

The next question that has to be dealt with concerns the problem whether there are net benefits from additional foreign investments induced by DES (assuming there are additional investments). The consumption benefits from these investments are by no means cost free. Therefore, a closer look at these costs is necessary. Generally these costs consist of the benefits from the best alternative use of the investor's capital and the government's resources for the subsidy.

In this context, one might first ask whether subsidies are a necessary tool for attracting investments in LDCs at all. According to the infant industry argument for protection, investors must be given a subsidy to induce them to build up new industries when private returns are inadequate. From a social viewpoint the subsidies are justified, for the new industries give rise to external economies. This argumentation does not discriminate between domestic or foreign investors – it applies to both in the same way. The underlying assumption of this argument is that the net present value of the net returns of capital outlays and subsidies together is positive, even though that of the private returns of the investment alone is negative.

However, in the case of foreign investments a qualification has to be made. The infant industry argument is in favour of the protection of new lines of production, where inefficiencies result from unexperienced workers, and where hopefully the disadvantages will diminish in a not too distant future, while the benefits accrue to others. Most foreign investments in LDCs, however, are made in a limited group of higher income countries, where a body of trained workers exists, and where returns of investments are usually higher than in the developed or other less-developed countries.[19] Therefore the infant industry argument for protection cannot really be considered to be in favour of subsidizing foreign investments in the highly-indebted countries.

The force of this argument is still greater in the case of DES, where transactions are often executed with the intention to acquire existing plants or firms instead of building up new industries. This at least holds true for Chile. Furthermore, subsidies implied by DES are rather unspecific as to the disadvantages that should be compensated for. Thus, they cannot really be seen as a compensation for losses in the early stages of production.

Therefore, subsidizing foreign investments cannot normally be based on market failure arguments as in the case of the infant industries. This result is troublesome, for it makes it more difficult for politicians to justify their subsidies at all.

Here one might point out that it is not correct to compare DES with a situation without any subsidies at all, but that they should be compared with a situation where subsidizing proceeds frankly and is of the same size as implied by DES. The assumption of subsidizing investments anyhow rules out the relevance of the argument that scarce government resources are wasted when a system of DES is introduced. Therefore, the question whether subsidies constitute a waste if foreign investors plan to invest in the DES country anyhow, does not help to evaluate DES. So far, the argumentation presented above is not an argument against DES but against all kinds of subsidies for foreign investments that do not accord with the underlying assumptions of the infant industry argument.

A different evaluation will result if one departs from the assumption that equivalent subsidies and political factors lead to higher subsidization through DES. Then additional current investments are either deducted from present investment in other countries or from future investment in the DES country. Apparently both cases differ in the opportunity costs of capital, which are equal to the sum of discounted future consumption streams out of the initial investment. In the first case (diversion from future to present investment) the opportunity costs are rather high if one assumes that the same investment without subsidies would have been carried out some periods later, generating the same stream of consumption and differing only in the weights used for discounting. Even if the net present value of the investment without subsidies is positive, it is likely to become negative if subsidies are paid.

In the second case, where an inter-country diversion of investment takes place, the opportunity cost of capital is zero as there is only a loss of consumption in another country. In order to result in a positive net present value, the returns net of all other costs must exceed the opportunity costs of capital and those of the subsidy.

Under *ceteris paribus* assumptions, this is more likely in the second than in the first case.

The positive result in the case of inter-country diversion of investments rests partly on the assumption that there are no repercussions from the country from which the investment is diverted, either because there is no trade in goods and/or factors between them and effects via third countries are negligible, or because the country from which the capital is diverted does not realize that a subsidy caused the diversion. However, once this has become obvious, the losing country may react in a beggar-my-neighbour manner. In both countries a waste of resources may ensue from increasing subsidies. DES-systems, by their very nature, imply incentives for debtor countries to profit from bad debt policies,[20] for they lower the price of their debts in the secondary markets. This seems to imply that the cost of higher subsidies are to be borne by banks. However, by applying this argument one neglects the fact that these benefits are gained at the expense of a lower ranking in creditworthiness. The ensuing costs may overcompensate for the gain from bad debt policies.

In sum, it is rather unlikely that a country will gain from DES. First it is very improbable that DES will increase investments; second – if they do – it is likely that costs exceed benefits. The only advantage is that DES can create positive external effects by increasing creditworthiness. This question will be dealt with in the next section.

The effects of DES on creditworthiness

Since the beginning of the debt crisis creditors have become more and more interested in studying the determinants of the debtor countries' creditworthiness. Although the methods applied in the studies published so far vary substantially, there seems to be some consensus concerning the main determinants of creditworthiness (debt-output ratio, debt-service exports ratio, reserves-GNP ratio, and so on). Table 5.1 shows determinants used in two of the more recent analyses as well as the signs of the regression coefficients expected from the theoretical reasoning and those obtained in the publications by Edwards[21] and McFadden *et al.*[22]

The following questions will be discussed in this section:

- What are the effects of DES on creditworthiness?
- Are there any reasons to prefer DES to the conventional financing of foreign direct investment?

Table 5.1 Determinants of creditworthiness: significant variables

Variables		*Sign*[a]		
Names	*Specification*[b]	*Hypothesized sign*	*Signs found in empirical analysis of* Edwards (1984)	McFadden et al. (1985)
1. Debt-output ratio	Public and publicly - guaranteed long–term debt outstanding and disbursed (DOD): GNP (WDT).	+	+	
2. Debt-service-exports ratio	Interest and principal repayments on DOD: exports of goods and services (WDT).	+	+	+
3. Debt-exports ratio	DOD: exports of goods and non-factor services (World Tables).	+		+
4. Reserves-GNP/GDP ratio	*Edwards*: reserves: GNP (IFS). *McFadden et al*: (reserves–gold): GDP (supposedly IFS).	–	–	–
5. Average propensity to invest	Gross domestic investment: GDP (*Edwards*: World Tables and World Development Report; own analysis: IFS).	–/+	–	
6. Current account-GDP ratio	Balance of current account: GDP (*Edwards*: see 5; own analysis: IFS)	–/+	+	
7. Income per capita	Real GNP per capita (World Tables).	–		–

8. Growth rate of real GDP per capita	(see 7).	−	−
9. Average propensity to import	Imports of goods and non-factor services: GDP (World Tables, IFS).	+	+
10. Loan duration	Weighted average from all loans per year (*Edwards*: in years, BICM; own analysis: in months, BCDC).	−/+	
11. Dummy	1976-81: 0; since 1982:1.	+	

Notes:

(a) Symbols: + (−) sign of regression coefficients.
no entry: variable has not been used or has been insignificant.

(b) WDT: Definition and data from World Bank (World Debt Tables).
IFS: Definition and data from IMF (International Financial Statistics).
BICM: Data from World Bank (Borrowing in International Capital Markets).
BCDC: Data from Banco Central de Chile (*Boletin Mensual*).

According to these questions two comparisons of creditworthiness can be made:

(a) a comparison before and after the debt swaps have been carried out; and
(b) a comparison between different ways of financing foreign direct investments in order to evaluate whether they lead to different changes in creditworthiness. The second comparison indicates which practice of finance should be preferred.

Table 5.1 clearly illustrates that DES influence creditworthiness in a variety of ways. Debt may decrease and so may the debt service. Investment may increase, causing a growth of production. Thus several determinants of creditworthiness will change as long as debt swaps continue. However, it must be recognized that the conventional financing of investment may change creditworthiness, too. There may be an increase in reserves if the central bank exchanges investors' funds at the official exchange rate. As in the case of DES, an increase in investment is likely to happen. Therefore, all variables of Table 5.1, with the exception of loan duration and the dummy, may be affected by DES and its competitive way of financing. A comparison of the situation with and without DES respectively shows that debt swaps will generally bring about higher creditworthiness. But the same is true for conventional financing. Unfortunately no more can be said at the moment. Detailed information on the weight of the determinants of creditworthiness is needed. For this reason an empirical analysis of the determinants of creditworthiness has been carried out on the basis of Chilean data. In order to execute the comparisons it was necessary to assume that a fixed amount of foreign investments will be financed either conventionally or by DES. In this case the assumption was that additional investments of 4 billion US dollars would be executed. The reason for choosing this sum is as simple as arbitrary – it is the (maximum) amount of DES the Chilean Minister of Finance, Mr Buchi, expects to be executed.[23] Because of data restrictions it was also assumed that these investments were executed at the very beginning of 1985.

The effects of these hypothetical DES on macroeconomic data are shown in Table 5.2. The second column (headed by '1985') contains the data of the 'without situation' as they are reported in *World Debt Tables* and *International Financial Statistics.* Column 3 (1985*) gives the data for the same variables after the completion of the swaps, with the assumption that capacity effects of the investment can be ignored.[24] Alternatively, column 4 (1985**) shows the data when hypothetical foreign investments of 4 billion US dollars lead to an additional capital stock of the same amount. A decrease in the Chilean foreign debt of 4,000 million US dollars leads to a stock of debt that prevailed at some time in 1984 (lines 1(a) and 1(b)). This decline reduced the debt service (lines 2(a) and 2(b)). According to the assumptions described above, the gross national product (GNP) and gross domestic product (GDP) are only affected by capacity effects in 1985**. The difference in GNP between 1985 and 1985* can be explained by a small change in net factor payments abroad, which resulted from the decrease in interest payments. As regards exports, it was assumed that they are completely determined by the import demand in the partner countries so that there is no change at all. The ratios which indicate the burden of indebtedness (debt-output ratio and debt-service-exports ratio) decline as a result of the reduction of debts and debt service (1985* and 1985**). Furthermore, the debt-output ratio is reduced as a result of the increase in the GNP. The average propensity to invest is the same for 1985 and for 1985*. However,

Table 5.2 Effects of a decrease in Chilean external debts by 4,000 million US dollars using DES (in millions of US dollars or in percent unless otherwise stated)

Effects	*1984*	*1985*	*1985**	*1985***
1. (a) Public and publicly-guaranteed long-term debt outstanding and disbursed	10,838.9	12,934.2	8,934.2	8,934.2
(b) Financial markets	8,785.2	10,381.0	6,381.0	6,381.0
2. (a) Service on debts defined in 1(a)	1,259.5	1,230.7	830.7	830.7
(b) Service on debts defined in 1(b)	892.0	960.7	560.7	560.7
3. (a) Implicit rate of debt service $= [(2b)_t : ((1b)_t + (1b)_{t-1})/2] \cdot 100$	12.9	10.0	–	–
(b) Implicit interest rate on 1(b)	11.8	8.9	–	–
4. Decrease of debt service by swaps of 4,000 million US dollars (10% of 4,000 million $)	–	–	400.0	400.0
5. Gross national product (GNP)	17,240.6	14,097.1	14,453.1	15,024.5
6. Exports of goods and services	4,814.0	4,669.0	4,669.0	4,669.0
7. Debt-output ratio	62.9	91.8	61.8	59.5
8. Debt-service-exports ratio	26.2	26.4	17.8	17.8
9. Gross domestic investment	2,615.1	2,192.7	2,192.7	6,192.7
10. Gross domestic product (in millions of US dollars)	19,191.2	15,995.8	15,995.8	16,567.2
(in billions of pesos)	1,893.4	2,576.6	2,576.6	2,668.6
11. Average propensity to invest	13.6	13.7	13.7	37.4
12. Reserves-GNP ratio	16.1	20.9	20.9	19.6
13. Imports of goods and non-factor services[a]	479.6	678.1	678.1	903.6
14. Exports of goods and non-factor services[a]	459.5	749.2	749.2	749.2
15. Correction for decrease in interest payments[a]	–	–	57.3	57.3
16. Balance of current account[a] (=(14)+(15)−(13))	−20.1	17.1	128.4	−97.1
17. Current account-GDP-ratio	−1.1	2.8	5.0	−3.6

Source: Own calculations from data in IMF (International Financial Statistics) and World Bank (World Debt Tables).

Note:

(a) Billions of pesos. For lack of data net factor payments abroad are excluded from figures in line 16.

it increases drastically if the capacity effects of DES are considered. The ratio of reserves to GNP is the same in all three columns for 1985, with the assumption that DES do not affect reserves. As the imports of goods and non-factor services weigh heavily in investment expenditures (for example, the average percentage share of imports in investment rose from 30 to 40 per cent between 1979 and 1982), imports increase strongly if the capacity effect is taken into account. Line 15 is the peso equivalent for the change in interest payments. After an examination of the changes which occur if DES-financed investments of 4 billion US dollars are executed, the next step will be to infer the weight of the determinants of creditworthiness as they are perceived by creditors. A model developed by Feder and Just,[25] and applied by Edwards[26] was used to analyze the determinants of Chile's creditworthiness.

The main idea of this model is that the spread is a measure of risk. The higher the probability of default, the higher is the risk and thus the spread, and the lower is creditworthiness. Specifically, it is assumed that the relation of the spread (s) and the probability of default (p) is given by

$$s = [p/(1-p)]g \tag{1}$$

where g takes into account all other influences on s except the default probability. Next the authors assumed a logistic function for p:

$$p = \exp(a + \Sigma\, b_i X_i)/(1 + \exp(a + \Sigma\, b_i X_i)) \tag{2}$$

with X_i as the determinants of the default probability.

Both equations yield

$$\ln s = a + \Sigma\, b_i X_i + \ln g. \tag{3}$$

Combining a and $\ln g$ to the intercept b_o yields the equation to be estimated:

$$\ln s_t = b_{0t} + \Sigma\, b_{it} X_{it} + \mu_t \tag{4}$$

where X_{it} are the determinants of creditworthiness at a time t and μ_t is the disturbance term assumed to possess the usual properties for OLS estimation.

Table 5.1 contains the variables that were used in the empirical analysis.[27] According to the small number of observations only a limited number of them was applied:

1. The debt-output ratio can be regarded as an indicator of a country's solvency, for the output is an indicator of a country's productive wealth. The higher the debt-output ratio, the less is a country's productive wealth in relation to its debts and the higher is the risk associated with indebtedness. Therefore, one would expect a positive sign in the regression analysis.
2. The ratio of debt service to exports of goods and services is usually regarded as a measure of the liquidity risk. Rising ratios indicate higher risks and, therefore, lead to higher spreads. As before, the sign should be positive. The same argument holds for the debt-export ratio.
3. An indicator of a country's existing liquidity is the reserves-GNP ratio. The higher the value of this ratio, the lower is the risk of becoming illiquid. The expected sign is, therefore, negative.
4. Some authors regard the average propensity to invest as an indicator of the country's future growth prospects. Thus, it seems reasonable to expect a negative sign. On the other hand, one might argue that with given domestic savings, foreign savings must increase to finance a higher volume of investment. Thus, both signs are theoretically plausible.
5. The current account-GDP ratio can show either a positive or a negative sign. The usual argument is that a given debt can be reduced the more, the higher the surplus on the current account is. This line of reasoning suggests a negative sign.

   A positive sign results from the following argumentation: with domestic savings given, a higher current account surplus or a lower deficit reduces a country's capacity to invest, which in turn reduces its growth prospects and therefore augments the risk associated with indebtedness. Thus, with this coefficient a positive sign could be expected just as well.
6. The per capita income is used to measure the relative size of a country. According to the debt-cycle hypothesis, one may expect that with growing per capita incomes the probability of getting current account surpluses increases, thereby reducing indebtedness. Thus, a negative sign may be expected.
7. A high rate of growth of the real gross domestic product is usually regarded as an indicator of a dynamic economy, which has less trouble with structural adjustments. A negative sign is hypothesized.

8. The average propensity to import is a measure of a country's openness. Open economies are usually affected more seriously than economies that are more closed. Therefore, one would expect a positive sign.
9. The sign of loan duration is ambiguous. Normally one would expect a positive sign because a longer duration implies a higher risk. On the other hand, one may argue that an extended duration is an indicator of a better standing, with all other variables being given. This would imply a negative sign.
10. Finally a dummy was applied in the empirical analysis. Banks may have changed their attitude towards their debtors immediately after the beginning of the debt crisis, associating a higher risk with given values of the determinants of creditworthiness. Thus, generally one would expect a positive sign.

The data used as regressors were taken from the IMF (*International Financial Statistics*), and from the World Bank (*World Debt Tables*). Data about the spread were taken from the Banco Central de Chile (*Boletín Mensual*). In its monthly bulletin, the Chilean central bank publishes a series on external loans entered through article 14 of the Chilean foreign exchange laws; this series contains data on the spread as the weighted average of those loans that were disbursed in the province of Santiago. In general these loans make more than 98 per cent of all the loans entered through article 14. From these loans, only those with a variable interest rate were used in the analysis. The data reveal more or less the general pattern of the spread for all debtor countries, although some Chilean properties can be observed. The series begin in 1976 with a very high level of the spread (2.5 per cent), which may be explained by the financial troubles Chile had in the first years after the *coup d'état*. After reaching its maximum of 2.57 per cent in 1977, the spread steadily declined until 1981–2 (1.11 per cent). As mentioned above, the banks may have changed their attitude towards debtors after the beginning of the debt crisis. Therefore, the spread may have increased to 1.56 per cent in 1983, then declined by 14 basis points in 1984 and finally reached a very high level of 2.25 per cent in 1986. Compared with the spread for all developing countries,[28] the spread on Chilean loans has generally been substantially higher, although the difference between both declined a bit in the course of time.

The results of the regression analysis are given in Table 5.3. The dependent variable is always the logarithm of the spread. Three types of equations were applied. The first is based on the debt-

Table 5.3 Determinants of creditworthiness: Chile, 1976–86[a]

	Equations							
Variable	*(5)*	*(6)*	*(7)*	*(8)*	*(9)*	*(10)*	*(11)*	*(12)*
Debt-output ratio	1.247	1.440	1.087	0.919	1.182			
	(5.47)	(6.59)	(4.59)	(3.11)	(8.56)			
Debt-service-exports ratio						3.073	1.756	2.477
						(4.39)	(3.19)	(3.48)
Reserves-GNP ratio	−6.240	−5.305	−3.857	−5.821			−15.690	0.016[c]
	(−4.46)	(−4.24)	(−3.22)	(−4.47)			(−3.88)[b]	(1.74)
Square of reserves-GNP ratio							57.514	
							(3.75)[b]	
Average propensity to invest				4.051	−6.912			
				(2.21)	(−6.74)			
Current account-GDP ratio			2.896	4.968		5.458	3.471	5.313
			(2.22)	(2.26)		(5.21)	(4.03)	(5.65)
Dummy [0: 1976–81]		−0.253	−0.332		−0.837			
[1: otherwise]		(−2.10)	(−3.23)		(−8.54)			
Intercept	0.803	0.712	0.739	0.315	1.457	−0.282	0.999	−0.268
	(5.47)	(5.48)	(7.05)	(1.19)	(7.89)	(−1.42)	(2.86)	(−1.52)
R^2	0.79	0.87	0.93	0.89	0.94	0.84	0.96	0.89
$\bar{R}^2$	0.73	0.81	0.88	0.82	0.91	0.80	0.93	0.84
F	14.63	15.40	19.23	12.23	34.94	20.89	31.87	18.46
DW	2.29	3.10	3.03	2.96	2.44	2.94	2.99	2.84

Notes:

(a) t-values in parentheses.
(b) F-values for both variables to be equal to zero is 15.445.
(c) Regression coefficient for reciprocal of reserves-GDP-ratio.

output and reserves-GNP ratio as regressors (equations (5)–(8)). The second type is characterized by the use of the debt-output ratio and the average propensity to invest as independent variables (equation (9)). The third type relied mainly on the debt-service-exports ratio and the current account-GDP ratio (equations (10)–(12)). The limited number of observations precludes the combined use of all or a larger set of variables in one equation. As a general rule, only those variables were included that yielded at least a 5 per cent significance level. There are only two exceptions to this: in equation (12) the reciprocal of the reserves-GNP ratio is significant only at the 12.6 per cent level, and in equation (6) the significance level of the dummy variable is 7.3 per cent.

In the first type of equation nearly all coefficients show the hypothesized sign with the exception of the dummy variable. Contrary to what was expected, its sign was negative and its coefficient was significant at the 7.3 or 2 per cent level. This can hardly be interpreted as a change in the creditors' attitude towards the debtors as a result of the debt crisis, for this change occurred one year earlier than hypothesized and in the opposite direction – with the other conditions remaining constant, the banks have been lowering their spreads on Chilean loans since the end of 1981. One explanation could be that foreign creditors honoured the attempts of the Chilean government to bring down the inflation rate from very high levels in the mid-1970s to less than 30 per cent, while there was a marked opening of the economy, a reduction of fiscal deficits, and an accumulation of reserves at the same time. This may be interpreted that banks were not fully aware of the problems to come. In all these equations the debt-service-exports ratio yielded insignificant results so that this variable was removed. Furthermore, these equations reveal that the banks attach a relatively great importance to the debtor countries' reserves. Equation (8) should be interpreted with caution. The average propensity to invest and the current account-GDP ratio are highly correlated. On the whole these equations show relatively stable regression coefficients for the debt-output and reserves-GNP ratios.

There is a reversal of the sign of the average propensity to invest in equation (9). As discussed earlier, both signs are plausible for this variable. Again, the influence of the dummy variable is opposite to what was expected, but this time it is significant at a higher than the 0.1 per cent level. As this variable is most significant when the propensity to invest is entered into and the reserves-GNP ratio removed from the equation, one may conclude that the dummy mainly reflects events that are not related to investment.

The last set of equations ((10)–(12)) is based primarily on the debt-service-exports and current account-GDP ratios. Both variables have the expected signs and are significant at a satisfactory level. In these equations the use of the unmodified reserves-GNP ratio never yielded satisfactory results. Therefore, transformations were applied. In addition to the original variable, its square was used (equation (11)), while its reciprocal was applied in equation (12). As indicated above, the significance level of the reciprocal was rather unsatisfactory.

The values of the summary statistics of the regressions are acceptable. If the limited number of observations is taken into account, the autocorrelation of residuals seems to be weak.

The fact that the debt-output ratio is significant when the debt-service-exports ratio is not (and vice versa) is troublesome because it is not clear whether the Chilean creditor banks regarded Chile's debt crisis as being caused by illiquidity or insolvency. However, as DES affect both the debt-output ratio and the debt-service-exports ratio in the same direction, the problem of diagnosing the nature of the debt crisis is only of secondary importance.

As can be seen from equations (5)–(8), the coefficient of the reserves-GNP ratio takes on a relatively high value. As Table 5.4 shows, the absolute values of the reserve-GNP elasticity are more or less equal to the debt service elasticity, and always higher than those of the debt-output ratio. This observation partly confirms a result obtained by Edwards, where '. . . countries that want to reduce the probability of being excluded from the international financial market, due to an increase in the perceived probability of default, should be particularly careful in managing their international reserves'.[29]

Table 5.4 Selected spread elasticities[1,2] with respect to changes in determinants of creditworthiness

Determinants	*Equations*						
	(5)	*(6)*	*(7)*	*(8)*	*(9)*	*(10)*	*(12)*
Debt-output ratio	1.04	1.20	0.90	0.76	0.98		
Debt-service-export ratio						1.66	1.34
Reserves-GNP ratio	−1.60	−1.36	−0.99	−1.49			
(Reserves-GNP ratio)$^{-1}$							0.29
Average propensity to invest				1.22	−2.08		
Current account-GDP ratio			−0.06	−0.10		−0.11	−0.11

Notes:

1 Evaluated at means.
2 Logarithm of spread.

Table 5.5 Probabilities of default: Chile, 1976–86

Equation	*1976*	*1977*	*1978*	*1979*	*1980*	*1981*	*1982*	*1983*	*1984*	*1985*	*1985**	*1985***	*1986*
(5)	0.522	0.510	0.444	0.367	0.322	0.355	0.394	0.394	0.445	0.460	0.370	0.382	0.508
(6)	0.555	0.535	0.480	0.408	0.362	0.388	0.371	0.384	0.450	0.490	0.384	0.393	0.539
(7)	0.574	0.515	0.465	0.416	0.371	0.349	0.359	0.402	0.425	0.485	0.420	0.367	0.529
(8)	0.673	0.614	0.569	0.504	0.476	0.454	0.476	0.509	0.534	0.580	0.539	0.677	0.640
(9)	0.392	0.339	0.292	0.280	0.224	0.198	0.207	0.257	0.262	0.332	0.259	0.062	0.338
(10)	0.767	0.719	0.745	0.660	0.609	0.586	0.625	0.670	0.678	0.724	0.694	0.587	0.760
(11)	0.488	0.473	0.409	0.331	0.308	0.289	0.318	0.343	0.351	0.449	0.430	0.337	0.454
(12)	0.779	0.743	0.732	0.652	0.604	0.579	0.630	0.670	0.666	0.707	0.686	0.582	0.740
Edwards (79)[a]	0.558	0.543	0.543	0.533	0.522	0.518	0.533	0.556	0.595	0.637	0.591	0.587	0.652
Edwards (80)[a]	0.610	0.582	0.584	0.570	0.551	0.541	0.569	0.611	0.679	0.749	0.676	0.668	0.769
McFadden[b]	0.510	0.480	0.350	0.570	0.470	0.440	0.650	0.950	0.660	0.570	—	—	—

Notes:

a Own calculations based on Edwards's regression estimates (in Edwards, (1986) p. S91.), including the variables with significant coefficients only.
b McFadden *et al.*, (1985) p. 197.

Table 5.5 contains the Chilean default probabilities from 1976 to 1986 according to equation (2), using the coefficients from equations (5)–(12). For the purpose of comparison, default probabilities from McFadden *et al.*[30] and those obtained by using the regression result from Edwards[31] and applying it to Chilean data are added. These data reveal that in the early years banks considered Chilean credits to be risky. From 1978 to 1980–81 creditworthiness improved significantly. However, the banks judged the situation to be worsening during the course of the Chilean boom period in the early 1980s. This development of declining creditworthiness continued until 1986. Against this background, one may ask about the possible effects of the DES of 4 billion of US dollars that were assumed to have been executed at the beginning of 1985. The results of this experiment are shown in columns 1985* and 1985**. The difference between both columns is caused by the inclusion (1985**) or non-inclusion (1985*) of the capacity effect of investments as explained above. The decline of the default probability between 1985 and 1985* is large in those equations that contain the debt-output ratio as a regressor.

Contrary to these results are those obtained from equations (10)–(12) in which the default probability decreases less and where the debt-service-exports ratio is used. If the capacity effect is accounted for (1985**), the probability of default changes less markedly in those equations that contain the debt-output ratio as an independent variable. It declines drastically when the average propensity to invest is negative and less dramatically when the debt-service-export ratio is used. The result of equation (8) is a little striking because the default probability increases. This is mainly due to the positive sign of the investment variable in that equation. However, as indicated above, this result should not be taken too seriously. The intercorrelation of the variables raises objections to it.

Thus, the decline of the default probabilities in columns 1985* and 1985** may be seen as a valuable contribution to the recovery of creditworthiness. Nevertheless, it would have been insufficient if the objective of DES had been to re-establish creditworthiness. With the exception of equation (6) and, if the capacity effect is taken into account, of equations (9) and (10), the probabilities obtained for 1985* or 1985** are significantly higher than those prevailing before the outbreak of the debt crisis. In addition, if one takes into account the possibility that the banks' attitudes towards their creditors might change, it seems not very likely that creditworthiness would have been re-established. This result is reinforced if the possibility is taken into account that there may be no complete correspondence between the DES and the additions to the capital stock. The Chilean DES system is organized in such a way that debt swaps are not automatically productive investments.

So far, the evaluation of DES in the empirical analysis has rested on a comparison of the situation with and without DES respectively. As was demonstrated in the theoretical analysis, a proper evaluation requires a comparison between DES and conventionally-financed investments. The result of this comparison is presented in Table 5.6. The underlying assumption was that in both cases investments of 4 billion US dollars with identical capacity effects were realized. The only difference between them consists in the way the subsidy is paid. It is furthermore assumed that DES affect creditworthiness only through the debt-output ratio, the debt-service-exports ratio and – where applicable – the current account-GDP ratio and average propensity to invest, while the reserves-GNP ratio remains nearly unchanged. Compared with DES, conventionally-financed investments increase the reserves-GNP ratio while leaving the other ratios unchanged. Furthermore, it is assumed that in the case of conventionally-financed investments, additional foreign exchange in the hands of the central bank will be invested in the financial markets rather than used to repurchase foreign debts (because this would yield the same result as DES). The resulting change in the spread (in percentage points) is given in the last line of Table 5.6. It demonstrates the superiority of conventional financing as compared with DES in the majority of the equations. Thus DES can improve creditworthiness, but the gain will usually be higher if investments are financed in a conventional manner. Only in those equations where the reserves-GNP ratio was not used, or where it was applied in a transformed way, conventional financing of foreign direct investment would result in somewhat higher spreads than DES financing would do. But as explained above, there are reasons for objecting to the use of equations (10)–(12).

Final remarks

The results of the last two sections contrast with the enthusiasm which is usually found in the financial press when DES are discussed. As has been shown, there is normally not much room left for optimism as far as additional investment is concerned. It has been demonstrated that additional investment occurs only if there are substantial illusions about the true nature of DES. But even if there are illusions, it is not altogether clear whether a country which engages in DES activities can reap appreciable gains

Table 5.6 Changes in spreads induced by swap-financed and conventionally-financed investments

Variable	*Equation*													
	(5)		*(6)*		*(7)*		*(8)*		*(9)*		*(10)*		*(12)*	
	DES financing	*Conventional financing*	*DES financing*	*Conventional financing*	*DES financing*	*Conventional financing*	*DES financing*	*Conventional financing*	*DES financing*	*Conventional financing*	*DES financing*	*Conventional financing*	*DES financing*	*Conventional financing*
Debt-output ratio	−0.403	−0.071	−0.465	−0.082	−0.351	−0.062	−0.297	−0.052	−0.382	−0.067				
Debt-service-export ratio											−0.264	0	−0.213	0
Reserves-GNP ratio	0.081	−1.585	0.069	−1.347	0.050	−0.980	0.076	−1.479					0.005	−0.042
Average propensity to invest							0.960	0.960	−1.638	−1.638				
Current account-GDP ratio					−0.185	−0.185	−0.318	−0.318			−0.349	−0.349	−0.340	−0.340
Change in l*n* *s*	−0.322	−1.656	−0.396	−1.430	−0.486	−1.227	0.421	−0.889	−2.020	−1.706	−0.614	−0.349	−0.548	−0.382
l*n* *s*, before changes	0.779	0.779	0.779	0.779	0.779	0.779	0.779	0.779	0.779	0.779	0.779	0.779	0.779	0.779
l*n* *s*, after changes	0.457	−0.877	0.383	−0.651	0.293	−0.448	1.200	−0.109	−1.241	−0.927	0.165	0.430	0.231	0.397
s, after change	1.580	0.416	1.466	0.522	1.340	0.639	3.320	0.896	0.289	0.396	1.180	1.537	1.260	1.487
s, before change	2.180	2.180	2.180	2.180	2.180	2.180	2.180	2.180	2.180	2.180	2.180	2.180	2.180	2.180
Change in *s*	−0.600	−1.760	−0.710	−1.658	−0.840	−1.540	1.140	−1.284	−1.891	−1.784	−1.000	−0.643	−0.920	−0.693

from DES. It may happen that the costs exceed the benefits of the DES system. Most likely a different evaluation of DES systems stems from the fact that usually an incorrect comparison is made.

Compared with traditional means of financing foreign investment, there is no reason to expect additional investments from DES if the present value of the subsidy is the same in both. The same idea applies to the argument that DES might facilitate the repatriation of flight capital. A result identical to the one reached by DES can be obtained by overt subsidization. Besides, the argument that the debtor countries might get better terms in the next rounds of reschedulings is not very forceful. It has been demonstrated that, although DES can improve creditworthiness, subsidy-induced direct investments with their accompanying increase in reserves will most likely increase creditworthiness even more.

Finally, the argument that DES represent a market approach to the solution of the debt problem is misleading. With yields of approximately 15 per cent[32] or 25 per cent as in the Chilean DES system, which last for some time, there must be something wrong with the state of the markets. As a matter of fact, such high profits are only possible if these markets are regulated. Indeed, the auction system of chapter 18 loan conversions and the case-by-case treatment of chapter 19 transactions give an idea of the regulations involved. Under these circumstances the market will possibly give the wrong signals for investment.

Notes and references

1. The author is grateful for comments on an earlier version of this contribution by Leonardo Auernheimer, Manfred Borchert, Helmut Hesse, Patricio Meller, Feli Nowak, and Heinz G. Preusse.
2. *The Wall Street Journal*, 26 October 1986.
3. Dornbusch, R. cited in Marton, A. (1987) 'The Debate Over Debt-For-Equity Swaps', in *Institutional Investor*, February, pp. 115–17.
4. Franke, G. (1987) 'Economic Analysis of Debt-Equity Swaps', Paper presented at the Symposium 'New Institutional Arrangements for the World Economy', in Konstanz (FRG), p. 4.
5. Franke, G., ibid., p. 13.
6. 'Profile of Debt-to-Equity Conversion Programs Worldwide', *Business Latin America*, 20 April 1987, p. 124.
7. Garces Garrido, F. (1987) 'Comentario sobre Conversiones de Deuda Externa en Chile', *Boletín Mensual*, no. 710 (April 1987), Banco Central de Chile, p. 865.
8. Garces Garrido, F., ibid., p. 867.
9. *World Financial Markets*, June/July 1987, p. 12; the same idea is expressed in several other articles, for instance, in Schubert, M.

(1987) 'Trading Debt for Equity', *The Banker* 137 (732):18.
10. *World Financial Markets,* ibid., p. 12.
11. Feldstein, M. (1987) 'Latin America's Debt. Muddling Through can be Just Fine', *The Economist,* July, pp. 21–5.
12. Marton, A., op. cit., p. 116.
13. *World Financial Markets,* op. cit., p. 13.
14. Franke, G., op. cit., p. 4.
15. Franke, G., op. cit., p. 3.
16. French, M. (1987) 'Swapping Debt – Just Hot Air?' *Euromoney,* May, p. 115; Ollard, W. (1986) 'The Debt Swappers', *Euromoney,* August, p. 73.
17. Becker, G.S. (1976) *The Economic Approach of Human Behavior,* Chicago: chapter 1.
18. French, M., op. cit., p. 115.
19. *World Bank,* World Development Report 1985, p. 135.
20. Franke, G., op. cit., p. 16.
21. Edwards, S. (1984a) 'LDC Foreign Borrowing and Default Risk: An Empirical Investigation, 1976 – 1980', *American Economic Review,* 74: 726–34; Edwards, S. (1984b) 'Deuda Externa y Riesgo de País', *Cuadernos de Economia* 62: 3–22.
22. McFadden, D. *et al.* (1985) 'Is There Life after Debt? An Econometric Analysis of the Creditworthiness of Developing Countries', in Smith, G.W. and Cuddington, J.T. (eds) (1985) *International Debt and the Developing Countries,* Washington, DC: World Bank, pp. 179–209.
23. Ollard, W., op. cit., p. 73.
24. This assumption can be justified if one assumes that swaps lead only to portfolio investments without any increase of the capital stock.
25. Feder, G. and Just, R.E. (1977) 'An Analysis of Credit Terms in the Eurodollar Market', *European Economic Review* 9: 222–43.
26. Edwards, S. (1984a), op. cit.; Edwards, S. (1984b) op. cit.; Edwards, S. (1986) 'Country Risk, Foreign Borrowing, and the Social Discount Rate in an Open Developing Economy', *Journal of International Money and Finance,* 5: 79–96.
27. Note that a higher spread means less creditworthiness.
28. *World Bank* (1985), World Development Report, p. 119.
29. Edwards, S. (1984a), op. cit., p. 731.
30. McFadden, D. *et al.*, op. cit., p. 197.
31. Edwards, S. (1986), op. cit., p. S91.
32. Feldstein, M., op. cit., p. 21.

Chapter six

The international debt crisis, its causes and possible solutions

Hans-Rimbert Hemmer

The meaning of international indebtedness

From a purely technical point of view, that is, with respect to its balance of payments effects, debt-service, which is to be treated as net capital outflow, implies a surplus of exports over imports by the same amount. As regards national accounts for such an export surplus, an excess of savings over internal investments is needed – the savings surplus provides a part of the actual production, which, as an export surplus, can be used abroad for the debt service. Therefore only those foreign debts which create not only additional net savings (that is, induced savings > induced investment) but also additional net exports (that is, induced exports > induced imports) do not entail economic problems. Only in that case will the internal utilization of foreign debt later on be able to finance the debt service. If this economic profitability condition is not fulfilled, the debt service on the foreign credit reduces the economic potential of the country in question; at least its future possibilities for capital formation are restricted.

At the same time an economic evaluation of the internal use of foreign credits should include both the identification of its profitability and an analysis of its liquidity effects. Otherwise, projects which are economically sound if profitable only in the very long run might break down owing to liquidity bottle-necks. In particular, this can happen when long-term projects are financed by short-term credits with relatively high annual interest and repayment obligations, or when foreign credits are used to finance economically-sound projects which, however, do not show a positive foreign exchange effect.

In other words, foreign debts are not negative by nature. Foreign capital may increase a country's resource availability and therefore accelerate its development process. In this respect foreign debt is nothing but an expression of the fact that a country has carried out or allowed a repayable capital import. But from a developmental point of view, this capital import is unobjectionable only if one assumes that the investment of the imported capital in the internal development process produces returns that are higher than the macroeconomic costs. And part of these costs are the debt-service payments.

In many cases, however, these aspects of economic profitability and liquidity have not yet been adequately considered. Several empirical investigations of the last twenty years suggest the following suppositions:

(a) The access to foreign credits has often reduced the recipient countries' efforts to raise the internal savings needed to finance their development programmes. Quite often the internal savings diminished. This means that either the foreign credits were at least partially used for more or less effective consumption purposes or they encouraged capital flight.
(b) In many countries large parts of short-term credits were used for long-term infrastructural projects whose growth effects lag behind quite considerably. Later on, the resultant liquidity bottle-necks may cause debt-service problems.
(c) Often the investments financed by foreign countries show a higher capital-output-ratio than internally-financed investments. In such cases, a capital intensification of production takes place, which is not in conformity with the macroeconomic factor endowments.
(d) Frequently foreign credits were used to postpone necessary corrections of internal economic policy because the governments did not consider themselves to be politically strong enough to carry out necessary though unpopular reforms. In other cases this type of financing was chosen in order to brush over lacking democratic legitimation by economic success.

Although the effect of the above-mentioned factors varies according to the respective country's situation, the factors as a whole contributed to the fact that foreign credits often brought about constellations which rendered the repayment of credits at a later stage more difficult, or sometimes even made it impossible. This criticism does not refer to special credits only; because of the set-free effects of foreign credits, the entire development policy has to be included. The set-free effect describes the following situation – the foreign credits are formally used to finance economically-sound projects which, without the credit, would have been financed by the respective country's own resources. These resources can be used for other purposes which are not directly linked to the foreign credit, although indirectly financed by it.

In other words, there is a close interrelation between the inefficiency of the national economic policy and the foreign debt burden.

The main causes of international indebtedness

The debt crisis from the point of view of LDCs

Independently of these aspects, external factors also contributed to a distinct, intensification of the debt crisis. Since 1978 at the latest, that is, the year of the second oil price shock, the world economic framework for the debtor countries has worsened remarkably (and sometimes not foreseeably).

The western industrialized countries slid into a far-reaching economic recession phase. This development had negative effects on the LDCs in several respects:

(a) When meeting internal demand deficits, many suppliers from industrialized countries tried to switch over to export markets to a larger extent than before. They supported this strategy by intensive credit provision programmes – with the result that several LDCs burdened themselves with debt in a relatively careless manner.

(b) The volume of exports for suppliers from LDCs was reduced, even if their competitive strength sufficed. Quite often, revenues (even in traditional markets) fell off drastically. In addition, the prices of raw materials came under pressure on a large scale and, as a consequence, the terms of trade for many countries deteriorated. This in turn led to reduced foreign exchange earnings, and therefore to an aggravation of the debt service.

(c) The same effects result from protectionism, which became stronger in the industrialized countries, owing to their weak internal growth. In the long run, protectionism aims at shifting the industrialized countries' internal economic problems on to their trade partners. Besides, it has aggravated the debt crisis.

(d) The United States's policy of high interest rates had a great impact too. This policy, which aimed at diverting the financial resources that were available world-wide to the United States in order to enable them to finance their budget deficit, affected the whole world financial market. As many LDCs had taken most of their commercial credits (about 80 per cent) at variable interest rates (which corresponded to the usages of the 1970s), they, too, were severely affected by the new interest rate development. Suddenly it became clear that a lot of investments financed by foreign credits were economically viable only with low or negative interest rates, but not with high positive ones. On account of the resulting macroeconomic waste of capital, the necessary returns for the debt service could no longer be gained.

The debt crisis seen from the point of view of international banks

The list of the causes of the international finance crisis would be incomplete without an examination of the private lenders' behaviour.

It is a well-known fact that the international banks pay attention to bonity when giving credits. This means that they consider the use of the credits from the point of view of rentability and profitability. However, the rapid expansion of commercial credits to LDCs, which in fact contributed strongly to the present debt problem, indicates a departure from the banks' traditional behaviour. Notwithstanding that after the first oil price explosion American and European banks were pushed to actively recycle the petrodollars, it is surprising to see how generously the international credit business has been carried out.

The reasons for this behaviour are manifold. Partly it is due to misjudgements, that is, the banks

(a) overestimated the development potential of the credit-seeking country, especially if it was richly endowed with oil or other raw materials;
(b) assumed that the credits would be utilized in an economically productive way and neglected the setting-free effect;
(c) either generally or partly misjudged economic misdevelopments in the country in question.

However, in view of the given framework and some other respects, the banks' behaviour was fully rational:

(a) some credits had been given to governments or had been guaranteed by them so that the risk of a loss to the banks was reduced;
(b) partly public political declarations could give the impression that

either the central banks in the creditors' countries or the International Monetary Fund (IMF) or the World Bank would compensate in case of credit losses (in some cases a country's creditworthiness was even identified with its relationships with the IMF or with the World Bank);

(c) partly the banks were forced to grant credits in order to get the licence for bank activities in the country in question; if the expected profits from these new activities were higher than the loss which the credit to this country involved, such a policy was still rational.

Prerequisite conditions to a solution of the debt crisis

In sum, the debt crisis is the result of a constellation in which several factors mutually reinforced each other:

- the oil-price shocks;
- inefficient economic policies on the part of the debtor countries;
- deteriorated world economic conditions;
- the United States's policy of high interest rates;
- the private banks' behaviour.

These factors contribute to an explanation and analysis of the development of external indebtedness. Besides, the world is confronted with the fact that since 1981 at the latest the debt service obligations have been a heavy burden for many countries. In the meantime, a continuously growing number of these countries was forced to take up debt renegotiations because the abovementioned factors have still their negative debt effects.

Surely such debt renegotiations are not always simple; on the other hand, the policy of the past cannot be continued.

The basic scheme of debt renegotiations is as follows – in a concerted action, the banks and the IMF lend fresh money to the debtor countries in order to satisfy their additional financial needs; besides, they lengthen the repayment time and grant some payment-free years. In this way, the liquidity pressure levied on the debtor is reduced so that he can make the necessary corrections for the solution of the economic profitability problem of the debts. Doubtlessly these corrections are often very painful because they are directed towards fundamental changes in a policy which has been practised for a long time.

In principle, the suggested adjustment policies should always be reconcilable with development, that is, they should contribute both to the growth objective and to the distribution objective. In fact, most of the duties levied upon the debtor countries in the last years in connection with debt renegotiations (and especially with these countries' consent) brought about positive growth results; the distribution component, however, was often not adequately considered. Several times this neglect had negative distributional consequences – mainly the middle and upper classes benefited from indebtedness, while the burden of the adjustment costs was levied mostly upon the lower-income classes, for no internal supplements were provided to compensate for the negative social effects of the necessary external policies. Thus, there is still a strong need for further reforms regarding the selection of appropriate adjustment policies.

Despite all the criticism of the structural adjustment policies suggested or agreed upon in special cases, it should not be forgotten that the people responsible for these problems are those who made a mess of the situation, namely the debtor countries, the Organisation of Petroleum Exporting Countries (OPEC), the creditor countries, and the banks in a more or less unholy alliance. And justice demands that all four together should feel obliged to sort things out again.

On the other hand, it should be kept in mind that the adjustment efforts on the part of LDCs will not restore or consolidate their creditworthiness if world economic activities are still on a decline. Furthermore, the subordination of economic policies to short-term needs regarding the balance of payments might produce a spiral of devaluations without contributing to a solution of the crisis. It is true that import reductions set free foreign exchange for the debt service; however, they also impair export production and therefore threaten the standard of living of the masses as well as the economic chances of survival for LDC enterprises. An increase in the internal interest rate as well as a currency devaluation can make many enterprises with foreign debts bankrupt. Therefore, in most cases debt renegotiations include the provision of fresh money in order to avoid the worst adjustment consequences.

Notwithstanding all the agreements about a restructuring of the debts, a solution of the debt crisis is only possible if world trade expands even stronger than in the last years, and if the indebted LDCs participate in that expansion. There are three prerequisite conditions for such an expansion:

1. Economic growth in the industrialized countries has to accelerate.

2. The industrialized countries have to reduce their protectionism in order to (re-)open their markets for exports from LDCs.
3. The LDCs' export orientation has to be strengthened by means of competitive products, which in turn generate macroeconomic profits for these countries.

At the same time, the US budget policy has a strong influence: A departure from the policy of high interest rates as a means of financing budget deficits could reduce the interest burden on the debtor countries considerably, thus diminishing the debt service problems of many countries.

Besides, the industrialized countries too, whose protectionist policies are also responsible for the debt crisis, should contribute to its solution. Until the debtors' export ability is restored, and the industralized countries' internal markets are reopened, the industrialized countries should grant low interest transitory credits which go beyond the IMF's stand-by credits, thus signalling that they are willing to participate constructively in a solution to the debt crisis. But mostly, such proposals are categorically rejected.

To avoid misinterpretations – I do not wish to recommend the use of official development assistance (ODA) credits – which should be given for development purposes only – for the restructuring of debts. In such a case macroeconomically unprofitable projects, the financing of which by ODA is first rejected, and which are then financed by credits from foreign banks, would afterwards still be financed by ODA. Besides, since the size of the ODA is more or less fixed by the industrialized countries, such a restructuring policy would have the following consequences – economic rationality (that is, the debtor countries' decision to accept foreign credits only when they are able to finance their debt service) would be punished by a reduction of ODA, whereas economic irrationality would be rewarded by an assignment of additional ODA. This would, of course, be absurd!

However, if the debtor countries, supported by guarantees of the industrialized countries, had easier access to the capital markets in the United States and Europe, they could take up medium- and long-term loans there. In this way the debtor countries' interest burden would be relieved quite considerably, for some of the interest rates in these markets are clearly below LIBOR (London interbank offer rate). This relief could be an important development impulse for these countries, provided that their internal economic policy changes fundamentally.

Last but not least, OPEC, that is, those countries which

basically set off the crisis by their oil price rises of 1973 and 1978, has made almost no constructive contribution to a solution of the debt problem. In fact, it is surprising that these countries are largely excluded from the international discussion about the origin of the debt crisis and the responsibility as far as its solution is concerned. The fact that at present two OPEC members themselves (that is, Mexico and Venezuela) belong to the six most indebted countries could be interpreted as a historical example of poetic justice.

The current oil price reduction cannot be taken as a full compensation for the OPEC policies of the 1970s, for instead of reducing the LDC's actual debt burden, it does no more than slow down the growth of the debt mountain.

Recent developments in the solution of the international debt crisis

In 1985 Latin America made two proposals regarding the solution of the international debt crisis. First, the Peruvian president Garcia announced that his country would use only 10 per cent of its export earnings (instead of 40 per cent in 1985) for interest payments to foreign creditors. Additionally he wanted the IMF to be excluded from debt restructuring negotiations. Second, Fidel Castro demanded that the United States's government should discharge the Latin American countries' foreign debts to US banks by a reduction of military expenses.

What would the consequences of such a 'solution' of the international debt crisis be like?

As regards Garcia's proposal, in those cases, where contrary to previous arrangements the debt service payments are not made, the source of fresh money will probably dry up, that is, the debtor will not obtain new credits. International trade, however, can only prosper if trade credits are used as 'lubricants'. Thus, the lack of such trade credits would affect the foreign trade of the country in question very seriously and would have consequences for its national economy, which would probably be more dramatic than those resulting from a correct fulfilment of its debt service obligations.

Furthermore, the refusal to service a debt does not mean that the debt volume will not grow any further. On the contrary, interest payments which are not paid in time will be added to the outstanding credit, and for them, too, interests will have to be paid in future.

Therefore Garcia wanted to manage the debt restructuring on

his own; this procedure, however, has a decisive disadvantage in comparison to an official restructuring in collaboration with the IMF – the fresh money component is omitted, which is an essential part of all debt restructuring arrangements managed by intermediation of the IMF. Thus the relevant alternative is 'debt restructuring with', or 'debt restructuring without, fresh money'. But any debt restructuring requires internal structural adjustments, and additional resources would make these adjustments much easier. If Garcia realized his intentions, he would impede the economic rehabilitation of Peru.

There are also several objections to a general debt remission – as it is finally implied in Castro's proposal:

First, important creditor countries fear that the international banks might interpret such a general debt remission as an indicator of the inability of many LDCs to meet their repayment obligations in future. This could reduce the creditworthiness of all LDCs – even of the newly-industrialized countries – on the international finance markets.

Second, it is doubtful whether subsequent debt reliefs would increase the total volume of net capital transfers from industrialized countries to LDCs. It seems to be more realistic to assume that such a debt remission would be compensated by a reduction of other positions in the industrialized countries' budget for development assistance. This reduction would lead to unfair redistribution of capital assistance among the LDCs; the result would be similar to the situation analysed in connection with the consequences of a debt substitution by ODA. Owing to internal reasons in the industrialized countries, a non-discriminating debt remission, which rewards financial failures and mismanagement of LDCs, would also make new grants of development assistance more difficult. In fact, unfair redistributions as a result of a global debt remission will meet strong disapproval.

In October 1985 a new proposal was put forward by the United States's Minister of Finance, Baker. This proposal included three elements:

1. From 1986 to 1988 western banks should extend an additional credit of 20 billion US dollars to the fifteen most problematic debtor countries.
2. The World Bank and regional development banks should add another credit of 9 billion US dollars.
3. The debtor countries, on the other side, should undertake to change their national economic policy towards a better acceptance of the market mechanism.

In spite of the international applause, some doubts about the rationality and consistency of the Baker plan have to be raised:

(a) The total amount of 29 billion US dollars within three years was arbitrarily fixed; nobody knows the exact amount of the actually needed financial flow to the debtor countries;
(b) the concentration on fifteen countries could imply a reduction of the credits to the other, more solid debtor countries: they would thus be punished for their solid repayment policy;
(c) the official approval of the Baker plan on the part of western governments can be interpreted as a recognition of the private banks' political obligation to give credits to 'bad' customers. In case of losses, the banks will hand on their bill to their governments: the banks' losses will be socialized;
(d) the inclusion of the World Bank and of the regional development banks again means a conversion of development funds to solvency funds; this policy would be to the detriment of those countries which Baker does not mention;
(e) Baker's concept is inconsistent because it means a restriction of the market regarding credits, while there is a general demand for an extension of the market;
(f) last, neither the United States's budget policy, nor the industrialized countries' trade policy, nor the part of OPEC are mentioned as important factors in the solution of the debt crisis.

In sum, there are still many unanswered questions – apart from the fact that the details about a fundamental rearrangement of the debtor countries' internal policy and the time needed for such a change were not sufficiently specified. These questions leave many doubts as to whether the Baker plan is really as good as its author claims.

Part three

Latin American debt problems

Chapter seven

The external indebtedness of Latin America

Miguel S. Wionczek

> Not only will the Latin American debt never be repaid; it will become larger, although at a reduced rate. But the US-government's debt also will not be paid, nor will the AT&T debt.
>
> Terence C. Carnavan, Executive Vice-President of Chemical Bank (New York)[1]

> The costs of moratoria or partial debt service to maintain minimum growth are perceived to be significantly lower than those incurred by meeting debt service commitments first, and striving to grow with whatever foreign exchange is left over.
>
> (Economic Commission for Latin America and the Caribbean (ECLAC) Latin America's Economic Performance, 28 September 1987)

Introduction

The US and Latin American literature on the Latin American external debt is by now enormous, albeit inconclusive. Since much less has been written on this subject in Western Europe, let us first present some data about the region's foreign indebtedness evolution and its impact on the Latin American economy (see Tables 7.1, 7.2).

Four clear trends can be observed in these tables:

1. over the past ten years (1975 to 1985) the total external debt of Latin America increased fivefold;
2. the indebtedness of the region during the same period was concentrated in the borrowing from private sources (82 per cent);
3. the average burden of the debt service measured by the ratio

Table 7.1 Latin America and the Caribbean: external debt, 1970–85

	Total debt	Debt from official sources		Debt from private sources	
	(billions of US dollars)	(billions of US dollars)	(as a % of the total debt)	(billions of US dollars)	(as a % of the total debt)
1970	23	8	36	15	64
1971	26	9	36	17	64
1972	30	10	34	20	66
1973	40	12	28	28	72
1974	56	14	25	42	75
1975	75	16	22	59	78
1976	98	18	18	80	82
1977	116	21	18	95	82
1978	151	25	16	127	84
1979	182	27	15	157	85
1980	223	31	14	198	86
1981	278	34	12	246	88
1982	318	40	12	278	88
1983	344	51	15	293	85
1984	360	57	16	303	84
1985	368	65	18	303	82

Source: UN Economic Commission for Latin America and the Caribbean (ECLAC): *The Problem of the External Debt: Gestation, Development, Crisis, and Prospects*, 6 March 1986, Table 4.8.

of goods and services exports for that purpose increased steeply from 15.7 per cent in 1978 to 35.1 per cent in 1986;

4. this increase affected with particular severity the largest debtors, whether oil-exporting (Mexico) or non-oil-exporting (Argentina, Chile and Brazil) countries – by 1986 their debt service exceeded 40 per cent of their respective exports of goods and services.

The above findings may or may not look alarming depending upon the degree of knowledge about the events which preceded, and the circumstances which surrounded, the external debt explosion in the region, which started officially in the late summer of 1982 with Mexico's announcement of its inability to continue servicing its debt. However, contrary to the conventional perceptions, the Latin American debt crisis had started much earlier, perhaps in the second half of the 1970s, because many serious international and domestic problems of a financial and non-financial nature converged at that time – large surpluses of idle funds in international financial markets, high interest rates, aggressive lending policies of great financial intermediaries, accompanied by mistaken

Table 7.2 Latin America and the Caribbean: ratio of total interest payments to exports of goods and services, 1978–86 (percentages)

Country	*1978*	*1979*	*1980*	*1981*	*1982*	*1983*	*1984*	*1985*	*1986*
Latin America	15.7	17.6	20.2	28.0	41.0	36.0	35.6	35.2	35.1
Oil-exporting countries	16.1	15.7	16.6	22.6	35.6	31.4	32.5	32.3	36.5
Bolivia	13.7	18.6	25.0	34.5	43.4	39.8	49.8	46.8	46.7
Ecuador	10.4	13.6	18.3	24.3	30.0	27.4	30.7	27.0	32.2
Mexico	24.0	24.5	23.3	29.0	47.3	37.5	39.0	36.0	40.0
Peru	21.2	15.5	16.0	24.1	25.1	29.8	33.2	30.0	27.3
Venezuela	7.2	6.9	8.1	12.7	21.0	21.6	20.1	26.3	33.3
Non-oil-exporting countries	15.5	19.3	23.7	33.6	46.7	40.7	38.7	37.9	34.2
Argentina	9.6	12.8	22.0	35.5	53.6	58.4	57.6	51.1	51.8
Brazil	24.5	31.5	34.1	40.4	57.1	43.5	39.7	40.0	37.7
Chile	16.9	16.5	19.3	38.8	49.5	38.9	48.0	43.5	39.2
Columbia	7.5	9.9	11.8	21.9	25.9	26.7	22.8	26.3	18.6
Costa Rica	9.9	12.8	18.0	28.0	36.1	33.0	26.6	27.3	22.7
Dominican Republic	14.0	14.3	14.8	19.1	22.7	24.5	18.1	22.2	27.1
El Salvador	5.3	5.7	5.9	7.8	11.9	12.2	12.3	12.6	10.3
Guatemala	3.7	3.2	5.3	7.6	7.8	8.7	12.3	14.9	14.9
Haiti	2.8	3.2	2.1	2.7	2.4	2.4	5.3	4.2	5.7
Honduras	8.2	8.6	10.6	14.4	22.4	16.4	15.8	15.3	12.7
Nicaragua	9.3	9.7	17.8	21.9	32.1	14.3	12.1	13.0	25.8
Paraguay	8.4	10.7	13.4	14.8	13.5	14.3	10.1	8.3	10.1
Uruguay	10.4	9.0	11.0	12.9	22.4	24.8	34.8	34.2	23.8

Source: UN Economic Commission for Latin America and the Caribbean, *Economic Survey of Latin America and the Caribbean, 1986*, Tables 16, 22.

domestic macroeconomic policies, and overvalued exchange rates in the borrowing countries.

Causes and consequences of the debt bubble

It may be worth recalling that while the external debt crisis, not only in Latin America but in most other less-developed countries (LDCs), appeared on the agenda of international financial institutions (the International Monetary Fund (IMF) and the World Bank) only after the Mexican crisis of 1982, by the initiative of the LDCs as a group, the subject has been on the agenda of the UNCTAD (United Nations Conference on Trade and Development) in Geneva since the early 1970s.[2] At that time, however, the stubborn opposition of the governments of creditor countries, and the vested interests of private financial intermediaries, did not even permit the serious discussion of the issues involved. The LDCs' debt problem simply did not exist at that time except for some academic observers and analysts and the LDC delegates to the UNCTAD meetings.[3]

Thus, it is not fair to concentrate exclusively, as is done now in the creditor countries, on the most recent unsuccessful attempts to solve the Latin American debt problem, that is, (a) the burst of the 'debt bubble' all over the region between the time of the Mexican announcement and the fall of 1983; (b) the merry-go-round of the increased number of reschedulings between the 1983 IMF-World Bank meeting and early 1986; and (c) the relentless crisis which presently affects practically all Latin American countries. Some well-meaning observers in the creditor countries sustain these days that each of the three recent phases of the Latin American debt crisis represents a realization of the creditors that the crisis has not been solved, but indeed, has worsened, and that it requires more elaborate responses. Such *ex post* appraisal indicates the absence of a historical memory and represents wishful thinking rather than reality. On the basis of the available evidence, one can sustain that the Latin American debt problem could probably have been managed without undue hardships and risks if, during the early stages of the debt gestation, in the final years of the past decade, a joint action by the creditors and the debtors had been agreed upon. If they did not reach such an agreement, these two parties are both responsible, but the responsibility of the creditors and international development finance agencies is much greater than that of the debtor countries.

What really happened was that neither the private creditors nor the IMF-World Bank were willing, either before or shortly after the bursting of the 'debt bubble' in Mexico, to accept the position that Latin America's and other LDCs' debt difficulties were more than a passing liquidity problem.[4] Later on, both international financial agencies and the private creditors continued clinging to their unfounded faith in the workings of the sequence of debt reschedulings on a case-by-case basis, which were supported by the IMF-designed adjustment programmes. By the autumn of 1985 the rapidly worsening LDC debtor countries' external and domestic situation resulted in the emergence of a rather unconvincing, but highly publicized, remedy known as the Baker plan.

This limited international financial gimmick assumed that – 'more of the same' – some insignificant financial contributions of the IMF-World Bank (9 billion US dollars over a three-year period) and the 'involuntary' assistance of international private credit and capital sources (20 billion US dollars over the same period) to a selected group of major well-behaving debtors would make the LDC debt problem disappear. The wrong diagnosis and the over-optimistic expectations underlying the Baker plan made it unworkable from the start. The plan ignored the earlier chain of events which led to the fall of most debtor countries into the 'debt trap', assumed incorrectly common interests between different groups of creditors and their governments,[5] and ignored the recessionary impact of the case-by-case adjustment programmes, not only on the individual debtors' economies, but also on the international economic situation.

As far as the first of these main factors responsible for the meagre – to say the least – results of the debtor countries' rescue operations of 1982 to 1987 is concerned, the fact is that in spite of the heroic efforts of the World Bank statisticians,[6] nobody seems to know – first, how much each debtor country originally borrowed, world-wide, for investment and development purposes, and second, how much of the present outstanding external debt corresponds to the accumulation of the overdue service payments on the originally-incurred capital borrowing of the lenders. It is not enough to point out that in the early 1980s international interest rates reached the highest levels in history in spite of the excess of liquidity in the international private financial system. It would be more relevant to remember that long before Mexico's fall from grace as a perfect borrower in the late summer of 1982, most, if not all, LDC countries engaged in a practice of informal external debt rescheduling by borrowing short at increasing interest rates, spread, and commissions, for the purpose of servicing their earlier debt and staying in the 'good boys' lenders' league.

While the Mexican case may not be typical, its misadventures prior to 1982 are highly illustrative of the way in which a country may become rapidly a semibankrupt lender with the most serious domestic, economic, and social difficulties. Mexico's outstanding external public debt increased from about some 5 billion US dollars at the end of 1971, to slightly over 21 billion US dollars at the end of 1976, and to close to 59 billion US dollars at the end of 1982. The country's ratio of the accumulated public debt to the gross domestic product (GDP) grew from 11.6 per cent in 1972 to 28.5 per cent in 1976 and to 65.1 per cent in 1982. Its payments of interest on the external debt as the ratio of total servicing of the debt (capital and interest repayments) expanded during the same period from 13.5 per cent (1972) to 24.1 per cent (1976), and to 34.9 per cent (1982). Finally, the ratio between the debt servicing and the balance-of-payments current account revenue rose from 49.6 per cent (1971) to 63.5 per cent (1976), and 72.6 per cent (1982).[7] Within these parameters of external debt behaviour,

Mexico's financial misadventures could not be stopped in the fall of 1982 by any instant rescue operation.[8] The country's three successive external debt renegotiations, and the allegedly generous help under the Baker plan left Mexico by 1986 with over 100 billion US dollars of the outstanding debt, which is equal to 3.6 times of its annual exports.[9]

The use of simple arithmetic offers a rather depressing picture of the evolution of Mexico's external total indebtedness: while from 1971 to 1986 Mexico's public and private sectors together probably borrowed something like 75 billion US dollars abroad for investment projects, their repayments of principal amounted to over 60 billion US dollars during the same period and their payments of interest to close to 70 billion US dollars. All these capital transfers abroad are made for the purpose of debt amortization and servicing, notwithstanding the country presently still owes over 100 billion US dollars (not including interest to be paid on the outstanding debt over the next 15 years) to foreign creditors. Despite the fact that the present worth of Mexican private assets abroad has been estimated at 40 billion US dollars, the Mexican debt trap worked with the utmost efficiency and a high degree of automatism to the advantage of the lenders.

Case studies of the external debt experiences of Argentina, Brazil, Chile, Peru, Venezuela and five Central American countries suggest that the accumulated results of the working of the 'debt trap' mechanism have been of a very similar nature and severity[10] in all of them. It could not have been otherwise because of the speed of debt accumulation, its record-breaking costs due to the workings of the compound interest rates mechanism, and the adherence to the IMF-designed adjustment programmes. While these programmes presumably aimed at reinstating the external and domestic financial stability of the region, they made Latin America a great net exporter of capital to the industrially-advanced creditor countries and brought hyperinflation to the region. Since the economic growth performance of the creditors slowed down perceptibly by the mid-1970s from the levels registered during the first three post-war decades, the capital transfer from the debtors helped the creditor countries to keep their own stagnation within politically- and socially-acceptable limits.

Requests for balance of payments improvements

Between 1982 and 1986 the net outflow of capital from the region averaged 30 billion US dollars a year, adding up to a total of 150 billion US dollars within the last five years. In order to finance such a capital (savings) outflow, one Latin American country after another was forced into a strait-jacket of domestic austerity programmes. As the adoption of the austerity programmes was made a precondition for a relief of the outstanding external debt burden through its rescheduling under allegedly more generous service conditions, these programmes contained a small carrot attached to the big stick: the promise of access for the practically bankrupt debtor countries to 'fresh money' from international private financial creditors. In practice, however, whenever 'fresh money' was made available to the debtor countries lately, it was used almost immediately to service external obligations. The correct description of such exercises in the criminal law language is the 'stay of execution' for the debtors.

For the purpose of a balance-of-payments improvement, the Latin American countries were advised by the IMF and World Bank missions, and by the private creditors, to expand exports while cutting imports to the bone. Their budget deficits were to be eliminated through a drastic compression of both current and capital public expenditures, accompanied by the elimination of subsidies in public services and in pricing of wage goods. How these exercises in external and domestic austerity were to be translated into action in face of the demographic explosion and the accelerating inflation was left to the political imagination of the debtor countries' governments. On the creditors' side nobody seemed to note the adverse impact on the debtors' economies of the deterioration of their terms of trade related to the shrinking international demand for commodities, the declining use of materials in response to technological progress, the growing weight of the services in international trade, and finally, the world-wide protectionist tendencies. The feasibility of the austerity programmes imposed upon the debtors could hardly be explained convincingly by the greatest Latin American creditor and the greatest world debtor at the same time – the United States. The current international and domestic United States' policies, which result in huge foreign trade and budget deficits, continue to be in full contradiction to the financial and economic policy advice offered to Latin American debtors.

Internal consequences

Within the framework of the 'stay of execution' doctrine, during the first half of the 1980s Latin America suffered an economic and social crisis which is comparable only to that in the industrial market economy world of the 1930s. While by 1985 the GDP per capita in the region fell to the levels of the mid-1970s, Latin American economists and social scientists started to describe the outcome of the crisis as the 'lost growth decade', characterized by a violent and accelerating inflation, a rapidly-expanding unemployment and underemployment, a fall of 40 per cent or more in real incomes of the salaried work-force, and a steady deterioration of the income distribution, which was unacceptable by the industrial countries' standards even in the earlier better times.

While a slight recovery took place in various Latin American countries in 1986, the ECLAC (UN Economic Commission for Latin America and the Caribbean) preliminary review of the situation during that year warned that:

> some advancements in economic recovery and the correction of certain principal macroeconomic disequilibria were not generalized enough and only counterarrested regression registered in the previous five years.[11]

Although some economic improvements took place in Peru, Brazil, Argentina, Colombia, Chile, and Uruguay in 1985–6, the most recent data indicate that almost all of these countries were again undergoing an economic and social deterioration during 1987.

Are international financial agencies and international private creditors aware of the Latin American economic and social crisis of the 1980s? There are reasons to believe that while the former lately started to learn what was going on in the region from their own internal studies and reports, the latter could probably not care less.[12] However, more serious is the fact that until recently large sectors of the public opinion in the creditor countries had no inkling about this situation. Only in the autumn of this year did the mass media on both sides of the Atlantic start to note the prolonged social and political costs of the Latin American deepening financial and economic crisis.

In late August, *The Wall Street Journal*, the newspaper with the largest circulation in the United States, published a long page one reportage about the capital of the Dominican Republic, Santo Domingo, starting with the following lines:

> The Third World debt crisis is not denominated in dollars alone. Here in the impoverished Dominican Republic, it is also denominated in blood.[13]

And, in a series of three detailed and long reports entitled 'The social strains in Central America' in the first week of September, a no-less influential US newspaper, *The New York Times*, discovered that

> Central America is in its worst economic crisis this century, and the working class, struggling to find work and largely unprotected by laws regulating working conditions, is suffering the most.
>
> Six straight years of recession, devaluation and political instability have forced the vast majority of Salvadorians, Hondurans, Guatemalans and even some Costa Ricans, traditionally the most affluent of Central Americans, to accept living conditions and wage levels that are equivalent to those of a decade ago.
>
> In most of Central America, steady employment is a dream for half the working population. Not being able to find a job is one of the most common and painful experiences facing millions of men and women in the region.[14]

Similar discoveries could have easily been made in Ecuador, Peru, Colombia, Venezuela and Brazil. While the IMF-World Bank group in their official reports and communiqués maintain that the Latin American economic recovery is around the corner, and that the region's external debt is almost under control, the less official but better-informed sources both in North and Latin America express increasing doubts in this respect. It seems to be quite easy to be optimistic, according to a recent analysis made by an impeccably conservative but knowledgeable British observer:

> The debt crisis has always been easy to solve on paper. Make the right assumptions about the future world growth, commodity prices and so forth and, hey presto, the crisis evaporates. Slightly vary these assumptions and it becomes obvious that the debt strategy outlined by the US Treasury Secretary, Mr James Baker, in Seoul in 1985 will not work.
>
> The idea was that commercial banks (in tandem with the official institutions) would increase their exposure in return for a shift to more market-oriented (and thus supposedly growth enhancing) policies in debtor countries. Nearly two years later, it is still improbable that private sector agents in the industrial world can be persuaded to provide finance and terms that permit sustained rapid growth in the developing world.[15]

In spite of no less than 100 proposals, elaborated by academic experts, politicians, and international finance practitioners over the past five years, the gap between the respective visions in the key creditor and the key debtor countries about the severity of the LDC's and, in particular, Latin American debt crisis is as great as ever.[16] It seems that much depends on whether one looks at debt through the eyes of creditors or debtors. From the standpoint of lenders in the industrial world, enormous progress has been made since 1982. What western financiers claimed to fear most was that a series of concerted defaults would result in a collapse of the international banking system. Such concerted defaults could have been possible only if the debtor countries had established a common front against their creditors and had consolidated their domestic political systems and assured themselves of strong popular support, including, if necessary, a willingness to accept further sacrifices, in the name of national self-determination. Such an unlikely danger was disarmed by the division of the debtors, the offer of some sort of 'special treatment' for each of them, and by the evolution of the treatment of heavy sanctions. Any student of the Latin American who attempts to co-ordinate their policies *vis-à-vis* the external creditors realizes that, while these dividing tactics had worked, the objective conditions were never present for a concerted group debt default in the region.

The interest of private lenders

Successive rounds of individual debt reschedulings have put to sleep the ghost of concerted defaults in Latin America and elsewhere. By 1987 the large private creditor banks, both in the United States and Western Europe, had built up a much more solid position to face individual country default than they had in the early 1980s. While their primary capital as a ratio of doubtful loans increased very fast, problem loans as a proportion of total bank assets declined sharply. It is the improvement in these two fundamental ratios that has made possible the rise in loan loss reserves of major lenders. By the end of 1987, partly as a result of the Citicorp's move last May, the majority of the world's large banks will have provided for at least 25 per cent of their doubtful LDC loans. In the case of Latin America, where the United States' loans are concentrated in less than fifteen banks, the coverage of the probably 'bad' loans will be even higher. Moreover, many European banks with exposure in Latin America have set aside proportionately much larger loss reserves.

Both in the United States and Western Europe the private lenders' internal rescue operations for Latin America were possible because of the very attractive overall banking profit levels, which are partly due to the recent diversification of the range of financial activities. This diversification reflects the steady progress of bank deregulation both at domestic and transnational levels. Contrary to the international banking community scare, international private financial institutions do not live on lending to less-developed countries alone. In fact, not only did they never do so, but their dependence on underdeveloped foreign lenders has lately been decreasing steadily in favour of retail banking at national level, foreign currency arbitrage, and foreign exchange transactions, fees for advice to industrial companies' mergers, and so on.[17]

While the stream of interest payments on the outstanding Latin American debt may still be of importance to these large international private financial conglomerates, they could comfortably live and prosper even if the Latin American debtors stopped borrowing from them, provided that the debtors continue servicing their external private debt, which in certain cases has been stretched over fifteen and more years. This brief analysis of the reasons for the international private banks' present negative attitude toward the proposal that they should continue lending to Latin American debtors is not just a far-fetched academic speculation. A little-known study which was written in mid-1986 by a staff member of the Joint Economic Committee of the US Congress, and deals with the impact of the Latin American debt crisis on the United States' economy, provides convincing evidence to the effect that, except in one case (Bank of America), none of the major US lenders to the region was seriously endangered by the region's debt crisis.[18] Moreover, when this writer asked a group of Scandinavian central and private bankers at a meeting held in Stockholm in the summer of 1986 what would have happened if by act of God all Latin American borrowers had presented themselves on the same day to the creditors to repay all their debt, the answer to that question was rather amusing, albeit not completely unexpected – the meeting was not exactly the place to ask 'perverse' questions. As long as the unlucky debtors were servicing their debts, if they did so with delays, everything was going more or less well.

Recent proposals for solving the debt problem

The foreign private creditors worked out, however, a new line of defence against the possible risks of their operations in Latin America. It consists of a brief list of the measures which the Latin

American debtor countries should adopt to get out of their present financial, economic, and social misery, accompanied by another list of what would not be acceptable for the creditors.

Their recipe for Latin America's salvation can be summarized in a few points, which coincide with the philosophy underlying the Baker plan:

(a) In the sectors of strategic importance for development, privatize the respective debt-ridden economies which are top-heavy on account of the presence of public enterprises;
(b) create a better climate for foreign private investment by eliminating all controls and restrictions upon profit remittances, foreign capital participation in economic activities and technology transfers;
(c) swap debt for equity investment; and
(d) do away with all existing limitations on the activities of foreign enterprises in the sector services (bank, insurance companies, communications, transport, and tourist facilities).

The list of prohibited actions contains the following:

(a) do not attempt to evade the IMF-World Bank controls over your financial, monetary, budgetary and other economic policies;
(b) do not expect either the remission of even a part of the outstanding debt or preferential interest rates for its servicing;
(c) abandon the idea of joint ventures unless fully controlled by foreign private investors.

The private international banking community insists that all liberalization and privatization measures should be supported by the reactivation of lending on commercial terms by governments, governmental export agencies, and international development financing bodies like the World Bank and Inter-American Development Bank. That such a reactivation of official bilateral and multilateral lending is not forthcoming is another story. On the basis of convincing evidence offered with disarming frankness, the reasons for this delay were analyzed in a special survey of the *The Economist* on the eve of the IMF-World Bank annual meeting in late September 1986.[19] While the IMF has lost most of its political clout in Latin America and elsewhere in the developing world, the World Bank has been undergoing a period of confusing reorganization of its bureaucratic structures and major functions. Neither its new *modus operandi* nor its goals have been clearly defined yet.

The situation seems to be somewhat uncertain since the Bank's new president Barber Conable, a professional US politician,

> comes to the job with no experience of banking and no experience of running a large organization.[20]

His principal asset has been, however, that he knows James Baker, the author of the Baker plan, well, and

> they are both veterans of Mr George Bush's campaign for the Republican party's presidential nomination.[21]

Against this background – according to *The Economist* 1986 survey – the new president of the World Bank is supposed to assure that the bank will play the leading role in efforts to deal with the developing countries' debt problem. The same source offered a small caveat: the World Bank's success in putting Latin America and other countries back on the track of development would depend mainly on the increase of its lending resources. Unfortunately, not only have new resources for the bank's lending not been forthcoming lately because of budgetary difficulties on the part of the treasuries of the major World Bank members, but the reimbursements to the bank from earlier loans exceed the volume of new loans. Moreover, it should not be forgotten that, first, processing of the bank's project loans in the past took three years on average, and second, that the borrowings from that body declined in the fiscal year 1986 to the levels of 1982 (5.7 billion US dollars distributed among 41 out of 125 underdeveloped member countries) after a considerable increase to over 7 billion US dollars a year in 1983–5.

The Baker plan

In view of the fact that in future the World Bank will probably concentrate on the policy-based lending in the form of sector-adjustment and structural adjustment loans, and by attaching various sorts of macroeconomic policy strings to old-fashioned projects loans, it can hardly be expected that the processing of a loans request can be speeded up by the bank's operational staff. All these factors give rise to a by-no-means-trivial question – can Latin America under the present circumstances wait and hope, let us say until 1990, for the World Bank to reappear as a powerful development lender, while the region has needed the immediate reversal of high capital transfers to the creditor countries over the past five years? This key question is particularly urgent, because – whether with or without the Baker plan and the efforts of Latin American debtors to provide the adequate climate for lenders and investors – the flow of new private bank lending to, and foreign direct investment in, the region has virtually dried up.[22]

It could not have been otherwise because the Baker plan, which received accolades all over the creditor countries, was a piece of improvisation as one of the high officials of the United States' Treasury who helped to design it and resigned shortly afterwards recently admitted:

> In fact, the plan was pasted together quickly in breakfast meetings between the Treasury Secretary, James A. Baker III and Paul A. Volcker then chairman of the Federal Reserve Board. It was simply an attempt to steal the thunder from the newly inaugurated Peruvian president, Alan García, who had the gall to unilaterally implement his own formula for cutting back Peru's unsustainable debt service without consulting the United States. Mr Baker's speech was calculated to regain the initiative.
>
> Accordingly, the Baker plan was primarily rhetoric – a good speech, but without follow-through. It called for substantial new lending to the 15 most troubled debtors between 1986 and 1988, particularly from the World Bank and private banks. But no one even asked the private banks in advance if they were willing to increase lending to the Third World. And the other creditor nations of Western Europe and Japan – whose banks hold more Latin debt than do American banks – weren't even consulted.[23]

Most of the Latin American countries were forced to accept three fashionable propositions about the wonders of foreign private investment:

1. Unlike interest on external debt, which must be paid under any circumstances, equity finance results in a foreign-exchange outflow only if the investment earns a positive return.
2. The bigger the share of foreign investment in a country's total external liabilities, the less vulnerable it is to external shocks.
3. The impact of new technology, and of technical and managerial expertise which accompanies foreign investment can be as useful as the actual inflow of capital itself.

But even the domestic policy changes following the acceptance of these propositions did not bring about any sizeable inflow of foreign private investment to the region. This is not only due to the generally chaotic economic and social conditions in Latin America but also, as historical evidence proves, to the fact that large companies, both in manufacturing and in other sectors, decide to invest in a foreign country only when they are attracted by its large domestic markets, or because cheap labour and available raw materials make it a good place from which to export. Unfortunately, the critical domestic conditions at present, and the deterioration of the income distribution patterns, do not permit an expansion of the domestic markets anywhere in Latin America. On the other hand, the prospects for exports to advanced countries' markets by the latecomers seem to be quite uncertain in view of world-wide protectionist tendencies and economic growth stagnation. South Korea's, Taiwan's, Singapore's, and Hong Kong's export achievements cannot simply be repeated overnight in Latin America.

While because of Mexico's geographical proximity to the United States, and the high managerial and marketing capacities of Brazilian industrialists, Mexico and Brazil may be put into a special category as prospective receivers of a certain amount of foreign investment, the remaining Latin American countries hardly provide the conditions which would convince foreign investors to engage themselves strongly in the region. The fall of private foreign investment has lately not been limited to Latin America alone. Since the beginning of the 1980s it has been taking place in almost the whole developing world. According to a very recent study, the share of foreign direct investment in the LDCs has fallen from two-thirds of the world total before 1939 to about a quarter in the mid-1980s, while foreign private investment among the industrial countries continues to expand mainly because of the Japanese and West European investment activities.

While US corporations still account for almost a half of the book value of foreign investment in the LDCs, their share is now declining. Since 1970 the stock of US investment outside of other industrial countries has risen by less than 10 per cent, while Japan's total foreign direct investment has risen by almost twice as much. During the present decade new foreign investment in the LDCs from all sources has actually been falling in absolute terms from a peak of 15 billion US dollars in 1981 to less than 8 billion US dollars in 1986. Against the background of the recent steep depreciation of the US dollar, this amounts to less than half its real level in the late 1970s.[24]

Principal objectives

Since in the framework of these secular trends the US and other foreign investors look only for real bargains in Latin America, debt-equity swaps became particularly attractive to foreign banks and manufacturing corporations. Their attraction arises from the fact that in the Latin American crisis-ridden countries real assets can be acquired at a fraction of their book value. Swapping debt for equity means buying debt instruments at the secondary markets for something like 50 to 60 per cent of their face value and exchanging them at full value in local currency at the debtor's central banks. In this way, the acquisition of real assets in Latin America through such swaps provides the buyer with large margins of immediate windfall gains, apart from larger-term gains via depreciation mechanisms.

While an increasing number of foreign investors seems to be enthusiastic about this particular item of the menu of financing options available to them in Latin America, and about 2 billion US dollars of debt-equity swaps were reported in Brazil, Chile, and Mexico in 1986, many US analysts have the strongest reservations about the overall soundness of these operations for the debtor countries. A recent report from the Group of Thirty, an international study group, expressed the opinion that such deals 'may distort trade and waste foreign exchange and, in the extreme, result in new capital flight'.[25] While on James Baker's initiative the US banks were recently permitted also to enter into the debt-equity swap business, although the proceeds can be held for four years only, the less successful bidders for bargains in the Latin American basements are reported to complain that the 'sound companies in the region can be bought only by cash'.[26]

But neither the increase of debt-equity swaps nor the expansion of in-bond assembly plants producing for export, which is another attempt of Latin Americans to attract foreign private capital, will not do the trick of compensating the constant huge transfers of financial resources to the creditor countries in connection with the external debt servicing. It seems that, although Latin America's default on the outstanding debt can be postponed for a while, it is unavoidable in the long run. If even such far from radical ideas as US Senator Bradley's proposal in April 1986 to offer Latin America debt relief by cutting both the outstanding debt and the interest rates by 3 per cent a year are not acceptable to the creditors, and if no reversal of the large capital outflow from the region will take place, such a default will eventually come.

While not necessarily resulting in a word-wide financial débâcle, a disorderly Latin American debt default would not only destroy the region's development prospects, but would affect the industrial countries themselves seriously albeit indirectly. It would deprive them, and particularly the United States, of sizeable export markets at a time when the global international trade has practically stopped expanding. Thus, instead of thinking of the Latin American debt-default apocalypsis, it would be better perhaps to start thinking about the instrumentation of a Latin American default on the initiative of the creditors and in agreement with the region's debtors and creditors.

Whereas such an idea may sound outlandish in view of the creditors' clinging to the concept of the sanctity of sovereign debts, it appeared at least in one serious study written in 1985 by a key contributor to the very respectable *Financial Times* of London.[27] It is so novel and appealing that it should be rescued from oblivion. The 'agreed default' would amount to a new round of long-term debt negotiations between the borrowers, the banks, and the creditor governments (acting perhaps through the IMF or other international institutions). The open presence of all three parties in such negotiations would be necessary. The government of the creditors, and particularly the United States' government, would have to abandon their disingenuous position that the debt problem involves the creditors and the debtors only. The creditors would also have to put aside the fictitious position that the debtors alone are responsible for solving the debt crisis.

While few debtors in Latin America can continue servicing their debt under the present conditions, most of them badly need some kind of a sizeable debt-burden relief, whether by putting a once-for-all limit on interest rates, capitalizing a part of the debt servicing costs, or transforming it into long-term fixed interest bonds. The principal objective of any default-cum-renegotiation exercise would be to distribute the costs of the post-default debt rescheduling more or less equally among the creditors, the debtors, and the governments of the creditors alike. Only then the uncertainty which is permanently hanging over the debtor countries would disappear. To devise workable proposals with these characteristics should be technically possible:

> Given the will, there clearly would be no shortage of ideas for dealing in a controlled and rational manner – either before or after a default. Only two elements are needed before this chronical malignancy in the international system can be cured. These elements, both critical, are realism and money.[28]

Perhaps the fact that after a long absence the international debt problem appeared as the central issue of the UNCTAD agenda, and that after the four most exhausting weeks of the UNCTAD VII negotiations at ministerial level in Geneva in July-August 1987, some sort of a basic agreement regarding its future management was achieved, illustrates that all parties involved begin to accept that the deadlock on the international debt handling must be broken. The section of the Final Act of UNCTAD VII which deals with debt and was accepted without reservations by the 140 member countries present, including all major creditor countries, starts with the following text:

> The debt crisis is complex and an equitable, durable and mutually agreed solution will be only reached by an approach based on development, within the framework of an integrated, co-operative, growth-oriented strategy that takes into account the particular circumstances of each country. The response to the debt crisis should evolve, through continuous dialogue and shared responsibility, and the strategy should be implemented with feasibility in an environment of strengthened international cooperation . . .[29]

While cynics may dismiss this statement as another piece of UN rhetorics, hopeful pessimists like this writer would like to assume that we are perhaps facing the beginning of the recognition that the sterile debt game of the past years cannot continue indefinitely. Otherwise it would not only make chaotic debt defaults unavoidable all over Latin America, but it would also contribute to the world-wide repetition of the 1930s despite the presumed strength of one of the major actors in that game – the international private creditors.

Notes and references

1. Pastor, R.A. (ed.) (1987) *Latin America's Debt Crisis – Adjusting to the Past or Planning for the Future*?, London: Boulder, p. 63.
2. See, among others, UNCTAD (1974) *Debt Problems in the Context of Development*, New York: Report by the Secretariat.
3. Wionczek, M.S. (ed.) (1978) *LDC External Debt and the World Economy*, Mexico City: El Colegio de Mexico; Abbot, G.C. (1979) *International Indebtedness and the Developing Countries*, London.
4. See the presentation in early 1983 of the World Bank position on this subject by the then chief economist of the Bank, Hughes, H. (1984)

'External Debt Problems of Developing Countries' in *Energy and Structural Change in the Asia-Pacific Region*, Papers and Proceedings of the Thirteen Pacific Trade and Development Conference, Manila, Philippines, 24–28 January 1983, Philippine Institute for Development Studies/Asian Development Bank, Manila, pp. 469–88.

5. Cohen, B. J. (1986) *In Whose Interest? International Banking and American Foreign Policy*. New Haven.
6. See the annual volumes of Debt Tables of the World Bank.
7. For details see CIEMEX-WHARTON (1987) *Perspectivas Economicas de Mexico*, Philadelphia: February.
8. Kraft, J. *The Mexican Rescue, The Group of Thirty*, New York.
9. If these last figures do not compare with those mentioned earlier about the country's indebtedness growth in the 1971–1982 period, it is due in part to the inclusion in the 1986 data of the private external debt guaranteed now by the Mexican state and estimated in the spring of 1985 at 13 billion US dollars.
10. Most of these individual Latin American countries case studies appear in Wionczek, M. S. (ed.) (1985) *Politics and Economics of External Debt Crisis – The Latin American Experience*, London.
11. CEPAL (ECLAC) (1986) *Balance preliminar de la economía latinoamericana*, Santiago de Chile, 18 December.
12. In 1985 the World Bank commissioned for its internal use a number of surveys of the socio-economic conditions in selected Latin American countries. A copy of such a study on Mexico, entitled 'Social consequences of the economic crisis: Mexico 1982–85', was made available to the writer on a confidential basis. It makes very grim reading.
13. McCoy, C.G. (1987) 'Beyond the Dollars-Debt: Crisis is Inflicting a Heavy Human toll in Dominican Republic (a dispatch from Santo Domingo)', *The Wall Street Journal.* 20 August.
14. LeMoyne, J. (1987), 'In Central America the Workers Suffer Most', *The New York Times*, 8 September (datelined from San Salvador), an article from a series, 'Roots of Turmoil – The Social Strains in Central America'. Two earlier articles from the same series, datelined from San Salvador and Guatemala and written by Larry Rother and Stephen Kinzer respectively, appeared in *The New York Times* on 6 and 7 September and carry the following titles: 'Central American Plight is People in Abundance', and 'The Hunger of Land Feeds the Crisis in Central America'.
15. Prowse, M. (1987) 'When Forgiveness Could Pay Off', *The Financial Times*, 23 July.
16. A very useful taxonomic survey of these proposals can be found in Grugman, P. (1981) *Prospects for International Debt Reform*, (report to the Group of Twenty-Four) New York, UNDP/UNCTAD, January (mimeo). The author is professor of economics at the MIT, Cambridge, Mass.
17. For the evidence that this process continues see 'America's Banks Struggle and Strive', *The Economist*, 19 July 1986, and Borg, E.N.

(1987) 'Debt Actions May Affect Bank Loans Dividends', *The New York Times*, 4 July.

18. The Impact of the Latin American Debt Crisis on the US Economy, a staff study prepared for the use of the Joint Economic Committee, Congress of the United States, Washington, DC, 10 May 1986 (mimeo).
19. Crook, C. (1986) 'The World Bank – A Change of Pace (Special Survey)', *The Economist*, 27 September.
20. Ibid., p. 20.
21. Ibid., p. 23.
22. 'Bridging the lending gap', *The Economist*, 20 June 1987.
23. Broad, R. (1987) 'How About a Real Solution to Third World Debt?', *The New York Times*, 28 September.
24. A very extensive literature originating in the developing world rejects such propositions as not applicable under conditions of underdevelopment. Moreover, they are criticized by such representatives of the structural economics school as Gunnar Myrdal, Ragnar Nurkse, and Hans Singer, among others.
25. Dunning, J. and Cantwell, J. (1987) *Directory of Statistics of International Investment and Production*, London.
26. Ibid.
27. Quoted by Michael Browse, 'When forgiveness could pay off', *The Financial Times*, 23 July 1987. A devastating analysis of the debt-equity-swaps for a debtor economy was written by a leading Chilean economist, Ricardo French-Davis, 'The impact of debt equity swaps: A view from the developing countries', *The CTC Reporter*, UN Center on Transnational Corporations, New York, no. 23, spring 1987.
28. Truell, P. (1987) 'Despite Progress, World Still Gropes for Debt Solutions', *The Wall Street Journal*, 18 August.
29. Kaletsky, A. (1985) *The Costs of Default*, New York: Priority Publications.

Chapter eight

Indebtedness, savings, and exports: prerequisite conditions to an expansive adjustment[1]

Carlos Massad

Introduction

Apparently the problem of external indebtedness is not being solved in the Latin American countries. The debt is steadily, if slowly, increasing, and both the export rate and the gross domestic product are practically stuck now. In 1982 and 1983 they even fell off violently, partly because of the debtor countries' own efforts to adjust themselves in order to fulfil their external obligations, and partly because of the recessionary international economy and the dwindling financial markets.

First, this article examines the recent development of the problem of indebtedness and the costs of the debt service. In the course of this examination, the present situation is compared with the Great Depression, with Germany's situation after the First World War, when it had to make reparations, and with the recessions that occurred in the past century. Second, a simulation model is developed in order to assess the extent of the efforts in the form of exports and savings that have to be made in order to service debt under different assumed circumstances as regards the rate of interest and external financing in a context of growth.

Third and last, various alternative ways of diminishing the burden of the debt service are presented, and all of them aim at reconciling adjustment and debt service with the requirements of economic growth.

The debt burden and adjustment

Expansive or recessionary adjustment?

If the debt service involves real net transfers of financial resources abroad, such transfers will diminish the financial resources for internal consumption and investments and force a trade surplus which corresponds exactly to the amount by which the internal savings exceed investments. This very surplus is transferred abroad.

The financial resources for such transfers have first to be put into a transferable form. This is done by producing a corresponding trade balance surplus. Thus the surplus of savings over investments is balanced by a corresponding *contra* entry in the external sector.

If the required surplus is achieved by an increase in savings, and if it is converted into transferable financial resources by means of an increase in exports and an efficient import substitution, the transfer can be carried out without lowering the level of activity and employment, and without curtailing investment. In this case the transfer would still imply costs in terms of prosperity, for part of the goods and services that were produced by means of the available financial resources would have to be transferred abroad. Nevertheless, this approach to the solution of the problems will minimize unemployment costs and the diminution of the growth potential.

In the Latin American countries the surplus to be transferred was achieved by a dramatic fall in capital spending, and its conversion into transferable financial resources was brought about by a drastic diminution of imports, employment, and the level of economic activity. The diminution of imports was meant not only to make the necessary macroeconomic room for a foreign transfer of the real financial resources that were raised for the debt service, but also to facilitate an adjustment to the falling Latin American exports. This unprecedented fall can be explained by the decline in the terms of trade and in the price of almost all the Latin American export products.

The Latin American imports, valued at constant prices, have fallen off by 40 per cent since they reached a peak in 1982; in 1986, they even showed a lower level than in 1974. In 1986 the per capita gross regional product (GRP) was 7.6 per cent lower than in 1980, and the decline in the national per capita income, a figure which takes into account the negative effects of the terms of trade and the export of capital by foreign enterprises on profits and interests, is much more serious.

The Latin American governments are interested in maintaining long-term relations with the financial markets abroad. Evidence of this can be seen in the fact that in order to keep up normality, they are quite willing to defray the high costs which the enforced adjustment process entails, provided that these costs are bearable in addition to the debt service. The Latin American governments did not seek a breakup, and one-sided steps were taken only in exceptional cases and when there was no other alternative.

The problem of indebtedness is on the increase. The international rate of growth does not reach a satisfactory level, and all the prognoses confirm an impression of general weakness. Despite the sudden devaluation of the US dollar on the international markets, the terms of trade, except those for crude oil, do not show a lasting recovery. Besides, protectionist tendencies are still prevailing. Apparently the present situation does not help to solve the problem, but only permits the creditors to strengthen their rights of ownership by means of commissions and capital increase so that they can meet risks in their respective line of business more easily. In the present circumstances some of the adjustment measures of the debtor countries might bear fruit; however, with a weak world economy and growing protectionism, the effect on the international economy and on the terms of trade of many countries adjusting at the same time in the same direction leave nothing much to expect.

The 1930s and the 1980s

In Latin America, the crisis of the 1980s shows characteristics that are just as bad as those of the crisis of the Great Depression of the 1930s, or even worse. In 1985, the terms of trade of the non-oil-exporting Latin American countries and the Caribbean were even more unfavourable than those of the years of the Great Depression. In 1986 the terms of trade of all Latin American countries as a whole were 4 per cent lower than the corresponding average figure for the period between 1930 and 1937 (see Figures 8.1 and 8.2). During the Great Depression, the major part of the debt consisted of bonds placed abroad. When the crisis drastically diminished the debtor countries' ability to pay off their debts to other countries, the debtor countries were forced to suspend payment completely or at least partly; as a result, the market price of the bonds dropped drastically. In 1939, for instance, that is, seven years after the worst moment of the crisis, the South American bonds, in a backlog of payments, were traded at 40 per cent of their nominal value, the Central American bonds at 30 per cent, and the West Indian bonds at 46 per cent of their value.

Between 1935 and 1939 Chile bought bonds of its own debt for 13 million US dollars, whereas originally they had had a nominal value of 88 million US dollars; in other words, Chile paid 15 cents for every dollar of its foreign debt.[2] This debt diminution amounted to a reduction of Chile's total debt expressed in bonds in

Figure 8.1 Terms of trade in Latin America 1930–86 (1970 = 100)

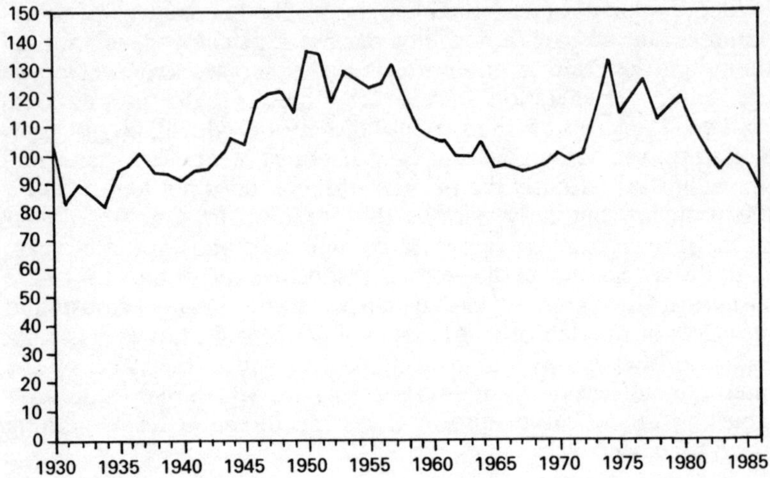

Source: CEPAL.

Figure 8.2 Terms of trade in non-oil-exporting countries 1930–85 (1970 = 100)

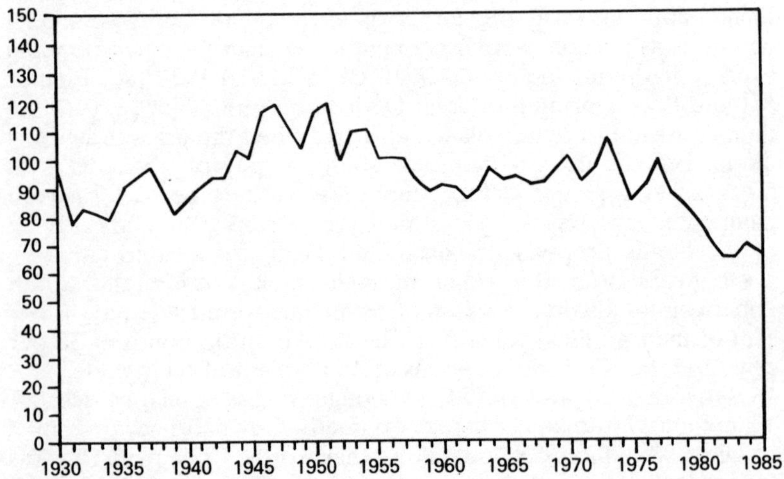

Source: CEPAL.

1935 by a third. By means of this mechanism, and the total or part suspension of the debt service payments, the burden was shared between the debtors and the creditors.

This is different in the crisis of the 1980s, when the non-fulfilment of a debt service is an exception, and the burden of the debt service is, except for some minor cases, not relieved by the circumstances of the market. The debt is a debt to the banks, and there is no broad and generally-used market for the documents that represent it.

During the crisis of the 1930s arrangements that diminished the amount of debt and fixed the rate of interest below the market level of interest rates were made between the creditors and the debtors. Besides, the time limits were extended. There are no similar agreements in the crisis of the 1980s. On the contrary, the Latin American debtor countries' interest payments on their foreign debts require a real transfer of resources to other countries that, in proportion to their exports, exceeds many times over the amount which, according to the Treaty of Versailles, Germany had to pay in the form of reparations, interest on its foreign debt, and profit transfers of foreign investors.

In fact, the total amount of profits and net interest payments as well as reparations to other countries never came to 25 per cent of the German exports, not even at the worst moment of the crisis. This is different in the case of Latin America, where since 1982 the interest and profit transfers have amounted to 40 per cent of the export of goods. And when in 1931 Germany's payments including reparations came to 23 per cent of the exports (or even 36 per cent, if the capital flight out of Germany is taken into account), a special commission of the Bank for International Settlements (BIS), which was to advise the banks regarding the control of the reparations, ascertained that Germany was right in stating that it was unable to fulfil a major part of its financial obligations.[3] In the following year the reparations dropped by 84 per cent, and in 1933 they were completely suspended. Besides, even at a time when Germany had to make extensive reparations, it was a net importer of funds from other countries; from 1924 to 1932 Germany's net capital imports exceeded the total amount of its interest payments, profit transfers, and reparations by 20 per cent (see Table 8.1).

In order to diminish the debt capital and to relieve the debt burden, Latin America's creditor banks have made arrangements with some enterprises whose liabilities were not hedged by the state. However, in proportion to the total debt, these amounts, which do not even come to 1 per cent, are too small to render

Table 8.1 Germany: current payments and net capital inflows, 1924–32 (in billions of RM)

Year	(1) Merchandise exports	(2) Reparations	(3) Interest and earnings[1]	(4) Capital injection[2]	(5) 2+3	(6) 5/1	(7) 4–5	(8) 7/1
1924	7.8	0.3	−0.2	3.1	0.1	1.30	3.0	0.38
1925	9.6	1.1	0.0	3.5	1.1	0.11	2.4	0.26
1926	10.7	1.2	0.2	1.1	1.4	0.13	−0.3	−0.03
1927	11.1	1.6	0.3	5.3	1.9	0.17	3.4	0.31
1928	12.6	2.0	0.6	3.8	2.6	0.20	1.2	0.10
1929	13.7	2.5	0.8	3.2	3.3	0.24	−0.1	−0.01
1930	12.2	1.7	1.0	1.0	2.7	0.22	−1.7	−0.14
1931	9.6	1.0	1.2	−1.3	2.2	0.23	−3.5	−0.36
1932	5.8	0.2	0.9	−0.2	1.1	0.19	−1.3	−0.22

Source: On the basis of data ascertained by the League of Nations (see League of Nations (1945) *Experiencia Monetaria Internacional. Lecciones del periodo de entreguerras* (*International Monetary Experiences. Lessons from the period between the two World Wars*), Geneva).

Notes:

1 Interest and net earnings transferred abroad. The minus sign indicates the net earnings.
2 Includes the net balance of other outputs, net capital earnings, mistakes, and omissions. The latter are mainly registered capital movements. The minus sign indicates the net outflow.

macroeconomic significance to these arrangements. At the same time new financing was drastically cut back, and is now only effected under strict conditionality. There are several historical precedents for these cut-backs in external financing.

The procyclical behaviour of external financing

A repeated lesson from history is that international financing shows a strongly procyclical behaviour. The sale of bonds in England made the loans possible which the Latin American republics raised during the past century in order to maintain their recently-won independence. Between 1820 and 1825 Argentina (Buenos Aires), Chile, Colombia, Guatemala, Mexico, and Peru placed their issues in London. At the end of 1825 the financial flows stopped completely because of a financial crisis in England – in the course of the two following years, the interest payments of all the debtors, with the exception of Brazil, were suspended. It took thirty years of permanent negotiations to normalize the situation. In the third and fourth decades of the past century, the debt of the United States increased by 15 times its value in 1820. The recession, which began in England in 1837, stopped the financial flows into the United States, and nine American States by turns stopped their interest payments in 1841 and 1842; two of them, Mississippi and Florida, rejected their whole debt, and one, that is, Michigan, rejected parts of its debt. The other six simply suspended interest payments without any official announcement.[4]

There was a new wave of non-compliance at the time of the recession of 1873; like the preceding recessions, it brought about a diminution of the international capital flows, which in turn caused a crisis of the debt service. Eleven states of the Union did not meet their obligations. Owing to the necessity of negotiations between the official debtors, the issuers of bonds, and the owners of these bonds in London, the British Corporation of Owners of Foreign Bonds was set up. This corporation represented the interests of the bond owners in negotiations which took place regularly, and which resulted in a diminution of capital and/or a modification of the capital and interest payments. The only overdue debtors who did not come to an agreement with the corporation during the five decades of its existence until 1914 were those states of the Union that had rejected their debt.[5]

In 1933 a similar commission named Foreign Bondholder Protective Council was set up in the United States.

Between 1931 and 1937, that is, in the worst years of the Great Depression, the most important debtor countries exported net capital, while most creditor countries received strong inflows of capital.[6] Both in the crisis of the 1930s and in that of the 1980s the United states imported capital from abroad. As to the latter crisis, before which the Latin American debt had increased by 20 per cent annually since the middle of the 1970s, it resulted in a drastic reduction of the rate of growth of debt: to 8 per cent in 1983, in 1984 to 5.6 per cent, in 1985 to 2.1 per cent, and in 1986 to 3.6 per cent. The rise in indebtedness is clearly below the level of the direct interest payment and of the profit transfers to other countries.

The phenomenon of the procyclical behaviour of foreign financing has been known for over 40 years now. It was generally expected that after The Second World War the World Bank would take over the task of anticyclical financing.[7]

Historical experience has repeatedly shown the necessity of considering the problem of indebtedness, not only from the point of view of the respective country's situation, but also from a systemic point of view. The fact that many people are under the delusion that measures which are appropriate for individual countries, but have a negative impact on all the countries as a whole are acceptable, is further proof of the necessity of such a systemic viewpoint. Therefore a solution to the debt problem requires both national measures, which promote the adjustment of the economy, and measures on the part of the creditors, which relieve the heavy debt burden, such as modifications to the international monetary and financial system and to trade.

The debt burden and growth: a simulation model

In order to assess the debtor countries' efforts to fulfil their debt obligations and achieve growth at the same time, a model was used which relates the rate of growth of indebtedness, the external rate of interest, the ratio of indebtedness to gross domestic product (GDP), and the foreign trade disequilibrium (or the difference between savings and investment) to each other.[8] The calculations were made for seven Latin American countries: Argentina, Brazil, Chile, Colombia, Mexico, Peru, and Venezuela.

The application of the model required an estimation of the necessary investment for an annual growth of the gross national product (GNP) of 4 per cent, a figure which was fixed as the lowest justifiable performance target.

An average growth of 4 per cent in all seven countries requires a propensity to invest of 23 per cent of the GDP. Nevertheless, a lower rate of 20 per cent was taken as the basis of the simulation, for it was assumed that there are unused capacities in these countries and that there is a relatively high rate of unemployment, which makes growth with less investments possible than it is on average required for a longer period of time. A more specific study might try to assess the prerequisites of cyclical investments.

Furthermore, the income elasticities for imports had to be assessed. The well-known estimations refer to average elasticities for long periods of time and do not permit an evaluation of what happens to the imports when the GDP falls or rises at a certain velocity. Therefore, estimates of the cyclical elasticities are assessed because they are significantly superior to average or tendential elasticities. The latter were also assessed for the purpose of comparison, and the resulting estimated values tally with the ones in other papers.[9]

On the basis of these estimates three groups with different relative levels of indebtedness were set up: high, that is, a level that comes close to the GDP; medium, that is, a level that corresponds to 70 per cent of the GDP; and low, that is, a level that amounts to only 50 per cent of GDP.

Four successive periods were simulated on a yearly basis, and the results were averaged. The values ascertained in this way are presented in Tables 8.2a, 8.2b, and 8.2c. The average values cover a leap, which appears in the first year of the simulation when the savings rate is adjusted to the required levels. In some cases this leap is so big that it could not possibly occur in reality. Therefore in practice the debt level would have to rise above the level indicated in the simulation.

For the highly-indebted countries (see Table 8.2a) the internal savings rate would have to be 27 per cent of the GNP and the average rate of growth of exports 12 per cent per annum in the first four years of the simulation. These values can hardly be reached as long as the nominal US dollar debt rises by 3 per cent annually and the external rate of interest, which includes all the costs of indebtedness, amounts to 10 per cent. With a growth of debt of 3 per cent per annum and an interest rate of 4 per cent per annum, the necessary savings rate for an economic growth of 4 per cent would be only 21 per cent of GDP per year, while exports would be required to grow at 6 per cent per year, on the average.

For all countries the best simulated situation is given with a rate of growth of debt of 7 per cent per annum and an annual interest rate of 4 per cent on the debt. The savings rate would then range between 17 per cent and 18 per cent of GDP; and the rate of growth for exports would go down to 3 per cent. Although this savings rate tallies with the recently ascertained actual one, the required rate of growth of exports exceeds the actual one by far.

In view of the presently obtainable facts, it seems highly improbable that the foreign indebtedness will increase by 7 per cent per annum. And even if it did, this would not change the present ratio of indebtedness to GDP. In the long run this situation is not at all desirable.

The results are even worse if a nominal growth of indebtedness of about 3 per cent per annum is assumed. At best, an internal savings rate of 20 per cent of the GDP and an increase in exports by 6 per cent to 8 per cent per annum would be necessary. It should be mentioned here that between 1981 and 1985 the average savings rate amounted to 17 per cent of GNP, while the exports went down annually by almost 1 per cent on average, a fact which illustrates the deterioration of the terms of trade.

Apparently a nominal growth of debt of 3 per cent cannot easily be achieved; this is why a situation in which the debt does not continue to increase is examined (in real terms it would even decrease). In such a situation and under the best possible simulated circumstances, that is, with a relatively low level of debt, a savings rate of 23 per cent of GNP and an average increase in exports by 7

Table 8.2a High level of indebtedness ($D/Y = 1$)

	I	*AMI*[a]	*AME*[b]	*AMX*[c]	*D IM*	*D EXMI*	*D EXME*	*D EXMX*	*TRMI**	*TRME*	*TRMX*
i	*Y*	*Y*	*Y*	*Y*	*M*	*EX*	*EX*	*EX*	*Y*	*Y*	*Y*
0.12	0.20	0.25	0.29	0.32	0.09	0.09	0.15	0.18	0.05	0.09	0.12
0.10	0.20	0.23	0.27	0.30	0.09	0.07	0.12	0.16	0.03	0.07	0.10
0.08	0.20	0.21	0.25	0.28	0.09	0.06	0.09	0.14	0.01	0.05	0.08
0.06	0.20	0.19	0.23	0.26	0.09	0.04	0.07	0.11	−0.01	0.03	0.06
0.04	0.20	0.17	0.21	0.24	0.09	0.03	0.06	0.08	−0.03	0.01	0.04

Table 8.2b Medium level of indebtedness ($D/Y = 0.7$)

	I	*AMI*[a]	*AME*[b]	*AMX*[c]	*D IM*	*D EXMI*	*D EXME*	*D EXMX*	*TRMI**	*TRME*	*TRMX*
i	*Y*	*Y*	*Y*	*Y*	*M*	*EX*	*EX*	*EX*	*Y*	*Y*	*Y*
0.12	0.20	0.23	0.26	0.29	0.09	0.07	0.11	0.14	0.04	0.06	0.09
0.10	0.20	0.22	0.25	0.27	0.09	0.06	0.09	0.12	0.02	0.05	0.07
0.08	0.20	0.20	0.24	0.26	0.09	0.05	0.08	0.11	0.01	0.04	0.06
0.06	0.20	0.19	0.22	0.24	0.09	0.04	0.06	0.08	−0.01	0.02	0.04
0.04	0.20	0.18	0.20	0.22	0.09	0.02	0.05	0.06	−0.02	0.01	0.02

i	*I* / *Y*	*AMI*[a] / *Y*	*AME*[b] / *Y*	*AMX*[c] / *Y*	*D IM* / *M*	*D EXMI* / *EX*	*D EXME* / *EX*	*D EXMX* / *EX*	*TRMI** / *Y*	*TRME* / *Y*	*TRMX* / *Y*
0.12	0.20	0.22	0.24	0.20	0.09	0.06	0.08	0.11	0.02	0.04	0.06
0.10	0.20	0.21	0.23	0.25	0.09	0.05	0.07	0.09	0.01	0.03	0.05
0.08	0.20	0.20	0.22	0.24	0.09	0.05	0.06	0.08	0.00	0.02	0.04
0.06	0.20	0.19	0.21	0.23	0.09	0.04	0.05	0.07	−0.01	0.01	0.03
0.04	0.20	0.18	0.20	0.22	0.09	0.02	0.05	0.06	−0.02	0.00	0.02

Notes:

a A nominal rate of growth for the debt of 7 per cent per annum is assumed.
b A nominal rate of growth for the debt of 3 per cent per annum is assumed.
c A zero growth of the nominal debt is assumed.
* The minus sign means: inflow of funds from abroad.

i = External nominal interest rate (includes all costs of the foreign debt).
I/Y = Requisite ratio of investment to GNP.
AMI/Y = Requisite minimum ratio of savings to GNP.
AME/Y = Requisite mean ratio of savings to GNP.
AMX/Y = Requisite maximum ratio of savings to GNP.
D IM/M = Rate of growth of imports.
D EXMI/EX = Required minimum rate of growth of exports.
D EXME/EX = Required mean rate of exports.
D EXMX/EX = Required maximum rate of exports.
TRMI/Y = Transfer of resources into other countries/minimum GNP.
TRME/Y = Transfer of resources into other countries/mean GNP.
TRMX/Y = Transfer of resources into other countries/maximum GNP.

per cent per annum are required, provided that the rate of interest per annum amounts to 6 per cent.

If the rate of interest rises to 8 per cent instead of 6 per cent, while the level of debt remains constant, the results are even worse – in the best possible case an internal savings rate of 24 per cent of GNP, and an annual increase in exports by 8 per cent on average would then be necessary.

The fact that in any case a high rate of growth of exports is required shows that a 'natural' solution of the problem of indebtedness is very much dependent on internal economic growth. Without a sufficient growth of the world economy, the required increase in exports is highly improbable. And even if such an increase were achieved, it would have an additional negative impact on the terms of trade.[10]

These calculations clearly illustrate the necessity to find formulas for relieving the debt burden, and these formulas should also reduce the savings and export efforts of the countries with a relatively low level of indebtedness.

The formulas should give relief without entailing costs, that is, they should not exhaust the financial resources of the debtor countries. There are only three ways of achieving this: a diminution of the real rates of interest (or the debt), an improvement of the terms of trade, and a rise in the productivity of investments. The first two cannot be influenced by the debtor countries' policy, at least not in the short term; their realization is on the creditor's hands. The third way is basically dependent on the debtor countries' internal policies, although it is also related to the price of export products: only a price rise can effect a fast increase in the productivity of investment measured in terms of imports; other measures would require further investments and structural reforms, which in turn would entail additional financing and take a lot of time. Therefore 'financing' and 'adjustment' are complements rather than alternatives.

It is worth mentioning that a diminution of the rate of interest by 2 per cent would facilitate the savings efforts by 1 per cent or 2 per cent of GNP and reduce the necessary rate of growth of exports by 1 per cent to 2 per cent.

A drop of the real rates of interest to the historical level of 1 per cent to 3 per cent per annum, or specific measures for lowering the existing debt costs to that level, would reduce the necessary investment efforts by 2 per cent to 4 per cent, and would limit the necessary rate of growth of exports to something between 2 per cent and 4 per cent. Apparently it is imperative that the creditors should make these contributions in order to keep the efforts on the part of the debtor countries within justifiable limits.

The evaluation of the debt through the market and the sustainable level of debt

Another way of ascertaining the degree of probability that the debtor countries will be able to meet their obligations regarding foreign indebtedness exactly as they had initially been laid down is to examine the evaluation of the debt on the market. During the past years both the creditors and the debtors thought it right to rearrange the credit and debit items with regard to individual debtors as well as to countries and to currencies. These rearrangements brought about a secondary market for the enforceable legal documents, the prices of which are established according to the conditions of demand and supply. Demand and supply vary according to the existing incentives or impediments to the re-arrangement of items; besides, they are dependent on how the economic participants who operate on the market, that is, the creditor banks, the foreign and the national investors, and the debtor countries' governments, assess the probability of non-compliance.

On this secondary market four different types of operations are carried out:

1. An exchange of one country's debt for another country's debt;
2. An exchange of enforceable legal documents for cash from the creditor country;
3. An exchange of a debt for investments in the debtor country;
4. An exchange of a debt for the debtor country's domestic currency.

The first of these operations aims mainly at the realization of one of the three other possibilities. The number of developing countries which have worked out strategies to arrange the third and the fourth operation is steadily increasing. Among these countries are Argentina, Brazil, Chile, Costa Rica, Ecuador, Mexico, Venezuela and the Philippine Islands. The debts of other countries, such as Nigeria, Poland, and Yugoslavia, are also traded on the secondary market.[11]

Table 8.3 shows that except for the extreme case of Peru, the foreign debts of the listed countries were traded on the secondary market with a mark-down between 25 per cent and 55 per cent of their nominal value, depending on the respective country. There is

Table 8.3 Market price of notes payable on the foreign debt (100 - nominal value)

	1985	*1986*			*1987*		
Country	*June*	*January*	*June*	*December*	*February*	*March*	*May*
Argentina	60–65	62–66	63–67	62–66	62–65	63	58
Bolivia	nd	nd	7[a]	nd	nd	55–10	11–13
Brazil	75–81	75–81	73–76	74–77	73–75	69	62
Chile	65–69	65–69	64–67	65–68	68	68	71–72
Colombia	81–83	82–84	80–82	90	nd	nd	nd
Costa Rica	nd	nd	nd	40	nd	45	nd
Ecuador	65–70	68–71	63–66	63–65	nd	62	50
Mexico	80–82	69–73	55–59	54–57	56–58	58	58
Peru	45–50	25–30	17–23	16–19	16–19	nd	14
Uruguay	nd	nd	64[a]	nd	nd	nd	nd
Venezuela	81–83	80–82	75–78	72–74	72–74	72	72–75
Philippine Islands	nd	nd	nd	72–76	74	74	70

Source: June 1985–December 1986 – Shearson, Lehman Brothers, Loan Transactions Group; February 1987 – 'Fortune', 30 March 1987; Shearson Lehman Brothers, in *The Economist*, 21 March 1987; March 1987 – *Business Latin America*, 20 April 1987.

Notes:

a May 1986 – Dornbusch (1986) 'The Debt Problems and Some Proposed Solutions', October.

also a dramatic drop of prices on the secondary markets observable. However, the latter tendency might be due to the specific nature of the traded credits and to the short-term assessment of the probability of payment by the market.

The simulation model developed in this article offers yet another way of looking at the same problem: a sustainable level of debt for a country with given expectations of economic growth, given rates of interest, and further costs in connection with its debt can be ascertained at any point of time. The faster the growth which a country with a given behaviour of its exports strives for, the lower the tolerable level of debt will be, for the keeping up of a higher rate of growth requires an increase in imports; the increase in imports will use up resources which could have been devoted to debt service. On the other hand, the higher the costs of indebtedness are, the lower the tolerable level of debt for any rhythm of economic growth will be. A calculation based on the assumption of an adequate real economic growth of 4 per cent per annum, and on the assumptions that the exports in terms of quantity have a similar rhythm of growth and that the costs in connection with the foreign debt amount to 10 per cent per annum, results in econ-

Table 8.4 Sustainable foreign debt, debt at market prices, and nominal debt (in billions of US dollars)

	1986	*1987*	*1988*	*1989*	*1990*
Argentina					
Simulated debt[a]	48 646	46 611	45 556	44 497	43 360
Debt in the market price[b]	41 360	38 253	39 915	41 144	42 348
Nominal debt[c]	50 300	51 809	53 363	54 964	56 614
Brazil					
Simulated debt[a]	102 937	99 120	94 126	90 064	87 608
Debt in the market price[b]	87 012	74 136	76 360	78 343	81 010
Nominal debt[c]	101 750	104 802	107 946	111 184	114 520
Chile					
Simulated debt[a]	18 263	16 285	15 334	14 915	14 163
Debt in the market price[b]	14 900	16 150	16 656	17 177	17 714
Nominal debt[c]	20 690	21 310	21 950	22 608	23 286
Mexico					
Simulated debt[a]	96 554	90 834	84 979	78 855	73 656
Debt in the market price[b]	72 192	70 987	73 116	75 309	77 882
Nominal debt[c]	100 000	103 000	106 090	109 272	112 550
Peru					
Simulated debt[a]	12 448	10 623	9 502	9 150	8 702
Debt in the market price[b]	9 850	10 169	10 466	10 787	11 111
Nominal debt[c]	14 300	14 729	15 170	15 625	16 094
Venezuela					
Simulated debt[a]	33 262	30 254	29 752	28 741	27 250
Debt in the market price[b]	27 161	30 395	31 037	32 248	33 215
Nominal debt[c]	35 880	36 956	38 065	39 207	40 383

Notes:

a Debt calculated by means of the simulation model used in this article.

b Calculated by an evaluation of the debt to banks at its market price plus the nominal debt to non-banks. The market price of 1986 corresponds to that of December 1986, while the market price from 1987 onwards corresponds to that of May 1987. Both were taken from Lahera (1987) op. cit. Information about the amounts due to the banks was obtained from the Bank for International Settlements, International Banking and Financial Market Developments, April 1987.

c CEPAL, 'Balance preliminar de la economía latinoamericana', 1986. Debt is assumed to grow by 3% nominally per year.

omically sustainable debt figures, which are considerably lower than the nominal value of the debt of 1987. If a period of time of five years is taken into account, and if both the nominal debt of 1987 and the market value of the debt of 1987 (given by the market price) remain constant in real terms, the economically-sustainable debt becomes lower than the other two in four of the six countries which were examined in this study. In three of these countries, the sustainable debt is already after two years of simulation lower than the nominal and the market value of the debt. The estimation through the market was based on the assumption that a country's total debt to the banks is assessed on the basis of the prices which were effective in the transactions of 1986, while the debt to non-banks, that is, mainly governments and multilateral institutions, is estimated at its nominal value (see Table 8.4).

Table 8.4 shows the result of an application of the simulation model to six Latin American countries. The calculations are based on the situation registered in 1985 and on the income, demand, and import elasticities that were ascertained for the phase of expansion in the business cycle.

These two ways of looking at the problem, that is, the assessment through the market and the estimation of an economically sustainable debt, leave no doubt that the solution of the problem of indebtedness requires that the debtor countries are partially relieved of the burden of their debt service. Both the measures to increase loan-loss reserves, on which the US banks have recently decided, and the increase in reserves that has already been effected by the European banks, show that this necessity is recognized on the part of the creditors who incurred costs by facing the situation. Paradoxically, these costs do not entail corresponding benefits for the debtors because they neither help to strengthen the creditors' remaining positions, nor enable the debtor countries to initiate a new stage of growth in safer circumstances.

In view of the present situation, the most important aspects of any solution to the debt problem is probably the search for formulas which relieve the debtors of their debt burden, thus permitting them to benefit from the fact that the market assesses their debts below their nominal value.

It remains to examine the nature of those solutions to the problem of indebtedness which aim at relieving the burden of the debt service. Not only the debtors, but also the creditors will benefit from a solution of the debt problem. On the one hand a solution would improve the quality of the creditors' asset items and facilitate a return to normality in the financial system. On the other hand, it would make the implementation of a normal economic policy possible, that is, a policy without the grave insecurities that accompany every crisis. Last, it would permit a higher rate of growth in the debtor countries, whole imports from the creditor countries are an important element in the dynamics of the creditor countries' economy. As far as the United States are concerned, half of any reduction of the Latin American debt service payments would bring about additional purchases in the United States.[12]

Suggested Solutions

The solutions which aim at relieving the debt burden are based on five premises:[13]

1. Both the debtors and the creditors have to take responsiblity for the fast increase in indebtedness.
2. The evolution of the problem of indebtedness towards an acute condition results both from the debtor countries' own policy and from factors which they cannot control, such as a set of policies in the industrial countries, international recession, and the procyclical behaviour of international financing. Nevertheless, the general scope of the problem stresses the importance of external factors.
3. The lasting recessionary adjustment of the debtor countries' economies is no longer tolerable.
4. As it takes time and money to reallocate real resources which could then produce a surplus that might be used for the debt service, adjustment and financing are not alternative reactions to the problem of indebtedness, but together they are part of its solution.
5. It is in the creditor and the debtor countries' interest to find a solution to the current crisis as soon as possible.

A lowering of the rate of interest and an improvement of the terms of trade are the decisive factors in the solution of the debt problem. In the absence of an appropriate solution by way of the market for these two variables, any alternative solution must necessarily aim at reducing the debt-service payments. There are two ways of tackling this problem – the first consists in a reduction of the debt-service payments in accordance with certain criteria of the capacity to pay, such as the total amount of exports, the price of a key export product, the total amount of exchange proceeds, or the GDP; the second way consists in a direct diminution without an accumulation of debt-service payments. If debt-service payments are limited according to some debt-service capacity criteria, and if service above the limit is accumulated indefinitely, the capacity criteria and the direct diminution of debt-service payments become equivalent financially.

The reduction of the payment of interest on the debt

The debt burden can be directly diminished either by lowering the rate of interest and other costs below the market price, or by reducing the basic amount of debt directly. Although these two procedures differ in accounting, they are equivalent in financial terms except for differences in tax treatments. A cut in the interest rate affects the creditors' balance sheet only after some time (whenever the norms of accounting permit it), whereas a direct diminution of the debt capital is at once fully reflected in the accounts.[14] This difference in accounting can have decisive influence on the stability of the creditor institution.

In this context, the norms of accounting are very important. In the United States, for instance, the interest rate cuts will only burden the capital if the total future repayments and interest payments are lower than the capital due at the time when the reduction was granted.[15] This means that even if the interest and the commissions fall off to zero, the debt capital must not necessarily be burdened, provided that the repayment of this capital can be guaranteed for the future. Thus, on the part of the banks, the negotiable range of interest between zero and the market rates is only limited by the necessity of an appropriate rate of return on their capital.

A reduction of the interest payment on the debt does not seem to have an overwhelming effect on the creditor banks' receipts. A study by the United States Congress points out that if in 1985 Latin America's interest payments had decreased by 12 billion US dollars, and if the banks had written off their loans to Latin America with 1 per cent in that year, the nine most important US banks would have had after-tax profits in 1985 above the level of 1984. The calculation assumes that US banks take on a part of the interest rate cuts in proportion to their loans to Latin America.[16] It is worth mentioning that the after-tax effects of an interest rate cut or a diminution of the basic amount of debt on the profits of the banks depend on the respective tax treatment.

A lowering of the rate of interest improves the debtors' situation, and at the same time the creditors' chances of getting their capital back. Therefore a bank prefers interest rate cuts to taking the risk of extending a new loan to the debtor, provided that the loans at risk with this debtor are relatively small in proportion to the balance sheet total. In this way the debtor's situation can be improved and the probability of getting back the capital can be heightened. According to bankers of private commercial banks in the United States, the local banks prefer this strategy to giving fresh money to external debtors.

Many formulas for reducing the rate of interest on the foreign debt have been proposed by now. One of them, a cut in or a reduction of commissions and other burdens, has already been applied to a limited extent in the round of negotiations that have been taking place since 1982. During the first round, both the spread over the reference rate and the commissions were raised considerably in comparison with the levels before the crisis. In this first round, the average spread came to 2.22 per cent above (LIBOR), and the average commission regarding the newly-negotiated conditions for the twelve countries came to 1.27 per cent. In the second round the average burden was reduced to 1.77 per cent above LIBOR for all the seven countries which were negotiating again in 1983 and 1984, while the commissions went down to 0.8 per cent. In the third round, the average burden above LIBOR and the commissions were further reduced, until they reached 1.44 per cent and 1.42 per cent respectively. In this last round, some countries succeeded in negotiating a complete writing off of their commissions; however, the spread over the reference rate of interest remained above the one before the crisis, which had sometimes been substantially below 1 per cent.

The reference rate of interest itself is far above its historical level. In some of the recent negotiations the traditional reference rates (LIBOR or PRIME) were replaced by rates related to the cost of funding of the banks which are below the traditional reference rates. The difference is minor, though, and can mean no more than a cost relief of 0.5 per cent per annum to the debtors.

The formulas that have been applied so far have not at all sufficed for a general relief of the burden of the debt service. Therefore further formulas, which include a diminution of the interest payments and a rearrangement of these payments, are taken into consideration. Among the formulas which are applied in order to lower the interest payments are the automatic capitalization of the interest at a rate considerably below the prevailing market rates, and the payment of interest in domestic currency, which is only afterwards exchanged for foreign currency.

A capitalization of the interest would make a normalization of the nominal interest payments possible: the amounts which exceed a certain maximum would be capitalized. In this way the interest payment is facilitated; besides, a stabilizing factor is introduced into the debtor's balance of payments, for the annual interest payments would then be independent of the fluctuations of the international interest rates. Such mechanisms would automatically regulate world economy. They would also facilitate a proportional distribution of the capitalization costs among the creditors.

An interest payment in domestic currency (indexed according to the currency in which the loan was obtained) is similar to the interest capitalization except for the fact that creditors may use the accumulated financial resources in domestic currency. They might, for instance, use these funds to buy certain goods and services or certain securities or other assets in the debtor country, or to extend them as credits to the same country again.

The conversion of these financial resources into foreign currency, and the corresponding payment to the respective foreign country, would be arranged according to previously fixed formulas, which in turn would depend on certain conditions, such as the totality of exports or the amount of exports of a product with strategic importance to the respective economy. This aspect, that is, the control of the interest payments to the respective foreign country, could also be arranged by means of a stable flow in the course of time.

If applied massively, any of these methods of paying in domestic currency, which can then be used in the respective country, have macroeconomic effects on the debtor country, such as an inflationary pressure and changes in the ownership structure.

The diminution of the debt capital

Another way of reducing the interest payments to other countries consists in directly diminishing the debt capital. However, the simple write-off of debt with a government guarantee might have a negative impact on the debtors' future access to the market. It should only be performed if the debtors can adapt themselves to an economic situation which does not permit them to fall back on the capital market for a longer period of time. In general, the Latin American countries cannot do so, and this is why it is hardly possible for them to diminish their debt capital in this simple way. There are, however, ways of diminishing the debt capital without affecting the debtors' access to the private credit markets. There is, for instance, a secondary market for debt, which has been developing since the end of 1984 and which allows debtors to buy their own debts at a rate below their nominal value, provided that they are valued at a rate by the market.[17] It is well known that some transactions were carried out at rates between 20 per cent and 90 per cent of the original nominal debt, depending on the respective country. Some countries, such as Chile and Bolivia, even suggested or laid down formal mechanisms for the acquisition of their own debt from commercial banks. It is obvious that a diminution of the debt capital implies a diminution of the interest payments. The transactions that have so far been carried out in this manner make a small percentage of the respective countries' total debt due to the banks.

It has also been suggested that the banks' asset items be transferred to multilateral organizations, which would buy them at prices below their nominal value and then take on the task of reprogramming the debtor countries' payments. In so doing they would pass on the advantages of the lower value of these asset items to the debtors. There is one difficulty about these suggestions though: the multilateral institution concerned would either need a capital increase for this operation, or it would have to exhaust its capital resources available for direct institutional loans. Therefore this kind of solution is perhaps no adequate formula for providing the debtors with an increased amount of net financial resources. The suggestion might appeal to the creditors though, for they consider their present portfolio to be very risky.

The conversion of the debt into an equity participation

One way of modifying the conditions of interest payments which can be combined with a repurchase of the debt is the conversion into participation capital. Through this procedure the nature of the obligation changes because the regular interest payments are carried out by means of a transfer of dividends. As the government does not take the risk of the investments, the conversion into equity capital practically means the elimination of the government guarantees which might be connected with the debts. Such a conversion could render the amounts that are annually transferred abroad more flexible, for the dividends depend on the economic results of the enterprises.

Owing to the high amounts involved, a conversion of debt into equity capital can bring about considerable changes in the ownership structure of the national assets and can have corresponding political consequences, if it is massively applied.

The repurchase of the debt and the conversion into equity capital can facilitate the return of national capital invested abroad. If the transactions of repurchase and investment hold attractive profit prospects, as the transactions which have been made so far suggest, it would not come as a surprise if the chances which the repurchase of the debt offers attracted back to the debtor countries funds of their residents invested abroad.

Indebtedness to public institutions

The approaches discussed above are mainly used in the case of indebtedness to private sources. The debts to official sources, which make only a small part of the debt that is relevant to the Latin American countries, should not be restricted in renegotiations by the same considerations about profitability as the loans by commercial banks. In recent negotiations of the Club of Paris, the commissions and spreads over the reference rates have been eliminated. Besides, in recent negotiations the creditor countries agreed to a reprogramming, not only of the capital due, but also – in the case of the Dominican Republic – of the interest. Nevertheless, when new negotiations on a debt due are necessary, many public institutions in creditor countries that provide export financing have begun to cut down on their financing so that their reaction resembles that of the commercial banks.

As far as the write-off of certain loans is concerned, the creditor countries' governments are not subject to the same restrictions as the commercial banks. The remission of the write-off of a debt on the part of a creditor government does not necessarily have the same effects on the additional financing facilities available to debtors as the same write-off of the debt on the part of the commercial banks would have. The same goes for the reduction of interest payments. Therefore, whenever a considerable release from the debt payment is required, the contribution of the external public creditors to this release is of special importance. At present, a third of the Latin American foreign debt comes from various official sources, especially from government institutions and official multilateral institutions.

Some specific suggestions

The suggestion of the chairman of the managing board of the Inter-American Development Bank

The chairman of the managing board of the Inter-American developing Bank, Antonio Ortiz Mena, has presented an ingenious suggestion. This suggestion, which has not been worked out in every detail yet, aims at an automatic refinancing and reduction of the interest payments on the debt in the following way – the creditor banks are to transfer the necessary amount to a special financing fund for capital investment projects that are meant to promote an increase in exports from the debtor countries. Later on, the increase in exports would facilitate the repayment of the financial resources due to the special fund, out of which the original credits could then be serviced. In this way, a kind of automatic refinancing of a part of the interest by the banks would be introduced; this procedure would exclusively be applied to projects for increasing exports.[18]

The Baker plan

In October 1985, the secretary of the United States's treasury, James A. Baker, presented some ideas, which aimed at establishing a general framework of the problem of indebtedness.[19] Baker shares the debtor countries' opinion that the problem of indebtedness can only be solved in a context of growth and co-operation between creditors and debtors. He pointed to the necessity of carrying out structural reforms in order to liberalize trade and the debtor countries' payments, and to promote private initiative in the debtor countries. In his view such reforms are prerequisite conditions to the extension of new loans on the part of commercial banks as well as multilateral financing organizations. At the time of its presentation the Baker plan suggested an additional financing of about 10 billion US dollars per annum for three years with 70 per cent of the money coming from commercial banks. This measure would permit a nominal growth of debt of about 3 per cent per annum in the countries included in the plan.

The Baker plan is the first statement of the United States's government that recognizes the fact that the creditor countries' governments must intervene in the solution of the problem of indebtedness. Although the multilateral financing organizations consider their future transactions to be reconcilable with the Baker plan, the financing which they and the commercial banks provided was far below the amounts scheduled in the Baker plan. Besides, the slump in the price of oil in 1986 makes the amounts under discussion in the Baker plan appear totally dated.[20]

The Agreement of Cartagena

Eleven Latin American countries, signatories of the Agreement of Cartagena, namely Argentina, Bolivia, Brazil, Chile, Colombia, the Dominican Republic, Ecuador, Mexico, Peru, Uruguay, and Venezuela, have put forward an emergency suggestion about negotiations on aspects of foreign indebtedness and growth. This proposal does not aim towards a collective renegotiation on the terms of the foreign debt due, but it confirms the necessity of creating an adequate international economic situation, which permits the solution of the debt problem. This situation should include a reduction of the rates of interest to their average long-run levels, an increase in financial flows, and a strengthening of the mechanisms which alleviate the negative effects of fluctuations in the terms of trade and the rate of interest on the developing countries. The member countries pointed to the necessity of distinguishing between the treatment of the debt already contracted and that of the new debt, so that the latter can better be dealt with on the market, thus permitting the application of more favourable conditions for the already contracted debt.

The agreement states the necessity of putting an end to protectionist measures because they impede the selling of the debtor countries' products on international markets; besides, it stresses the necessity of fixing a limit for net transfers of financial resources in connection with the debt service, and this limit should be in tolerable proportion to the growth of GDP. The countries which signed the agreement tried to bring about a dialogue between debtors and creditors on topics in which all the participants are interested; they insisted that the precise terms of a renegotiation over the debt as such should be settled between each individual debtor and his creditors.

Suggestions in the Congress of the United States

The fact that a relief from the debt burden is necessary and would be advantageous for both the debtors and the creditors is gradually being recognized at a political level in the creditor countries. Senators and representatives of United States's Congress have recently made statements in this sense.

In his declarations of April, May, and June 1986, Senator Bill Bradley pointed to the advantages of a relief in the form of a reduction of interest and the amount of debt; this reduction should be negotiated between each debtor country and the creditor organizations of the banks and the governments as well as the international organizations.[21] The negotiations should result in supporting measures for those indebted developing countries that were prepared to carry out reforms to promote growth, increase the internal savings, and stop the flight of capital. One of the elements which would have to be taken into account is the start of democratic processes in order to guarantee wide domestic support for the debtor countries' economic reform plans.

Senator John F. Kerry, for his part, favours the introduction of an international development programme which should state a maximum limit for debt-service payments in percentage of the exports, combined with a progressive relief from the liabilities, depending on the degree of disequilibrium of the debtor countries' trade balance.[22] This programme would be financed by means of contributions by all developed countries. It would be controlled by a managing board with seven members, four of which would be elected; the remaining three would be representatives of the International Monetary Fund (IMF) the World Bank, and the General Agreement on Tariffs and Trades (GATT). The members of the board would choose a chairman out of the group of the elected members.

Charles E. Schumer, a member of the United States's House of Representatives, suggested a maximum limit of 25 per cent of the debtor countries' exports for the debt service. Besides, he suggested that the banks should write off debt until their claims reached a tolerable amount for the debtor, the level of which would be ascertained by the US government on the basis of an estimation of the debt amount which the debtors should normally be able to repay. The necessary write-offs would be spread over a longer period of time so that no shortage of capital would arise for the creditor institutions.

Rohatyn's suggestion

Felix Rohatyn, the chairman of the managing board of the Corporation for the Support of the New York Administration has pointed to the necessity of a significant relief from the debt burden, both by means of a considerable reduction of the rate of interest, and by a renewal of the payment dates. This relief would be accompanied by a flow of fresh capital into the developing countries. The capital would not come from the banking system but from countries with a high trade surplus, especially from Japan. The programme would be controlled by the World Bank, and the debtor countries would commit themselves to internal reforms which would improve efficiency and heighten the importance of the private sector.[23]

Debt, adjustment, and the monetary system

The above-mentioned suggestions aim at finding formulas for the relief from the present debt burden, but they are not directed at repairing faults of the economic system, which might cause a relapse into the external financing problems of the developing countries and aggravate the negative internal impact on them. These weaknesses are mirrored in a procyclical external financing

– as already shown – and in an asymmetrical adjustment process, which only those countries that are dependent on a financing by the IMF will carry out in an effective and disciplined manner.

The monetary system and the debt: stabilizing mechanism

A lack of symmetry in the international monetary system can already be seen in connection with the adjustment policy. This fault of the system increases the burden on the debtor countries, which become subject to mechanisms of incentive or punishment. The problem of asymmetry amounts to a problem of power which the international official organizations have over their members. It is therefore difficult to solve it in practice. Nevertheless, it is important to recognize the existence of the above-mentioned asymmetry in order to find ways of alleviating the debtor countries' problems without impairing the creditor countries' interests. Owing to the nature of the problem it is desirable to strengthen the existing mechanisms and to develop others for two purposes:

1. An increase in the available financing facilities on the part of the official multilateral organizations.
2. An improvement of those mechanisms which alleviate the negative effects of disruptive external factors on the developing countries' economy.

An increase in the multilateral organizations' disposable funds would permit them to offset the current financial flows and would offer the private institutions incentives to make supportive contributions on the international market in the debtor countries' favour. At the same time it would permit the stipulation of more rational conditions for the extensions of credits.

The latter aspect is most important of all, for the conditionality which the official multilateral organizations define for the use of their funds is clearly dependent on the amount of financial resources that they have at their disposal. The smaller this amount is, the severer and more recessionary the applied conditionality will be. And the smaller the amount is, the shorter the period of time will be within which the adjustment has to be carried out, and the more violent the adjustment process will be. As long as the creditor countries do not contribute to symmetry in the adjustment process on their initiative, the remaining financing, meant to relieve the burden of the debtor countries, is all the more important.

As regards the generally-applied alleviating mechanism, it

should be recalled the following two facilities which were set up after the Second World War, and both of them by the IMF: compensatory financing facilities for a loss of receipts from exports earnings, and oil facilities for the financing of oil after the Organization of Petroleum Exporting Countries (OPEC) I and OPEC II. The latter, which provided financial resources in 1974 and 1975, was meant to be an interim solution and was stopped in the middle of 1976.

The subsidy account is another mechanism for curbing costs; its purpose is to cut down the costs that the use of the IMF's additional financing service involves for countries with a low income.

A fourth mechanism, the service for the financing of buffer-stock facilities, was applied to a limited extent only, that is, to two products, namely tin and sugar.

Since the disposable funds are limited, all these mechanisms involve a combination of very restrictive conditions for their application. All of them were developed in order to solve the problems of individual countries or products, on the basis of the assumption that the world economy as a whole would keep up its normal financing. The situation requires additional mechanisms which will serve as automatic stabilizers in case of general problems. Among these additional mechanisms the following three would be particularly important – the fluctuations in the international rates of interest, the terms of trade, and the procyclical behaviour of external financing.

The fluctuations in the international rates of interest surpassed all expectations. From 1980 to 1981 they first rocketed up to a level three or four times above that of the preceding years and then fell off to slightly less than half of their maximum. The real rates of interest followed the fluctuations in the nominal rates of interest, although levels that exceed the historical ones three times are registered today. With the given growth of foreign indebtedness of the developing countries, and especially the Latin American countries, in comparison to almost any scale variable, and with the change in the composition of the debt towards a debt at a variable rate, the fluctuations in the rates of interest strongly influence the external and internal equilibrium of the debtor countries.

The mechanisms for alleviating the effects of fluctuations in the rates of interest on the debtor countries' economies can take various shapes. The financial resources of the IMF's extended fund facilities could be increased, for instance, so that the rise of the international rates of interest is covered even beyond a fixed norm, such as a moving coverage over a period of ten years. By the end of 1985, any fluctuation in the interest rate of 1 per cent meant a burden of 6 billion US dollars to the group of the developing countries. One could also apply mechanisms at a national level. Thus interest payments which exceed a certain limit might automatically be capitalized. Such formulas at a national level have already been mentioned in this contribution.

Three mechanisms can be applied regarding the fluctuations in the terms of trade. The first, which has already been mentioned, consists in extending the covering of the IMF's compensatory financing facility. Fluctuations in the terms of trade have far-reaching consequences, as the following figures illustrate – from 1981 to 1986 the decline in the terms of trade of the Latin American countries and the Caribbean amounted to 20 per cent, so that these countries suffered a shortfall in exports receipts of more than 100 billion US dollars in that period.

The second mechanism works towards making the access to the world markets easier for products made in the developing countries, thus facilitating a productive export-promoting diversification of these countries and saving them the costs that the protectionism on the market of the industrialized countries involves.

Third, as regards the procyclical behaviour of external financing, it should be investigated whether the debt-capital ratio of the multilateral financing organizations, which promote the development of the debtor countries, can be made more flexible, so that these organizations become able to extend their lending as soon as the private markets are dwindling, and to cut them back when the private markets expand more dynamically. With a more flexible debt-capital ratio, the international organizations could procure funds on the markets which the developing countries themselves would not obtain in this stage of the business cycle, as historical experiences have shown.

Of course, the introduction of stabilizing mechanisms would be less urgent, or even not at all necessary, if a symmetry in the adjustment of the debtor and the creditor countries' economy could be achieved. Since it is difficult to establish the required symmetry, the existence or the lack of stabilizing mechanisms will strongly influence the world economy in the next few years.

The monetary system and the conditionality

The discussion about the conditions on which the multilateral financing organizations are willing to allocate financial resources to member states becomes more aggressive and tense at the very moment when these financial resources run out. On the other hand, the debtor countries' willingness to carry out an adjustment policy based on the traditional rules of these institutions varies according to their need for additional financial resources.

From 1975 to 1982, that is, while there was a surplus on the international financial markets, the discussion about conditionality subsided, whereas it regained importance when the net financial flows into the debtor countries dried up.

From the point of view of the multilateral organizations, the conditionality should be such that the debtor countries' economy is allowed to function at a level of activity compatible with the available financial resources on the market, that is, to the given international economic situation. From the point of view of the countries which enlist the multilateral organizations' aid, this way of looking at the problem is apt to result in a considerable and often intolerable lowering of economic activity and the level of employment. Since a higher level of economic activity generally requires additional external funds, this conflict of opinion is quite understandable. A policy which allows for different ways of using resources can make some leeway for growth and economizing at the same time, although in general this leeway will be limited and temporary. In an international economic and financial system in which the willingness and ability to carry out adjustment policies consistently differs among the countries concerned, the availability of financial resources determines the nature of the conditionality; as a result, it is very difficult for the multilateral organizations to take into consideration the debtor countries' growth requirements. A conditionality on the basis of limited financial resources must be recessionary. Even if it aims at structural changes towards more efficiency, it will be recessionary, for such changes require both time and an adequate financing.

In a world with an asymmetrical adjustment mechanism, the recessionary effects of the conditionality can only be minimized by an increase in the availability of financial resources and the introduction of stabilizing mechanisms.

The lack of financing on suitable conditions unavoidably brings about a recessionary conditionality. The conditionality, which should be worked out on the basis of actual workings of the international economic system, could be modified if the multilateral financial organizations act in an anticyclical way, and if adequate economic stabilizing mechanisms can be introduced into the system. Just as the IMF did in the past years, the multilateral financing organizations must take an active part in procuring financial resources for the financing of those adjustment programmes which do not entail a sharp decline in the per capita income and a rise of the unemployment rate. These programmes will certainly not be homogeneous because they have to take into account the economic and social priorities of each individual country that asks for financial resources.

With sufficient financial resources, conditionality and growth will no longer be irreconcilable alternatives.

Notes and references

1. This contribution is based on a revised version of the article 'The Relief of the Debt Burden: Historical Experiences and Present Requirements', which was published in the *CEPAL Review* (no. 30, December 1986). The author would like to thank Daniel Titelman for his collaboration and Gert Rosenthal, Roberto Zahler, and the seminar of the Institute of the Universidad de Santiago de Chile for their comments.
2. Feuerlein, W. and Hanna, E. (1941) *Dollars in Latin America*, New York: Council of Foreign Relations.
3. Haberler, G. von (1950) *The Theory of International Trade*, London.
4. Solomon, R. (1983) *International Economic Letter* III (1) 18 January.
5. Feis, H. (1930) *Europe, the World's Banker 1870–1914*, Yale.
6. North, D.C. (1962) 'International Capital Movements in Historical Perspective', Mikesell, R.F. *U.S. Private and Government Investment Abroad*, University of Oregon.
7. League of Nations (1945) *Economic Stability in the Post-War World*, part II, Geneva.
8. Massad, C. (1985) 'Debt: An Overview', in C. Massad (ed.) 'The Debt Problem. Acute and Chronic Aspects', *Journal of Development Planning* no. 16, New York: United Nations; Massad, C. (1986) Debt and Debt Crisis in Latin America. Document prepared for the World Bank, Washington, DC.
9. For the seven above-mentioned countries the estimated values concerning the product elasticity of imports show an average cyclical elasticity of 2.2 per cent and a tendential elasticity of 1.6 per cent. These estimates are approximate values, and their confirmation requires additional elaboration.
10. Massad, C. (1984) 'Ajuste recesivo, ajuste expansivo y condicionalidad', Conference of the Banco Central de Reserva de El Salvador, San Salvador; *Bank for International Settlements* (1986) Fifty-Sixth Annual Report, Basle 1986; Joint Economic Committee of the Congress of the United States (1986) 'The Impact of the Latin American Debt Crisis on the US-Economy', Washington, DC.
11. Lahera, E. (1987) 'La conversión de la deuda externa: Antecedentes, evolución y perspectivas'. PNID/CEPAL manuscript; Roberts, E. and Remolona, E. (1987) 'Debt Swaps: A Technique in Developing

Country Finance', Group of Thirty Finance for Developing Countries, New York.
12. Joint Economic Committee, op. cit.
13. Massad, C. (1986) op. cit.
14. If the burden on the creditor caused by a diminution of the debt capital could be spread over a period of time, the diminution of the debt capital would be preferable to a reduction of the rate of interest because it would permit a faster return to normality in credit markets.
15. Joint Economic Committee, op. cit.
16. Ibid.
17. One might only argue that the debt assessed under its nominal value and the new loans can only coexist because the latter are granted voluntarily. However, it is impossible to distinguish clearly between 'voluntary' and 'involuntary' loans.
18. Montagnon, P. (1985) 'IDB Urges Fund to Aid Latin American Countries', *The Financial Times*, 21 September.
19. Baker, J. (1985) Statement by the US Secretary of the Treasury to the Joint IMF-World Bank Annual Meeting in Seoul, Korea, October.
20. CEPAL, (Comision Economica para America Latina) (1986) 'El problema de la deuda: Gestación, desarrollo, crisis y perspectivas', 10 March.
21. Bradley, B. (1986) LDC Debt Testimony Before the Senate Banking Committee, 14 May.
22. Kerry, J.F. (1986) 'A Way Out of the Debt Crisis', *Congressional Record* 132 (60), Washington, DC.
23. Rohatyn, F. (1986) 'Address Before the Overseas Development Council's Conference on the Future of the World Bank', Washington, DC, 23 June.

Appendix: the applied simulation model

A The model

The most essential formulas for the GDP are as follows:

$$Y = C + I + EX - IM \tag{1}$$

with Y = gross domestic product
C = domestic consumption
I = internal gross investment
EX = non-factorial exports of goods and services
IM = non-factorial imports of goods and services

$$Y - C - I = EX - IM, \text{ and} \tag{2}$$

$$Y - C = A \tag{3}$$

with A = total domestic savings,

$$I - A = IM - EX. \tag{4}$$

On the other hand,[1] the increase in debt is defined as a function of:

$$dD = INT + IM - EX$$

with D = total foreign debt
INT = interest payments to other countries
dD = annual increase in D.

Inserting equation (4) into equation (5) and dividing by D leads to

$$\frac{dD}{D} = \frac{INT}{D} + \frac{I}{D} - \frac{A}{D} \tag{6}$$

with $\frac{INT}{D}$ = effective interest rate on the debt (and other costs). An extension of equation (6) by Y results in

$$\frac{dD}{D} = i + \frac{Y}{D}\left[\frac{I}{Y} - \frac{A}{Y}\right] \tag{7}$$

with $i = \frac{INT}{D}$.

B The basis for simulation

A simulation was made on the basis of equation (7) with

$$\frac{A}{Y} = \left(i + \frac{YI}{DY} - \frac{dD}{D}\right)\frac{D}{Y}$$

This simulation was done according to the following assumptions:

(a) Rate of growth of the GDP, 4%.
(b) The proportion of investments to GDP, 20%.
(c) Alternative external rates of interest, 12%, 10%, 8%, 6%, and 4%.

(d) A ratio of debt to GDP, 1.0, 0.7, and 0.5.
(e) Rates of growth of debt, 7%, 3%, and 0%.
(f) The rate of growth of imports is given by

$$\frac{\Delta IM}{IM} = n\frac{\Delta Y}{Y}$$

The (cyclical) elasticity n was ascertained through an econometric estimation for the period from 1970 to 1985.[2]

The increase in exports according to equation (4) depends on:

$$\frac{I}{Y} - \frac{A}{Y} = \frac{IM}{Y} - \frac{EX}{Y}, \text{ or} \tag{4.1}$$

$$\frac{EX}{Y} = \frac{IM}{Y} - \frac{I}{Y} + \frac{A}{Y}. \tag{4.2}$$

We know that:

$$\frac{EX_1}{Y_1} = \frac{EX_0(1 + \widehat{EX})}{Y_0(1 + \hat{Y})} \tag{8.1}$$

$$\frac{EX_1}{Y_1}(1 + \hat{Y}) = \frac{EX_0}{Y_0}(1 + \widehat{EX}) \tag{8.2}$$

$$EX_1 = \frac{EX_0}{Y_0}(1 + \hat{Y})^{-1}Y_1 \tag{8.3}$$

with the ˆ sign indicating the rate of growth. All variables are expressed in current US dollars.

C Estimation of the sustainable debt level

A variable of the above model, which resulted from the division of equation (5) by D, was used in order to estimate a sustainable debt level for the debtor countries:

$$\frac{dD}{D} = \frac{INT}{D} + \frac{IM}{D} - \frac{EX}{D} \tag{5.1}$$

with INT = interest rates (and other costs) on the debt.

Division by D and extension of equation (5.1) by Y leads to

$$\frac{dD}{D} = i + \frac{Y}{D}\left(\frac{IM}{Y} - \frac{EX}{Y}\right), \text{ with } i = \frac{INT}{D}. \tag{7.1}$$

The sustainable level of debt was ascertained by reformulation of equation (7.1):

$$\frac{D}{Y} = \frac{\frac{IM}{Y} - \frac{EX}{Y}}{\frac{dD}{D} - i}. \tag{7.2}$$

The simulation, then was based on the following assumptions:

(a) A real rate of growth for the GDP, 4%.
(b) A real rate of growth for the exports, 4%.
(c) A real growth for the debt of zero.
(d) A rate of growth for the real imports which can be expressed by the following equation: $m = n \cdot y$,
with m = rate of growth of imports
n = cyclical product elasticity of imports
y = real rate of growth of the GDP.
(e) An interest rate (plus other costs) for the debt, 10%.
(f) A constant real exchange rate.

The elasticities used in this simulation amount to:

Argentina	$n = 1.8$
Brazil	$n = 2.0$
Chile	$n = 1.6$
Mexico	$n = 1.9$
Peru	$n = 1.5$
Venezuela	$n = 2.1$

The reference year for the simulation was 1985. Due to difficulties in the calculation of the GDP on a US dollar basis (difficulties which were mainly due to the strong devaluations in 1985), the ratio of debt to GDP in the reference year is an overestimate. Therefore, and as equation (7.2) expresses a ratio rather than an accounting identity, it was necessary to assess an implicit rate of interest, which kept up the consistency of the empirical values in equation (7.2) and the estimation of the ratio of debt to GDP for the reference year.

This does not distort the result of the simulation because an interest rate of 10 per cent had been assessed for the simulation. The adjustment of the equation for the reference year just permits a correction of those distortions which might result from an overvaluation of the ratio of debt to GDP.

It is worth mentioning that the simulation was carried out for five periods of time. As the simulated equation shows, the sustainable level of debt depends on the behaviour of imports and exports. This behaviour shows an asymptotic downward tendency of the trade balance. The more the positive difference between exports and imports decreases, the more the sustainable level of debt will drop.

Appendix notes and references

1. It is assumed that there is either no change both in the international net reserves and in foreign investments (joint property), or that both change by the same amount or sign. The first of these options is given in case of a crisis in the external sector of the economy.
2. The estimated function was:

$$M = a + b1\ GDP + b2\ GDPREC + b3\ TC$$

with M = real imports
GDP = real gross domestic product
$GDPREC = DUMMY \cdot GDP$ with $DUMMY = 1$ if $GDP < 0$ and $DUMMY = 0$ if $GDP > 0$
TC = real exchange rate applicable to imports.

All variables were measured in logarithms.

Chapter nine

Agriculture in the GATT system: Latin America's interests in the Uruguay rounds[1]

Alberto Valdés

Introduction

Agricultural trade conflicts are likely to dominate the Uruguay Round of the Multilateral Trade Negotiations (MTNs) under the auspices of the General Agreement on Tariffs and Trades (GATT). This Round offers a unique opportunity to introduce adjustments in domestic frame programmes, in which the major actors (United States, European Community, and Japan) could act in unison to reduce protectionism because the adjustment required would be much smaller than if countries acted unilaterally.

This contribution first highlights some of the traditional and emerging issues of interest to LDCs related to negotiations in agriculture in the GATT framework. This is followed by a presentation of the results of models simulating trade liberalization and its effects on developed and developing countries. The Third World is made up of many countries – imports and exports of both tropical and temperate zone products, and the complex pattern of the incidence of agricultural protection in OECD countries against less-developed countries (LDC's) are central themes in the second section of this paper. The third section presents a brief overview of the trends and structure of agricultural trade between Latin America and the European Economic Community (EEC) from 1962 to 1984, that is, the European Community (EC) of today. The last section presents some thoughts on approaches to negotiations by LDCs in the Uruguay round of the MTNs.

The background

Agriculture in the GATT system

It is now generally recognized that developed countries give significantly greater protection to agriculture than to manufacturing. While the degree of protection tends to rise and fall with world market prices on average, domestic food prices in Western Europe and Japan are often twice as high as international prices.[2] In most industrial countries, agricultural trade policy has become an instrument to validate price-support policies aimed at redistributing income to agriculture.[3]

In many developing countries, however, agriculture is taxed and manufacturing is usually protected from import competition. But there is further contrast. In developed countries agriculture is explicitly protected, aided by its exclusion from the discipline of GATT from the beginning. On the other hand, many LDCs have followed an import-substitution strategy, with agriculture often neglected because industralization was explicitly or implicitly favoured. This intra-industry contract will be important later on when we discuss 'reciprocity' in trade negotiations.

Agriculture in temperate products has been a problem since the beginning of multilateral trade negotiations. In contrast, many of the tropical products when exported as raw materials face relatively low levels of protection in the Organisation for Economic Co-operation and Development (OECD) countries and the constraint to expand exports lies more on the (slow) growth in demand than on trade barriers. As such, a large volume of agricultural trade in tropical products as raw materials operates under GATT rules. However, exporters of temperate, subtropical products, and processed goods from tropical products, face several restrictions of market access to OECD countries. This is due to protection against close substitutes in consumption, tariff escalation to processing (oil, seeds, coffee, and others) and the fact that several products such as sugar, livestock, rice, and others are produced in both temperate and tropical regions. In fact, much of the trade in the main temperate and subtropical agricultural products is beyond GATT rule on the argument, pressed by the United States in the past, and the European Communities (EC) and Japan today, that domestic frame policy measures should not be subject to international limitations and scrutiny. Exceptions have frequently been sought from the GATT Code, such as the waiver granted to the United States in 1954, and more recently, the tacit acceptance of the Common Agricultural Policy (CAP) of the EC.

The launching of the Uruguay Rounds in 1986 is an encouraging sign that many governments intend to strengthen GATT's authority on agricultural trade. During the last few decades agricultural trade has been drifting towards bilateral agreements and market-sharing arrangements, with the tactical acceptance of generous 'safeguards' against so-called 'unfair practices'. It is common belief that the international agricultural trade environment is worsening. There has been a dramatic increase in subsidies to agriculture in industrial countries compared to the levels prevailing ten years ago.[4] In terms of levels of protection, world agriculture has become more restrictive than at the beginning of the Tokyo Rounds in 1973, and there has been no clear stand against the prevailing system of managed trade in agricultural products. In the past, the major actors in trade did not show a commitment to freer multilateral trade, nor to a stronger GATT with power to establish rules and to enforce them. The relative ineffectiveness of GATT in dealing with temperate and subtropical agriculture products in the past has been recognized by most analysts. For example, the 1985 'Leutwiler Group' Report, written by an independent study group appointed by the Director-General of GATT, contains fifteen principal recommendations that clearly identify potential trade reforms that governments need to address in the coming years. Some of the recommendations are solely for agriculture and include 'clearer and fairer rules for agricultural trade, with no special treatment for particular countries or commodities', and 'greater integration of developing countries into the trading system, with all the accompanying rights and responsibilities'. However, while there is hardly any disagreement on the need for a reform of agricultural policy, the definition of and approach to agriculture in trade negotiations remains a major challenge.

Agricultural trade issues are at the centre of the developing countries' relationship with industrial countries. For instance, cereal imports by LDCs are the major growth area in world agricultural trade. LDC agricultural exports are also important in the relationship; more than 65 per cent of LDC's agricultural exports revenues came from exports to OECD countries. More generally, the rate at which many LDCs grow is a function of their export earnings, most of which are from agriculture.

A harsh reality for LDCs in agricultural trade is that adherence to multilateral trade rules by major economies (the EC, the United States, Japan) has far greater ramifications than adherence by smaller economies (most LDCs), because the consequences of their actions on agricultural trade flows and world prices are so much more widespread. In no other major sector is such a high proportion of production sold on world markets at less than domestic prices. This is, to a great extent, a direct effect of the domestic frame policies of developed countries.

What can LDCs do? In terms of market power, LDCs are individually fairly weak in bilateral bargaining. And there is no unified LDC representation in trade negotiations. Thus, it is in the interest of the weaker countries that the international rules are accepted as binding on the strong countries. In this sense, the GATT could serve as a safeguard for the weaker powers. It would appear that LDCs have no real alternative to the GATT system.

Looking beyond measures applied at the border

This issue has two related dimensions. One is defining what constitutes a 'trade' measure, considering the various forms of domestic assistance to agriculture and the widespread use of non-tariff barriers (NTBs). The other relates to the increasing influence on agriculture of macroeconomic policies affecting the exchange rate and thus the competitiveness of agriculture.

In the past, much of the international effort to improve the trading system focused on measures applied at the border, such as tariffs, quantitative import restrictions, and export subsidies. However, non-border domestic policies do indeed affect trade flows, particularly in agriculture, where often domestic frame policies include financial assistance, input subsidies, and tax policies. The total level of support (subsidy) to the production of some frame activities can be considerably higher than the nominal levels of protection to that activity.

Thus trade policies can be viewed as 'supporting' domestic prices in that, without frontier barriers on the same products, the fiscal cost of supporting frame income would rise significantly. Up to now, domestic policies have not been subject to GATT's trade rules, although the concept of 'trade effects' was introduced via subsidies at the Tokyo Rounds. Thus, even if the negotiations focused on the border measures required to operate domestic policies, the elimination of border measures is a threat to any domestic programme; thus the negotiators inevitably face the question before their own constituencies of whether domestic policy can and should be the subject of international negotiations, and what mechanism can be devised to offset the impact of national policies on world markets where such effects are 'negative'.

Furthermore, in recent years most new trade instruments have been NTBs, which create a problem of negotiability since their effects on trade flows are hard to assess. Several studies have documented the widespread use of NTBs in agriculture trade, although NTBs are in violation of GATT principles when used as protection devices. Indeed, there has been an upsurge in the proportion of agricultural trade subject to NTBs, such as quantitative restrictions, government procurement policies, technical barriers to trade (including health and sanitary, packaging, and labelling regulations), state trading, customs valuations and nomenclature, and more recently, voluntary export restraints. Many of these NTBs, such as state trading, could render most of the current rules of GATT virtually ineffective. Given the form that protection is taking, predominantly as NTBs, and their lack of consistency with GATT rules, the GATT system is not only having increasing difficulty in furthering trade liberalization, but also in safeguarding previously negotiated levels of market access.[5]

NTBs are more diverse, less visible, add a considerable uncertainty to exporters, and are more selective than tariffs. They can frustrate not only trade but also trade liberalization efforts. One must first determine which NTBs can be equated to an import quota for which the tariff equivalent can be computed, but in fact the effects of some NTBs are not quantifiable.

A further important implication for the MTNs is that trade negotiations conducted on the basis of trade flows – as implied by reciprocity – are unlikely to be productive. Reciprocity requires some kind of valuation of the mutual concessions on offer, but with so many NTBs in effect, it would be impossible to quantify concessions on either side.[6]

A second dimension of the problem is related to the exchange rate. The macroeconomic influences on agricultural markets have perhaps intensified, and have a strong effect on agricultural trade through the exchange rate in particular. As an illustration from the experience of industrial countries, the rise in the value of the US dollar in 1983 to 1985 brought international wheat prices close to the artifically higher domestic prices of the EC (in EC currencies), thereby reducing their rates of protection and their export subsidies, and relieving the financial pressure on the CAP. In this case, macroeconomic policies pursued in the United States had a significant impact on the fiscal cost of the EC's grain policy. A related question is the use of an index of protection in the negotiations. Measures such as nominal rates of protection or producer subsidy equivalents (PSEs) are likely to raise some resistance from farmers. They would argue that they buy and sell in their local currencies and hence should not be asked to adjust production based on measures which depend so much on the exchange rates at the time of measurement. This objection is not, of course, specific to agriculture. More generally, one would anticipate that the link between protection and exchange rate misalignment will become a major issue, particularly for LDCs, as they are more integrated into GATT.

Liberalizing OECD agricultural policies in the Uruguay round

Effects on world prices and trade flows and implications for LDCs

The direct effect that industrial countries' farm policies have on other countries has three dimensions: they depress world prices and thus LDC export revenues; second, they result in savings in LDCs' import costs; and third, they induce greater instability in world prices. Indirectly, the threat of protection in developed countries is an important deterrent to the opening of LDC economies. The current levels of protection and the unilateral unpredictable nature of access to industrial country markets reduces the willingness of policy-makers and producers in LDCs to assume the risks associated with a more trade-oriented strategy. Most economists agree that a major step that must be taken to achieve more rapid economic growth in developing countries is to make their trade regime among industrial and agricultural tradables more neutral. However, in the medium term, the current slow growth of the international economy, combined with the high rates of protection in the principal agricultural markets, makes it more difficult for LDC policy-makers to hold the line against domestic pressure groups who demand a more inward-looking trade policy. Furthermore, there is no real prospect for LDCs in debt to reduce their foreign debt substantially without a rapid expansion of foreign exchange receipts, which come from agriculture in many countries.

The trade restrictions imposed by developed countries include tariffs and NTBs, and they vary considerably in severity among countries and products. They all tend to lower world prices by artificially reducing domestic consumption and raising domestic production. As a consequence, the volume of exports from non-subsidizing countries is reduced. Price and volume effects together translate into a loss to LDC exporters of foreign exchange and welfare. On the other hand, many LDCs have benefited from trade restrictions on cereals in developed countries, as protection has led to lower world prices of their cereal imports.

A few studies available now (Table 9.1) have assessed the effects of agricultural protection in developed countries on world market prices, export earnings and import costs, and the resultant welfare gains and losses of developed countries and LDCs.

Some of these studies analysed the geographic distribution of the benefits and costs that would accrue to LDCs from trade liberalization and identified the products with the greatest potential for export growth. As expected, these studies show that the main beneficiaries of unilateral liberalization would be the liberalizers themselves. The efficiency gains OECD countries would get by liberalizing their agriculture were estimated to be 48.5 billion US dollars per year in 1980 dollars.[7] They also show that the potential net benefits for Latin America are substantial.

Although exact measurements are virtually impossible, estimates provide an approximation of the extent of protectionism and its effects on world prices. None the less, these studies present apparent discrepancies in the measurements of the effects on world market prices and on LDC exports and imports. For instance, it is questionable whether trade liberalization in temperate-zone products would benefit LDCs at all.[8] In comparing the findings of different studies, problems arise because of differences in commodity coverage, base years, the calculation of protection levels, and at times even in their general focus. Table 9.1 presents a classification of the agricultural trade liberalization literature discussed in this section.

In 1980, this author and J. Zietz[9] published a study on this subject, reporting the results of a hypothetical 50 per cent reduction across the board in tariffs and other trade barriers for ninety-nine commodities in seventeen developed countries belonging to the OECD.[10] The effects on export earnings and import costs of fifty-six LDCs, classified by both region and income, were quantified, and the most promising products for these countries were identified.

In a more recent study by the same authors, protection and trade values were updated for four commodities (wheat, maize, beef, and sugar), and adjustments were introduced for trade reversal.[11] The study examined a hypothetical removal of trade barriers (instead of a 50 per cent reduction). *Ad valorem* tariff equivalents for 1979 to 1981 were derived from a comparison of domestic wholesale prices and the corresponding border process for each commodity. As a check on the sensitivity of the results to different elasticities, four rounds were reported for sugar, and two each for beef, wheat, and maize.

Table 9.2, from the 1980 study of Valdés and Zietz, presents an overview of the effects on LDCs expressed in 1986 US dollars. Developing countries would have increased their export revenue by an additional 6 billion US dollars in 1985 prices. This is an 11 per cent increase for LDCs, as a whole, and the export revenues of low-income countries, taken separately, would have increased by 8.5 per cent. These figures were computed on the basis of 1977 to 1979 levels of protection and trade flows.

Trade flows and OECD protection has increased since 1977 to 1979, so that the benefits of liberalization would be substantially greater in 1985.

the impact on developing countries

	Valdés and Zietz	*Tangerman and Krostitz*	*Koester*	*Koester and Schmitz*	*Anderson and Tyers*	*Kirmani, Molagoni, Mayer*	*Matthews*	*Schiff*	*Zietz and Valdés*	*Tyers and Anderson*	*Parikh and Tims*
Year of publication	1980	1982	1982	1982	1983	1984	1985	1985	1986	1986	1986
Who liberalizes	OECD	Global	EC	EC	USA, EC Japan Canada N. Zeal. Australia	USA EC Japan Canada	EC	EC Japan USSR Canada Australia Argentina	OECD	Global OECD only LDCs only	Global
Which crops are liberalized	99 commodities	beef	cereals	sugar	grains, livestock products, sugar	meat, cereals, sugar	sugar, meats, cereals, oilseeds, dairy products	wheat	wheat, maize, beef, sugar	grains, livestock products, sugar	cereals, beef, dairy products
Percentage reduction in trade barriers	50	25, 50 100	100	100	100	100	100	[c]	100	100	100
Years for trade-flow matrix and protection levels	1975–8	1977–9	1975–7	1978–9	1980	1977–81	1981	[c]	1979–81[a]	1980–82	1980[b]

Notes:

Other studies include Roberts (1982) on sugar policies in the EC. All studies listed above liberalize tariffs and non-tariff barriers.

a Effects based on 1983 protection levels were also computed.
b Based on data for 1961–76, updated to 1980 where necessary.
c Approach different from the other studies; estimates free trade market clearing world price based on econometrically-estimated trade equations for 1960–80.

Table 9.2 Change in export revenue, import cost, and efficiency for selected commodities of developing countries caused by a 50 per cent decrease in OECD tariff rates, 1975–77

	Absolute increase		
	All developing countries[a]	Low-income countries	Middle- and high-income countries
	(millions of 1985 dollars)		
Change in export revenue			
Sugar	2,108	394	1,714
Beverages and tobacco	686	191	495
Meats	655	33	620
Coffee	540	123	417
Vegetable oils	400	60	339
Cocoa	287	21	265
Temperate-zone fruits and vegetables	197	60	137
Oilseeds and oil nuts	109	19	90
Other commodities	883	96	788
Total increase of all exports	5,865	997	4,865
Change in import costs			
Cereals	−876	−530	−345
Other commodities	−497	−152	−345
Total increase of all imports	−1,373	−682	−690

Note: Results of further work on a later period reported in Zietz and Valdés (1985) for sugar and beef indicate somewhat larger gains in export revenue than shown here.

a Includes developing countries with populations of more than 4 million in mid-1975.

Source: Table compiled for inclusion in The World Bank, *World Development Report 1986*, p. 128, from data found in Valdés, A. and Zietz, J. (1980).

For most commodities the price change ranged between 2 and 10 per cent. As expected, for the few commodities that faced little or no protection in the OECD markets, the world price change was nil. These commodities include cotton lint, jute, natural rubber, sisal, and hemp tow. At the other extreme, the calculated price change of wine, roasted coffee, malt, and cocoa paste cake fluctuated between 10 and 15 per cent. Apart from the change in world price, which reflected the degree of protection, the other factors that determined the size of the increase in export revenues were the initial market share of LDCs and their relative export supply elasticities.

The study identified many other commodities with a significant potential, including green coffee, wine, tobacco, maize, and others. Two criticial commodity groups, capturing approximately 47 per cent of the potential increase in export revenues in LDCs, were

Table 9.3 Range of values of the effect of trade liberalization on world prices, export revenues, and welfare for beef, wheat, sugar, and maize: sensitivity to different values of the domestic supply elasticity

	Percentage world price	*Change in world exports*	*Absolute change in developing country* Foreign exchange earnings	Welfare (exporters only)	Import bill	Net welfare
			(billions of 1980 US dollars)			
Sugar[a]	16.7	12.4	2.75	0.60	−0.33	0.08
Sugar[b]	13.6	10.4	2.19	0.46	−0.31	0.03
Sugar[c]	29.4	31.3	5.11	1.25	−0.42	0.39
Sugar[d]	12.9	16.8	3.04	0.49	−0.48	0.09
Beef[e]	18.5	167.7	5.10	0.54	−0.33	0.32
Beef[f]	16.2	143.2	4.38	0.43	−0.28	0.22
Wheat[g]	12.7	10.2	1.17	0.13	−0.25	−0.66
Wheat[h]	11.5	10.5	1.37	0.13	−0.58	−0.58
Maize[i]	11.7	35.6	0.61	0.14	−0.57	−0.07
Maize[h]	10.8	35.3	0.84	0.14	−0.74	−0.04

Notes: World exports are defined as the sum of net exports of all net exporting countries.
a Supply elasticities for all individual countries, set at 0.6.
b Supply elasticity of all European Community members set at 0.06.
c Supply elasticity of all European Community members set at 6.0 and of all other developed countries except Australia at 4.0.
d Supply elasticity of all developing countries doubled to 1.2.
e Supply elasticities by individual country varying from 0.38 to 1.02.
f Supply elasticities of all EC countries and Japan are reduced to 0.4.
g Supply elasticities by individual country ranging from 0.4 to 0.90.
h Supply elasticities of all developing countries is doubled to 0.8.
i Supply elasticities by individual country ranging from 0.19 to 0.91.
Source: Zietz and Valdés (1986).

sugar and its derivatives (36 per cent) and meat (11 per cent). Latin American captured 63 per cent of the total benefit from sugar and its derivatives, followed by Asia with 34 per cent. Smaller countries not included in the sample, such as Cuba, Mauritius, and Jamaica, would benefit substantially from liberalization.

It should be noted that the LDCs' studies capture a very high share of the increment in world trade in most commodities; they capture 50 and often as much as 70 to 80 per cent of the additional overall trade resulting from liberalization. As expected, the expanding exports of the developed countries are commodities such as wheat, pork, mutton and lamb, all of which represent the other end of the spectrum. The sample LDCs capture only 8.5 per cent of wheat exports, and 7.8 and 14.7 per cent of pork and lamb, respectively.

Table 9.3 presents the effects of a complete removal of trade barriers in sugar, beef, wheat, and maize, as well as a prediction of the changes in the world market price, based on the 1986 study by this author.[12]

The price increases predicted by the model for sugar vary between 13 and 30 per cent, depending on the supply elasticity used. The percentage price changes predicted using 1983 protection levels are more than twice as large as those estimated using the 1979 to 1981 protection levels. The percentage changes of world beef exports are predicted to increase even more dramatically. World exports of beef would more than double following a trade liberalization by OECD countries. The third column of Table 9.3 presents the predicted changes in foreign exchange earnings.

At 1979 to 1981 protection levels, an increase of approximately 10 billion US dollars per year is predicted in foreign exchange earnings for the four commodities (in 1980 US dollars).

The considerable increase in the export earning of LDCs reported in Tables 9.2 and 9.3 does not imply that all LDCs share equally in the gains from trade liberalization in either absolute or relative terms. One way to break down the distributive effects is presented in Table 9.2, which analyses the potential effect of liberalization on a group of low-income countries only. Low-income countries are those with a 1981 per capita GNP of 400 US dollars or less.

According to Table 9.3, low-income countries as a group would suffer a welfare loss from trade liberalization in cereals. This conclusion coincides with the one derived in Valdés and Zietz.[13] It also suggests that a small percentage of the foreign exchange gains from beef accrues to low-income countries; in other words, liberalization for beef exports is mainly in the interest of middle-income developing countries, particularly those in Latin America. At the same time, the gains to both low- and middle-income LDCs from trade liberalization in sugar are large. Moreover, only a fraction of the total increase in export earnings attributable to sugar is captured by developed-country exports. This is somewhat different for beef, for which the increase in export earnings is split almost equally among developed and developing countries. Most of the gains from a liberalization of trade in wheat and maize would accrue to the large developed-country exporters, namely the United States, Canada, and Australia, at the expense of the EC, and to Argentina, Thailand, and a few LDC cereal exporters which are the exceptions. But LDCs as a group would suffer a net welfare loss. The results suggest how interests among the LDCs diverge on this, as they do on other fronts in the MTNs.

The IFPRI and World Bank studies by Valdés and Zietz include only developing countries with more than five million inhabitants. However, many major sugar producers, which are exporting a considerable portion of their production under a preferential quota system to the EC, have populations of less than five million. Among this group of Atlantic Caribbean Pacific (ACP) countries are Mauritius, Guyana, Fiji, Swaziland, Jamaica, and Trinidad. A removal of all trade barriers would eliminate their rents, which they derive from selling their exports to the EC at internal EC prices. From data for 1978–9, Koester and Schmitz[14] estimate that the foreign exchange equivalent of the monopoly rent for the six countries mentioned above is about 380 million US dollars. Kenya, Madagascar, Tanzania, Uganda, and India, which also belong to the ACP group, are included in the study. However, none of them is actually treated as an ACP country in this study, an omission that does not seriously affect the results. The quota for Kenya, Madagascar, and India is small when compared to their total exports, and hence their export unit values for the years 1979 to 1981 are not significantly affected.

It is unlikely, however, that all the potential benefits from trade liberalization to LDCs are captured by these model simulations. Permanently reducing trade barriers in developed countries would lead the LDCs to develop new export products, and to expand their processing operations. In addition, such a development would probably encourage LDCs to direct more resources towards increasing agricultural production, helping to break the current climate in LDCs of 'export pessimism' that inhibits the adoption of export-oriented policies in agriculture, as well as in other sectors.

While the general thrust of the above conclusion is shared in other studies, the findings as to the effects on specific commodities do present apparent discrepancies. Their identification and implications for the analysis of the potential effects of liberalization is addressed next.

Comparison with findings in other studies

Several problems arise with a comparison of studies. Commodity definitions often differ. Kirmani, Molajoni, and Mayer,[15] for example, used broad aggregates such as meat or cereals rather than specific commodities such as beef or wheat. Similarly, Anderson and Tyers[16] study coarse grains rather than maize and ruminant meat instead of beef. Valdés and Zietz[17] distinguish between raw sugar and refined sugar, whereas their 1986 study is confined to total sugar in raw equivalents. Also, few studies use the same base

Table 9.4 Calculated world price increases from trade liberalization in selected commodities

Valdés & Zietz (1980)	Meat:	World price of beef and veal, beef preparations, pork, mutton and lamb, and chicken, increases by 7, 4, 9, 4, and 4 per cent respectively.
	Cereals:	World price of wheat, wheat flour, maize, rice, barley, and sorghum, increases by 5, 7, 2, 0.4, 8 and 0.6 per cent respectively.
	Sugar:	World price of raw, refined, and confectionery sugar, increases by 8, 6, and 9 per cent respectively.
	Others:	World price of roast coffee, cocoa powder, wine, soya beans, tea, palm-oil, increases by 11, 14, 16, 1, 3 and 3 per cent respectively. Several other products included.
Tangermann & Krostitz (1982)	Beef:	World price increases by 7 per cent.
Koester (1982)	Cereals:	World price of wheat, barley, maize, rye, oats, and sorghum, increases by 10, 14, 2, 9, 20, and 0.6 per cent.
Koester & Schmitz (1982)	Sugar:	World price increases by 12 per cent.
Matthews (1985)	Sugar:	World price increases by 11 per cent.
	Cereals:	World price of wheat, barley, maize, and rice, increases by 0.7, 3, 0.5, and 0.1 per cent respectively.
	Meat & dairy:	World price of beef, pork, mutton, poultry, butter, and milk powder, increases by 4, 4, 5, 3, 11, and 8 per cent respectively.
Schiff (1985)	Wheat:	World price increases by 15 per cent.
Zietz & Valdés (1986)	Meat:	World price of beef increases by 16–18 per cent.
	Cereals:	World price of wheat and maize increases by 12 and 11 per cent respectively.
	Sugar:	World price increases by 13 to 29 per cent.
Tyers & Anderson* (1986)	Meat & dairy:	World price of beef and lamb, pork and poultry, and dairy products, increase by 16, 2 and 27 per cent respectively.

	Cereals:	World price of wheat, coarse grains, and rice, increases by 2, 1, and 5 per cent respectively.
Parikh & Tims (1986)	Meat & dairy:	World price of bovine and ovine products, increases by 17 per cent.
	Cereals:	World price of wheat, coarse grains, and rice, increases by 18, 11, and 21 per cent respectively.

Note: Estimated effects on world price in percentages.
* In a more recent study, these authors have significantly revised their estimates of the price effects of protection. The same authors provided estimates of price effects in their 1983 study.

period. Valdés and Zietz[18] is based on 1975 to 1977 averages, as is the work by Koester[19]; Anderson and Tyers[20] take 1980 as their reference year; and the Zietz and Valdés[21] study uses an average of the years 1979 to 1981, as do Kirmani, Molajoni, and Mayer. Another problem is that large differences in the level of protection can show up, as Kirmani, Molajoni, and Mayer[22] reported for a number of surveyed studies. Finally, the methodology employed for a study of trade liberalization can be different enough to make comparisons of results meaningless. In the light of the above problems, most of the comparisons that follow have to be viewed with caution. A list of the studies and some of their characteristics are presented in Table 9.1, and a comparison of these studies and some of the calculated world price increases are presented in Table 9.4.

The long-run steady-state results reported by Anderson and Tyers[23] are similar in spirit to the comparative static results of the two studies by Valdés and Zietz.[24] Furthermore, they chose 1980 as their base year, which is very close to the average of the years 1979 to 1981 used in Valdés and Zietz's second study.[25] They report world price increases for ruminant meat, wheat, and coarse grains of 24, 20, and 16 percent. These are somewhat larger than the price increases given in Table 9.2 for beef, wheat, and maize, that is, the commodities that match the more aggregated commodity groups chosen by Tyers and Anderson. Almost identical numbers are generated for the projected increase in world exports, however. Anderson and Tyers report export increases of 3.9, 7.5, and 24.4 million tons for ruminant meat, wheat, and coarse grains. The corresponding figures from the Zietz and Valdés[26] study are 3.7, 8.2, and 25.4 million tons if the benchmark elasticity results are taken.

In their study for FAO on the beef market, Tangermann and Krostitz[27] find that a complete removal of trade barriers would result in a world price increase of 47 per cent, a value considerably greater than reported in Table 9.2. In addition, Tangermann and Krostitz estimate that world exports would increase by 300 per cent, which is about double the values found in the Zietz and Valdés[28] study. One reason for the larger percentage changes predicted by Tangermann and Krostitz is their assumption that trade barriers are removed, not only in OECD countries, but also in certain developing countries with high protection levels, such as South Korea.

Koester[29] uses the methodology and basic data base of Valdés and Zietz[30] but concentrates his analysis on cereals. Assuming a complete removal of trade barriers in the EC, Koester predicts an increase in the world price of wheat and maize of 9.6 and 2.2 per cent respectively. Both percentage increases are less than those of Table 9.3. However, they are based on the assumption that trade barriers are removed only in the EC. Koester, like Valdés and Zietz,[31] finds that trade liberalization in cereals as a whole results in a net welfare loss to developing countries.

In 1982, two studies, Koester and Schmitz[32] as well as Roberts,[33] analyze the effects of liberalization in sugar trade. They examine the protection given to sugar production in the EC. When they take into account the gains from higher export prices and the loss in the income transfers derived from preferential access to the high-price EC market under its Sugar Protocol, Koester and Schmitz conclude that a removal of EC trade barriers would actually result in a new loss to the ACP countries, except for Kenya and India. Roberts calculates that developing countries as a whole could expect an increase in welfare of between 370 million US dollars and 570 million US dollars, compared with a loss to the ACP countries under the Sugar Protocol of about 170 million US dollars. Roberts' results cannot be compared directly with the figures in Zietz and Valdés[34] because of different assumptions regarding the scope of trade liberalization. Generally a good deal of the attention of Robert's work is also devoted to the potential gains from liberalization to the developed countries. The effects predicted for LDCs are similar to those of OECD trade liberalization discussed below, although smaller. More recently the 1986 World Development Report of the World Bank presents estimates of the effects of the Lomé Convention on the income transfer from EC sugar quotas to ACP countries.

The studies reported above isolate the effects of liberalization by developed-market economies. A new and interesting dimension has been added to the trade liberalization literature by Tyers and Anderson,[35] and by the authors of the International Institute for

Applied Systems Analysis (IIASA) model, Parikh and Tims.[35] Both try to quantify the likely effects of global trade liberalization including liberalization of the LDCs' agricultural trade. The results are similar to those for OECD trade liberalization reported in Tables 9.2 and 9.3, apart from the fact that the LDCs' loss of welfare from liberalization in cereals does not occur. Also, Tyer and Anderson[37] predict a substantial loss in foreign exchange earnings rather than an increase. This is a result of the positive nominal protection rates found for several LDCs. In the author's opinion, however, the protection given to agricultural importables is overestimated in that it does not appropriately account for the fact that positive nominal protection in many LDCs can be viewed as a partial compensation for significant discrimination against agricultural importables as a result of an exchange rate misalignment, the consequence of high industrial protection and certain macroeconomic policies.[38] The degree of exchange rate misalignments in most developed countries has been, it is ventured, considerably smaller.

In addition to model specification and commodity coverage, the selection of the countries which liberalize their agricultural trade makes a major difference in the potential trade effects. Hence, there can be no single value for the potential effects of agricultural trade liberalization.

However, all studies that analyse OECD trade liberalization in agriculture predict an increase in the world price if part or all of the barriers to trade are removed; Table 9.4 presents the estimated effects on world prices. The extent of this increase varies by commodity. It is highest for the most protected commodities, such as sugar, beef, and dairy products. Sugar prices are predicted to increase between a low of 5 per cent[39] and a high of 13 to 17 per cent.[40] Results from both Tyers and Anderson[41] and Zietz and Valdés[42] suggest an increase in the world price for beef of between 16 and 20 per cent. For dairy products, Tyers and Anderson[43] put the increase at 27 per cent. We should emphasize that in comparing levels of protection, the base year chosen can be very important. For example, the world price of Caribbean sugar in 1980 was approximately 29 cents per pound and the New York spot price was 30 cents per pound, including a duty of about 2 cents per pound. In 1985 the world price was 12 cents and the New York spot price was 27 cents.

These world price increases accord well with the results reached by the linked system of national agricultural policy models developed at IIASA.[44] Using ten commodity classifications, including cereals, beef, and dairy products, the IIASA model predicts a long-run increase of world prices of about 9 per cent. This figure translates into a foreign exchange gain for LDCs of about 7 billion US dollars for all commodities taken together. Compared to Zietz and Valdés,[45] and Tyers and Anderson,[46] this overall foreign exchange gain seems low. Both these studies arrive at a figure of about 8 billion US dollars for sugar and beef alone, evaluated at 1980 prices. But according to Anderson and Hayam,[47] trade liberalization in dairy products would generate an additional 7.8 billion US dollars of foreign exchange for LDCs. Another reason why IIASA's estimate of 7 billion US dollars may be a likely underestimate is that neither they, nor Tyers and Anderson,[48] analyze the potential benefit to LDCs of a liberalization of trade in the major non-stable export crops, as opposed to the subset of foods and feeds from temperate zones. As Valdés and Zietz[49] have shown, however, LDCs would probably realize substantial gains in foreign exchange if trade barriers on products such as tobacco, roasted coffee, coffee extracts, cocoa derivatives, or oils and seeds were lowered or removed. Indeed, the authors have shown that the likely gains on these products (for LDCs as a whole) would also more than compensate for the losses LDCs could expect from the price increase in cereals, which many of them currently import. Seen from this perspective, it does not follow from the results of the IIASA and Tyers/Anderson models that LDCs would suffer a net welfare loss from OECD agricultural trade liberalization because the commodity coverage of these studies is limited.

A second benefit likely to be obtained through liberalization is a reduction of world price instability. This effect results from the removal of some NTBs, specifically variable levies, which insulate domestic markets from border prices. Both Schiff's[50] recent study of wheat in the EC, and the Tyers and Anderson[51] study arrive at the conclusion that changes in the system of protection would contribute significantly to world price stability. For example, Schiff[52] estimates that the variability of the world prices of wheat would fall from a coefficient of variation of 0.46 to 0.32 if the EC alone were to remove its trade barriers on wheat. If less price instability is valued highly, as the discussion of commodity price stabilization and buffer stocks seems to indicate, then the increased price stability resulting from liberalized trade should be included as a benefit in an overall evaluation of trade liberalization.

Two additional points should be made regarding these trade liberalization models. First, none of them includes adjustments for the exchange rate. Some policy simulations might affect the exchange rate, which could in turn affect the domestic responses to the initial change in world prices.

Second, the increased uncertainty of world prices and of market access (for example, NTBs) due to current OECD policies may also affect the trade response of LDCs. If OECD countries were to liberalize their agricultural markets, there would be lower and perhaps less stable food prices in the high protected industrial countries but higher and more stable food prices in the rest of the world. This change may stimulate LDC governments both to reduce their explicit or implicit taxation of agricultural prices and to expand public investments in agriculture, to take advantage of the more profitable and less risky opportunities that would become available for more LDCs to earn export income in international agricultural markets.

Trends and structure of agricultural trade between Latin America and the European Communities

The analysis of potential benefits to LDCs from trade liberalization presented above show significant differences in potential gains between major commodities and individual countries. The potential benefits would be particularly significant for Latin America, in terms of increases in export revenues and welfare gains.[53] Commodities like beef, sugar, roasted coffee, temperate fruits, and vegetable oils, are high in Latin America's agenda for their negotiations with the EC.

In this section we present a brief overview of the trends and structure of agricultural trade between Latin America and the EC. Table 9.5 identifies the evolution of the value of exports (in 1984 prices) from Latin America to the EC during 1962 to 1984. Coffee and animal feed (excludes feed grains) are by far the two major items in 1981 to 1984, with a very significant rise in animal feeds since 1975, a beneficiary of protection in the EC. The latter results from the expansion of the European livestock sector, an activity which is over-expanded as a result of high EC protection in livestock products. The other side of the coin is the reduction of Latin American exports of meat since 1975. Other significant items include oilseeds and nuts, tobacco, meat, fruits, wool, and others. In terms of import, penetration of Latin America's exports in the EC (relative to world exports to the EC), in Table 9.6 we observe important increases in Latin America's market share in the EC in animal feed (excluding feed grains), tobacco, fruits (preserved), and significant reductions in market shares in sugar, fixed vegetable oil, maize, and animal oils and fat, and fresh meat. Finally, Table 9.7 presents the pattern of agricultural exports from the EC to Latin America in 1984 US dollars. Milk (part as food aid) and alcoholic beverages are the biggest single items and are growing rapidly, but there are many others of significance. Overall, Latin America's agricultural exports to the EC have been considerably higher than Latin America's agricultural imports from the EC (for example, in 1981 to 1984), and Latin America now represents a relatively small market share for most of the EC agricultural exports. From the point of view of the GATT negotiations, the potential benefits of agricultural trade liberalization in the EC are of considerable interest to Latin America, while the EC commercial interests in Latin America's agricultural markets are quite limited. A corollary of the above is that self-contained negotiations to sector-by-sector negotiations are unlikely to yield much. If Latin America is to provide bargaining chips (to the EC) they will have to come mostly from the non-agricultural sector, primarily in industrial products. To this we turn in the following section.

Approaches to negotiations on agricultural trade in the Uruguay Round

What LDCs should ask for and offer

In the light of the discussion about this point, one might then ask, what should LDCs be seeking from the MTNs, what could they offer, and what should they watch for that would probably be against their interests? However, a reference to 'LDC views' should be interpreted with caution. The previous section showed that, like industrial countries and the LDCs, the Latin American countries have conflicting interests with regard to particular commodity markets, as, for instance, in the case of importers and exporters of cereals.

In this section, three sets of issues are discussed. These are (a) direct actions to increase market access to LDCs, (b) strengthening GATT rules and disciplines, and (c) reciprocity and what LDCs could offer. We now turn to these issues.

Direct action to increase market access to LDCs

The quantitative evidence presented above has several implications which are of relevance for negotiating strategies for LDCs. Broadly, the survey presented above underscores the need for LDCs to ensure that agriculture is high on the agenda in the Uruguay Rounds. Another feature worth highlighting is that the literature on the trade liberalization model suggests that the adjust-

Table 9.5 Value of agricultural exports from Latin America to the EC from 1962–5 to 1981–4

Commodity	*1962–5*	*1966–70*	*1971–5*	*1976–80*	*1981–4*
	('000s of 1984 US dollars)				
Coffee	1,344,470	1,685,861	1,740,965	2,348,912	2,045,201
Animal feed	568,828	736,824	857,386	1,321,626	1,911,976
Oilseeds, nuts	37,597	142,405	620,713	725,052	446,134
Meat, fresh	688,006	805,568	885, 974	453,669	366,579
Tobacco, unmanuf.	111,853	138,282	186,320	226,978	285,471
Meat prep.	137,046	186,429	176,541	195,232	246,294
Fruit, fresh	212,258	304,955	216,849	209,681	243,548
Fruit, preserv.	11,623	31,121	89,763	136,696	219,431
Wool, animal hair	301,681	217,709	177,050	256,226	214,446
Cotton	558,131	559,606	375,800	305,553	186,632
Maize	423,642	727,690	600,256	401,274	156,233
Cocoa	85,741	129,382	144,582	300,538	145,993
Fixed veg. oils	59,113	100,057	133,123	170,594	124,999
Sugar and honey	295,718	76,682	471,517	154,443	92,844
Other fixed veg.	170,380	135,455	159,006	124,180	75,679
Vegetables, fresh	30,941	20,158	42,949	100,501	66,674
Fruit, dried	2,845	1,776	2,499	4,035	63,571
Cereals, others	84,043	123,558	116,176	90,222	59,622
Crude veg. material	25,835	24,800	31,411	38,169	42,553
Rice	15,749	56,653	27,318	54,133	37,124
Animal oils & fats	52,939	76,798	75,478	23,558	29,805
Crude animal mat.	22,641	29,506	32,021	24,247	25,064
Hides and skins	101,210	132,781	75,777	38,532	23,343
Spices	4,498	9,443	15,940	12,630	18,926
Food prep.	1,483	3,844	16,313	21,314	18,913
Wheat and meslin	228,907	133,113	72,677	58,751	14,181
Veg. fibres	62,956	33,004	55,096	23,457	12,693
Animal and veg. oil	15,399	19,657	19,564	15,136	12,289
Tea	10,838	10,200	11,336	11,655	11,989
Crude rubber	995	6,303	4,660	4,764	11,758
Fertilizers, manuf.	1,199	1,969	5,092	9,746	10,534

ment costs to producers in the major trade liberalizing countries would be lower under multilateral liberalization, *vis-à-vis* unilateral reduction in trade barriers.

The loss in producer's welfare in the liberalizing countries is smaller if other countries liberalize at the same time. This is politically important, given the enormous influence of farm lobbies in the OECD countries. The larger the number of protected markets which liberalize trade in a given product, the larger the increase in the world price and so the smaller the reduction in the producer price required in the protected markets.

As to the questions of who liberalizes (OECD, EC, Japan,

Table 9.6 Latin America's exports of agricultural products to the EC as a percentage of world exports to the EC from 1962–5 to 1981–4

Commodity	*1962–5*	*1966–70*	*1971–5*	*1976–80*	*1981–4*
Coffee	59	61	56	52	56
Animal feed	29	27	23	30	34
Meat, prep.	22	22	18	20	25
Cereals, others	19	29	30	23	23
Tobacco, unmanuf.	7	7	12	17	20
Fruit, dried	1	1	1	1	16
Cotton	26	31	24	23	16
Fruit preserv.	2	3	7	10	13
Spices	6	11	13	10	13
Wool, animal hair	12	10	11	14	13
Cocoa	5	7	8	11	13
Sugar and honey	25	10	31	17	11
Veg. fibres	12	11	21	17	11
Fixed veg. oils	9	12	10	16	11
Oilseeds, nuts	2	3	15	17	10
Other fixed veg.	35	23	16	12	8
Fruit, fresh	8	10	6	6	8
Rice	9	12	9	11	7
Maize	24	28	17	12	7
Animal oils & fats	15	18	13	4	6
Crude animal mat.	7	7	7	5	6
Meat, fresh	21	18	13	7	5
Tea	1	1	3	2	3
Animal and veg. oil	11	10	6	4	3

LDCs), what trade barrier is lifted (quantitative restrictions, and/or tariffs), and which crops are to be affected, two major consequences follow from the previous sections.

One is that what really matters for LDCs and for world trade in agriculture more generally, is trade liberalization in industrial countries. The industrial countries are the dominant actors in most of the agricultural trade and, as argued earlier in the text, are thus the major contributors to the 'disarray' of world agricultural markets, to use Johnson's[54] all-too-appropriate terms.[55] Hence, what really matters are the levels of protection in these industrial countries.

High domestic prices are the basic problem behind the current overcommitment of resources to agriculture in OECD countries.

A second problem is that the importance of NTBs and non-border types of intervention strengthen the argument for concentrating less on trade flows and more on domestic price levels. Ideally, emphasis at the MTNs should be on NTBs and on all domestic policies that may have trade effects. Exports subsidies,

Table 9.7 Value of agricultural exports from the EC to Latin America from 1962–5 to 1981–4 (thousands of 1984 US dollars)

Commodity	*1962–5*	*1966–70*	*1971–5*	*1976–80*	*1981–4*
Milk & cream	88,687	100,808	124,913	179,472	187,775
Alcoholic bev.	71,114	110,171	170,553	236,412	180,212
Fertilizers, manuf.	90,632	85,770	210,236	143,124	76,864
Cereal prep.	12,816	15,635	35,324	52,980	55,610
Butter	7,220	23,263	17,799	42,669	46,448
Crude rubber	17,815	22,016	39,666	37,032	41,453
Sugar & honey	8,883	1,647	2,015	15,028	34,424
Crude veg. material	16,718	21,159	24,910	24,595	31,093
Vegetables, roots	10,082	19,255	24,551	33,879	23,997
Wheat & meslin	2,199	99,439	14,894	18,207	23,577
Food prep.	6,597	6,297	10,759	20,510	23,544
Cheese & curd	9,349	6,618	13,499	17,219	21,617
Vegetables, fresh	11,919	14,028	25,625	22,142	15,480
Wheat: meal, flour	4,373	4,641	5,422	6,316	12,586
Fixed veg. oils	26,611	32,892	51,043	17,970	12,497
Meat, fresh	9,778	10,251	14,522	11,282	11,742
Animal feed	2,682	5,485	10,383	7,011	10,795
Rice	4,077	8,869	14,823	8,823	10,171

variable levies, and other interventions, are an integral part of domestic policies aimed at farm income support. To effect any substantive change, negotiations must not be restricted to tariffs, although the 'tariff escalation' phenomenon is an important element on the agenda.

It is suggested to concentrate international negotiations on frontier barriers, which for agriculture means non-tariff barriers – rather than on domestic subsidies. While recognizing the influence of non-border domestic subsidies on trade flows, we choose to focus on frontier barriers because, as argued persuasively by Richard Snape,[56] trade barriers and more harmful policy instruments for other countries form non-frontier barriers, and the definition and measurement of the trade effects of non-frontier barriers is extraordinarily difficult and could cause considerable delays in reaching agreement.

What is suggested is a method that relies on a border measure of protection and, for the next three to four years, a binding of domestic supports based on a direct comparison of domestic and international reference prices. This would be followed by a gradual reduction of some percentage of protection every year.

Measures of nominal protection, or producer and consumer subsidy equivalents, are candidates for index of protection, capturing the effects of most types of protection on domestic prices.

The trade effects of import quotas, variable levies, tariffs, acreage diversion payments, and export subsidies result from domestic protection. However, while input subsidies cannot be captured by nominal protections, direct measures of them on tradable inputs could be estimated. This is desirable if measures of effective rates of protection are unsatisfactory or difficult to agree upon.[57] Some direct income transfers to farmers (such as social security, but not deficiency payments as currently used in the United States) could be left out of the calculations to the extent that they influence neither the level of protection to producers nor prices paid by consumers.

The question of commodity coverage in the negotiations raises a thorny issue for LDCs. The above results show how interests among LDCs diverge with respect to which commodities should be given priority. Most LDCs would benefit from priority being given to products other than cereals, such as sugar, meat, and other products. Cereals is the most controversial commodity group among LDCs, given how the dependent countries' negotiating positions could be weakened if they each press individually for their 'preferred' products in the negotiations, and a practical consideration is that cereals appear to be high on the priority list of developed countries in the negotiations (and certainly a high priority for a few LDCs like Argentina, Thailand, and Uruguay). Thus OECD countries are likely, at the very least, to address cereals.

But more generally, the question arises whether the negotiations should proceed commodity-by-commodity, which might be preferred by some developed countries. Sugar, cereals, and dairy products are often singled out as obvious candidates. Such an approach is attractive as a practical way of getting the process started, if the alternative of engaging in a battle against protectionism in many sectors appears politically very difficult. However, for LDCs this would be a bad deal. Individual commodity conventions, for example, wheat, dairy, and meats, have been tried in the past and they have been unsuccessful. They are too narrow for deals across sectors (a point presented below) and therefore unlikely to get the level of political commitment commensurate with the task. As a result they end up being negotiated by sectoral representatives, whose political support comes from the farm lobbies in their own countries. Furthermore, such an approach increases the likelihood of deals among the major industrial countries, with little attention being paid to the needs of LDCs.

Strengthening GATT rules and disciplines

Rule-making for agricultural trade in the 1990s is expected to become a critical issue at the Uruguay Rounds. It requires agreement on new rules to be followed. This includes deciding on the abolition of permanent agricultural exceptions, and whether to ban or limit certain policy instruments such as subsidies.

GATT negotiations have been successful in reducing industrial tariffs and enforcing these reductions. Unfortunately, this was not the case with non-tariff barriers, which are the dominant form of protection in agriculture. For agricultural exporters, the critical problem about GATT rules and disciplines has always been the question of how to deal with quantitative restrictions and domestic subsidies, with the selective safeguards by which countries can be singled out as targets for protective measures (very dangerous for LDCs), and the weakness of GATT mechanisms for surveillance and dispute settlement. The disputes panel, which handles the enforcement of the decision reached, has no real power to put the recommendations into effect. Hence, strengthening GATT's capacity and authority to evaluate, expose, and sanction violators of agreed-upon accords becomes a very important indirect way to increase market access.

Developing countries should be particularly interested in becoming active participants in an international system which provides a framework of norms, rules, and procedures. The alternative for small economic actors could easily result in discriminatory protection and bilateralism, which is much less promising. A strong monitoring mechanism within GATT could implement surveillance of national trade policies, increasing each government's accountability for its own trade-related practices. This would be particularly useful for small countries, and thus for most LDCs.

Reciprocity and what LDCs could offer

The major trading powers, the three 'giants' – the EC, the United States, and Japan – have to reach agreement among themselves if anything significant is to happen during the MTNs. The risk for LDCs is that the three big powers could strike a deal among themselves before starting negotiations with LDCs, which could have disastrous effects on the long-term interests of LDCs and on the GATT system as a whole. LDCs and developed countries other than these three biggest ones must offer some 'incentive' to the trading powers in order to be considered and become influential.

This incentive could come from two sides. First, LDCs must be prepared to reciprocate in trade concessions, on the premise that developed countries would then be more willing to make additional 'concessions'. The other side is related to preferential treatment and graduation. We will examine them both briefly.

The application of GATT rules is more lenient for LDCs than for industrial countries. In the past, GATT rules allowed LDCs to be free riders and hence not to make concessions themselves. This was supported by a tacit acceptance of import substitution as a development strategy. The economic importance of LDCs in trade negotiations was diminished as a result.

Industry in most LDCs is highly protected while agriculture is not. Industrial protection therefore helps industry at the expense of agriculture. A policy that protects industry raises the cost of tradable inputs, such as fertilizers, machinery, and other inputs.

Indirectly, and possibly more importantly, the resulting changes in the exchange rate penalize producers in other import-competing sectors as well as those producing exportables. As a result, resources move from the traded agriculture sector to the protected and home-goods sectors.[58] The impact of protection as implicit taxation of unprotected activity depends on the way it influences the prices of non-tradable goods.

Recent research has provided evidence of this phenomenon. In the Philippines the foreign trade regime between 1950 and 1980 discriminated heavily against agricultural exports. In Colombia, in the 1960s and 1970s, the implicit overvaluation of the peso resulting from the combined effect of exchange rate and industrial protection more than offset the nominal protection given to some agricultural products. Similar results were obtained for Argentina, Chile, Nigeria, and Peru.[59] Thus, the losers from industrial protection are consumers of industrial goods and the non-protected activities. This depresses the potential exports in general and particularly of agriculture, which is a highly tradable sector compared to the rest of the economy in most LDCs.

One way of cutting the cost of discrimination against agriculture and other exportables in LDCs is to reduce the protection of industry. Liberalization of industry could be used to provide additional leverage for LDCs for agricultural negotiations during the MTNs, and in the process, help to promote the growth of agriculture in LDCs. Greater freedom in agricultural trade could be the price demanded by the LDCs for a future prospect of freer trade in industry (and services) and better terms of foreign direct investments in the LDCs. A direct implication of the above is that agricultural negotiations should not be self-contained. In order to gain in agriculture, LDCs would have to provide bargaining chips from the non-agricultural sector, which is not compatible with negotiations about a single sector. Of course, in a commodity-by-commodity approach (for example, wheat being treated separately from dairy products) the risks for LDCs are even greater.

The second incentive LDCs could offer in the MTNs relates to preferential treatment. A critical issue is whether the growth and adjustment of LDC economies call for more or less preferential treatment in trade policy. Some LDCs still believe that their leading objective in any GATT negotiation should be to preserve their special preferential access to developed-country markets. Most trade economists argue, however, that greater benefits to LDCs have come from the reduction in tariff barriers under GATT rather than from preferences under the Generalized System of Preferences (GSP). The GSP is restrictive at best, and many agricultural products are excluded in the United States scheme, while most are excluded by both the EC and Japan. The effect of the Lomé Convention on sugar exports is significant for only the smallest economies among the eighteen ACP countries that have quotas to export sugar to the EC.

The Leutwiler Report, like others, concluded that special and preferential treatment has been of limited value for most LDCs. And there is a risk that insistence on preferential treatment could have a high opportunity cost in terms of concessions made and that it would only detract attention from other more important issues. On the other hand, preferential treatment of the smallest and poorest LDCs seems appropriate. Perhaps rather than emphasize a political alignment on North-South lines, the LDCs should focus negotiations on issue alignment, with the decision on where to align, based on the selection of those specific measures and rules that are of high priority for the LDC's own self-interest, such as export subsidies and quantitative restrictions. In this regard, the initiative by the Cairns Group, which includes some developed countries, is a very positive development for export-oriented LDCs, both as a mechanism to help keep the negotiations within a multilateral framework, and to focus the negotiations on an issue alignment.

The approach implied a differentiation between the rights and obligations of smaller lower-income LDCs and those of middle-income larger LDCs, including newly-industrialized countries. The argument is based on the fact that, first, the rent these small, low-income LDCs derive from trade preferences represents a significant amount of their foreign exchange supply, second, these economies are highly vulnerable to foreign trade fluctuations in one or two commodities, third, the 'cost' to preference-giving countries is relatively small, and fourth, the opening of the trade regime in the graduating LDCs would, it is presumed, represent an additional force to help these poorer LDCs.

The graduation from reciprocity and from trade preferences for middle-income LDCs would probably influence the coalition building between them and low-income LDCs. Is this inevitable? This differentiation between low- and middle-income countries does not imply that low-income LDCs have no incentive to support middle-income countries in their new (hypothetical) stance in the negotiation. On the one hand, if the same level of implicit income transfer from non-reciprocity and preferential treatment is now reserved exclusively for low-income countries, this would presumably be considered to be a benefit for them. Furthermore, the product mix of their exports is changing, and the pressure of middle-income countries for more access to OECD markets and to other middle-income countries products such as sugar and derivatives, vegetable oils, beverages, tobacco, fruits, and others, is also of great potential interest to low-income countries as exporters. But in the end, the formation of coalitions involves many variables, of which interest on agricultural negotiations is only one.

The Uruguay Round of the MTN offers a historical opportunity to tailor domestic farm programmes to GATT requirements. Latin America and consumers in the EC have much to gain from such policy reform.

Notes and references

1. I wish to thank Jagdish Bhagwati, Suzanne Gnaegy, D. Gale Johnson, Panos Konandreas, Edward Rossmiller, and Maurice Schiff for helpful comments on an earlier version, and Jim Gilmartin for some data processing.
2. Anderson, K. and Hayami, Y. (1986) *The Political Economy of Agricultural Protection*, Boston.
3. There are good reasons for doubting the effectiveness of current policies in raising small farmers' incomes. Empirical work supporting this conclusion is reported in GATT (1986) *Prospects for International Trade*, GATT/1392, Geneva, p. 29.
4. For example, farming support in the United States has increased from 2.7 billion US dollars in 1980 to a record 25.8 billion US dollars in 1986. The EC taxpayers are spending about 21.5 billion US dollars on farm support in 1986, as opposed to the 6.2 billion US dollars ten years ago, and these figures only include payments from the EC Commission, excluding direct payments from national governments.

5. GATT (1986) op. cit.
6. Dell, E. (1986) 'Of Free Trade and Reciprocity', *The World Economy* 9(2): 125–40.
7. World Bank (1986) *World Development Report 1986*, Washington, DC, p. 131.
8. Matthews, A. (1985) *The Common Agricultural Policy of the Less Developed Countries*, Dublin.
9. Valdés, A. and Zietz, J. (1980) 'Agricultural Protection in OECD Countries: Its Cost to Less-Developed Countries', *Research Report*, no. 21, Washington, DC: IFPRI.
10. Ibid.
11. Zietz, J. and Valdés, A. (1986) 'The Costs of Protectionism to Developing Countries: An Analysis for Selected Agricultural Products', *World Bank Staff Working Papers*, no. 769, Washington, DC (January).
12. Ibid.
13. Valdés, A. (1980) op. cit.
14. Koester, U. and Schmitz, P. (1982) 'The EC Sugar Market Policy and Developing Countries', *European Review of Agricultural Economics* 9: 183–204.
15. Kirmani, N., Molajoni, P., and Mayer, T. (1984) 'Effects of Increased Market Access on Exports of Developing Countries', *IMF Staff Papers* (December), pp. 661–84.
16. Anderson, K. and Tyers, R. (1983) 'European Community's Grain and Meat Policies and U.S. Retaliation: Effects on International Prices, Trade and Welfare', *Center for Economic Policy Research*, Discussion Paper no. 83, Canberra, Australia: Australian National University, October.
17. Valdés, A. and Zietz, J. (1980) op. cit.
18. Ibid.
19. Koester, U. (1982) 'Policy Options for the Grain Economy of the European Community: Implications for Developing Countries', *Research Report*, no. 35, Washington, DC, IFPRI, November.
20. Anderson, K. and Tyers, R. (1983) op. cit.
21. Zietz, J. and Valdés, A. (1986) op. cit.
22. Kirmani, N., Molajoni, P., and Mayer, T. (1984) op. cit.
23. Anderson, K. and Tyers, R. (1983) op. cit.
24. Valdés, A. and Zietz J. (1980) op. cit. and Valdés, A. and Zietz, J. (1987) 'Export Subsidies and Minimum Access Guarantees in Agricultural Trade Negotiations: A Developing Country Perspective', *World Development Report*, Washington, DC.
25. Valdés, A. and Zietz, J. (1987) ibid.
26. Zietz, J. and Valdés, A. (1986) op. cit.
27. Tangermann, S. and Krostitz, W. (1982) 'Protectionism in the Livestock Sector with Particular Reference to the International Beef Trade,' Paper prepared for the Ninth Session of the UN Food and Agriculture Organization's Intergovernmental Group on Meat, Rome, December.

28. Zietz, J. and Valdés, A. (1986) op. cit.
29. Koester, U. (1982) op. cit.
30. Valdés, A. and Zietz, J. (1980) op. cit.
31. Valdés, A. and Zietz, J., ibid.
32. Koester, U. and Schmitz, P. (1982) op. cit.
33. Roberts, I.M. (1982) 'E.E.C. Sugar Support Policies and World Market Prices: A Comparative Static Analysis', Canberra: Australian Bureau of Agricultural Economics, Working Paper 8213.
34. Zeitz, J. and Valdés, A. (1980) op. cit.
35. Tyers, R. and Anderson, K. (1986) 'Distortions in World Food Markets: A Quantitative Assessment', Paper Prepared for the World Bank, *World Development Report*, Washington, DC, January.
36. Parikh, K.S. and Tims, W. (1986) 'From Hunger Amidst Abundance to Abundance Without Hunger', Summary Finding by the International Institute for Applied Systems Analysis, Luxemburg, Austria, February.
37. Tyers, R. and Anderson, K. (1986) op. cit.
38. Valdés, A. (1986) 'Impact of Trade and Macroeconomic Policies on Agricultural Growth: The South American Experience', *Economic and Social Progress in Latin America*, Washington, DC.
39. Tyers, R. and Anderson, K. (1986) op. cit.
40. Zietz, J. and Valdés, A. (1980) op. cit.
41. Tyers, R. and Anderson, K. (1986) op. cit.
42. Zietz, J. and Valdés, A. (1980) op. cit.
43. Tyers, R. and Anderson, K. (1986) op. cit.
44. Parikh, K.S. and Tims, W. (1986) op. cit.
45. Zietz, J. and Valdés, A. (1980) op. cit.
46. Tyers, R. and Anderson, K. (1986) op. cit.
47. Anderson, K. and Hayami, Y. (1986) op. cit.
48. Tyers, R. and Anderson, K. (1986) op. cit.
49. Valdés, A. and Zietz, J. (1980) op. cit.
50. Schiff, M. (1985) 'An Econometric Analysis of the World Wheat Market and Simulation of Alternative Policies, 1960–80', *US Department of Agricultural Economic Research Service*, October.
51. Tyers, R. and Anderson, K. (1986) op. cit.
52. Schiff, M. (1985) op. cit.
53. Valdés, A. and Zietz, J. (1980) op. cit.
54. Johnson, D.G. (1973) *World Agriculture in Disarray*, London.
55. Trade policies of the two other actors are also influential in the final outcome. The USSR, not a member of GATT, has become a major importer in the world markets for grains, butter, sugar and, to a lesser extent, poultry, beef, and pork. Developing countries are now the fastest growing market for grains, at what I would argue have been low levels of protection, with a few exceptions like South Korea and Taiwan. But barriers to imports in LDCs are influential in several other products (jute, fruits, and others) and their trade policies should be addressed in the Uruguay Rounds. Still, as far as we can tell from the available research, the OECD countries are clearly the dominant

actors in terms of the world price effects of agricultural protectionism.

56. Snape, R. (1987) 'The Importance of Frontier Barriers, in Protection and Competition in International Trade', in Kiearkowsky, H. (ed.) *Essays in Honor of Max Corden*, Oxford.
57. T. Josling's work on consumer (CSE) and producer subsidy equivalents (PSE) is relevant here as a possible measure of an overall intervention. More recently the OECD member countries came up with measures of CSEs and PSEs. The United States and EC are currently in 'hot debate' internally about how to use these measures in trade negotiations. The advantage of nominal protection is its simplicity as a concept and as a measure and its effectiveness in terms of implications on trade-flow changes. Agreeing on what to include in the PSE measures could risk a main delay in the negotiation – see Josling, T. (1982) 'Developed-Countries Agricultural Policies and Developing Country Supplies: The Case of Wheat', *Research Report*, no. 14, Washington, DC.
58. Valdés, A. (1986) 'Exchange Rates and Trade Policy: Help or Hindrance to Agricultural Growth', in Maunder, A. and Renborg, U. (eds) *Agriculture in a Turbulent World Economy*, Proceedings of the 19th International Conference of Agricultural Economists, held in Malaga, Spain, published in England.
59. Dell, E. (1986) op. cit.

Part four

International monetary fundamentals

Chapter ten

External debt, a view from the Third World

Eduardo Lizano

Introduction

The external debt of the developing world, particularly that of Latin American countries, has been a topic in vogue during the last few years. Notwithstanding all that has been said, discussed, and analyzed, it remains, currently, one of the most serious problems facing less-developed countries, as it has major effects, not only in the development possibilities of debtor countries, but also in the relationship between debtors and creditors. Thus, in spite of the substantial efforts made, there is still much to be done.

Four questions will be addressed in these pages – first, what is the origin of the problem?; second, what has been done to encounter it?; third, which are the main lessons that can be derived from this effort?; and fourth, in what direction should further action take place?

The origin of the problem

The external debt problem was generated in the late 1970s. Some external factors, and others of a domestic nature, contribute to explain the genesis of the problem.

External factors

Among the external factors are the following:

(a) The second oil shock caused serious distortions in the international economy. For oil-importing developing countries, it represented a substantial increase in the petroleum bill. The total value of imports grew, in some cases, dramatically.
(b) The international economy suffered severe inflationary pressures, which reflected rapidly both in oil by-products, and

in the price of goods to which oil is an input. This, in turn, contributed to raising even more the value of imports.

(c) The effect was rapidly felt also in the financial markets, as international inflation pushed interest rates up in such a way that the cost of servicing the foreign debt increased significantly.

(d) A recessive economic policy was adopted in most industrialized countries. In order to encounter the cost-pushed inflation that had originated in the rise of fuel prices, domestic demand was reduced. This gave way to the phenomenon known as 'stagflation', that is, stagnation of production accompanied by inflation. It provoked a general decrease in export prices of developing countries. These were caught in a trap: increased foreign exchange requirements (oil prices, international inflation, interest rates), and, simultaneously, a decreased availability of foreign exchange (terms of trade).

(e) Given the abundance of petrodollars in oil-exporting countries, and the need of them in oil-importing countries, in a first stage, the recycling of balance-of-payments surpluses of the former to cover the deficit of the latter took place within relative normality. Borrowing abroad became fast and easy. Commercial banks played a very important role, although not fully responsible, given their inability to determine the real country risk. When the banks began to perceive an upsurge of debt-service difficulties in developing countries, the flow of resources ceased abruptly. Briefly thereafter, the external debt became a huge problem.

Domestic factors

Countries in trouble by the rise in oil prices and the additional consequences already mentioned had several alternatives at their disposal:

(a) to face the decrease in their standards of living because of the worsening of their terms of trade.

(b) to increase external borrowing with the purpose of expanding domestic investment, output capacity and exports; in this way, in the medium term, it would be possible to recuperate the standards of living enjoyed before the oil shock, and simultaneously, to service the debt which the country had incurred to expand its exportable production.

(c) not to face the situation and search for external resources that would enable the country to maintain the standards of living artificially; that is, borrowing abroad, not with a view to increasing exports, but to keeping the prevailing levels of consumption, military expenditures, and capital flight.

Most developing countries, particularly within Latin America, took this latter alternative. Once petrodollars became scarce, and confidence weakened, the stage was set for serious difficulties. They began with Mexico, and persist nowadays in all heavily-indebted countries.

The efforts made

The growing difficulties countries faced in servicing their external debt in contractual terms became evident in several ways: first, they resorted to a deferral of principal payments; then, to the building up of arrears, and, finally, to the suspension of principal, and even of interest payments. What has been done about this situation, that has rapidly spread among debtors?

Institutional aspects

In view of the general default of debtors, creditors decided to co-ordinate their action. Official creditors organized themselves in the Paris Club, and commercial banks, in advisory committees, membership varying according to the country case. The creditor clubs permitted the harmonization of points of view among governments and among commercial banks, thus avoiding a proliferation of positions, despite the diversity of opinions which, in the case of the government, was due to different political perspectives and, in the case of the banks, to different financial positions.

Contrariwise, the debtor countries were unable to co-ordinate their points of view. Numerous meetings took place among them, and statements and manifestos were subscribed to, but they were not reflected in the negotiations. It was virtually impossible to unite criteria, particularly in the case of big debtors. Once they reach an agreement, they easily forget about other debtors, relegating previous statements as one more evidence of tropical rhetoric.

The terms and conditions of debt rescheduling have gradually been improving

(a) Tenor and grace periods have gradually expanded; currently, nobody is surprised with sixteen to twenty years of amortization periods, and five to seven years' grace periods.

(b) The option of the United States prime rate as a base rate has been eliminated in most cases, the prime rate being usually around one percentage point higher than LIBOR.

(c) The spread over LIBOR has been slowly reduced. Gone are the days in which spreads of 2–2½ per cent over LIBOR were charged. Today normal spreads of 13/16 per cent and 7/8 per cent over LIBOR are paid.

(d) Costs, fees, and other expenses related to rescheduling have also descended over time.

Rules and regulations

Rules and regulations in the home countries of commercial banks have become more flexible, thus easing their participation in debt restructurings. Thus, rules for creating reserves, accounting for losses, and for the treatment of arrears of principal and interest, have been facilitated.

This has enabled creditor banks to make more realistic decisions based on the requirements of the debtor countries, without jeopardizing their own financial position.

The only way out

The only way out for commercial banks, specially for United States Banks, was by supplying new money to debtor countries. This situation has gradually changed, and as regards the concept of a menu of options, the following points can be mentioned:

(a) capitalization of interest, widely used in European countries, but, as of very recently, unacceptable for United States monetary authorities; this allows the banks to participate in debt reschedulings without having to disburse fresh money, which can become an important advantage to the banks, depending upon their financial position;

(b) the exchange of nominal and non-transferable documents issued in favour of each creditor bank for securities, promoting, in this fashion, the formation of a secondary market for debt documents, and allowing banks to get out of the deal through the sale of their notes; Argentine 'exit bonds' respond precisely to this rationale;

(c) the conversion of debt-denominated paper in foreign exchange into local-currency-denominated documents, or directly into local currency (debt for equity), is a measure already adopted by several countries; it aims at transforming external debt into investment in the corresponding country, a process which can be done directly by the creditor, or indirectly when the bank sells its notes to investors interested in the country in question. This procedure has created more expectations than it should. Actually, although of some use, the risks it implies are very high risks for monetary and credit policy so that its real utility, as a means of coping with the external debt problem, is very limited.

The responsibility for the debt problem

Through the years it has become evident that the debt problem for heavily-indebted countries could not have been the responsibility of only one of the concerned parties – neither commercial banks and governments of industrialized countries, nor of international financial institutions. The active participation and concurrence of all of them, in a simultaneous and co-ordinated way, is required. Hence, the necessity of guaranteeing the participation of all external agents in the rescheduling process. First it was necessary to establish generally-accepted methodologies in order to determine the size of the financial gap, based, among other things, on a given rate of growth of gross domestic product (GDP). Second, to determine the amount of the foreign exchange deficit. Third, negotiations then proceeded, in order to ensure the participation of each of the involved parties in what is known as the 'financial package'. It is not surprising that this negotiation has frequently produced a great deal of struggle and armtwisting among creditors, particularly in the case of large 'financial packages' such as the Mexican, in which the amount reached 12 billion US dollars.

The main lessons

Measures taken to cope with the debt problem allow us now, after five years, to examine the main lessons from past experience.

In the first place

In the first place, the great ability of the international financial system to avoid a crisis has to be recognized. In spite of the serious difficulties presented by the two largest debtors, Mexico and Brazil, no major crises have actually occurred in the international financial markets, although Brazil reached the extreme situation of unilaterally suspending interest payments on its commercial bank debt.

How has the crisis been avoided? – through the procedure known as 'muddling through'. Three elements should be mentioned:

1. Case-by-case approach. In spite of the frequent discussions about the necessity of establishing procedures of general application to all debtor countries, this point of view, in fact, has not been accepted. On the contrary, separate treatment for each case was followed. This allowed the consideration of each country's own problems, as well as the specific circumstances surrounding each negotiation.
2. The topic of the precedent has been always present. Commercial banks and Paris Club creditors have tried, again and again, to avoid the establishment of precedents that could subsequently be used by other countries in their own negotiations.

   Avoiding precedent-setting has been of crucial importance for domestic and external credit policy. The United States monetary authorities have therefore been constantly concerned about the possibility that rescheduling agreements approved by United States banks could eventually affect domestic monetary and credit measures, if banks gave similar conditions to troubled national activities, such as, for example, the agricultural or petrochemical sectors.

   It should be considered, however, that even when the case-by-case treatment is applied, precedents inevitably arise. Thus, conditions which refer to tenor, grace period, interest rate, spreads, and fees and were obtained by 'big' debtors in their negotiations, affect the conditions obtained by medium and small debtors. The important thing, in effect, is not avoiding the establishment of precedents, but favouring those that are propitious and convenient.
3. Avoiding the crisis required the active participation of different actors. Concretely, it was necessary to call commercial banks, governments, and international organizations, such as the International Monetary Fund (IMF), the World Bank, and the Bank for International Settlements (BIS) to stage. The co-ordinated consensus of all parties has been required to avoid the crisis. As may well be imagined, this concerted participation was always difficult to achieve and assure. As already said, a certain degree, frequently substantial, of armtwisting was indispensable. The need to reassure the contribution of all the parties, with predetermined amounts, pre-established

> dates, and prenegotiated conditions, led to a rather new phenomenon known as cross-conditionality. A party, not only all, sets certain conditions for a certain financing to a borrower. Now, each party also demands, as a prerequisite condition to participating in the negotiation of the financial package of a particular country, that the country agrees to comply with all the obligations and conditions established by the other parties. So, each party will participate and commit itself only if all of the others accept its own conditions at the same time. This means that the country cannot definitely conclude its negotiations with any of the creditors in absence of a definition, at least in principle, of the negotiations with each of them. Negotiations are thereby transformed into a set of simultaneous equations.

So, muddling through has provided the opportunity for obtaining the financial resources required every time, that, during the last five years, a serious problem has come forth. So the system has proven capable of avoiding financial panic, in spite of the very large and complex problems encountered.

The second lesson

The second lesson is that, notwithstanding the important efforts and the substantial achievements, the situation of heavily-indebted developing countries has not improved as main debt indicators, such as the stock of the debt as a proportion of GDP, interest payments as a percentage of exports or GDP, show. As of today, supplying oxygen to the patient's bed has been efficiently achieved, but there is still no possibility of the sick getting up and walking on the horizon. Furthermore, the solution seems to be still more remote than five years ago. The uncertainty and anxiety of the situation frequently cause tensions and confrontation between debtors and creditors. Neither have systematic procedures to approach the problems and solutions based on a real understanding of the problem been found yet, nor has the legitimate long-term interest of the various parties involved been duly recognized.

Several reasons can be pointed out to explain this evolution:

(a) It took a long time for creditors – industrialized countries, commercial banks, and international financial institutions – to accept the thesis presented years ago by developing countries, that debt-service problems were closely linked to the process of economic development. It is not just a short-term financial problem, but, on the contrary, a long-term development problem. This idea was only widely accepted when United States Treasury Secretary, James Baker, so established it in Seoul, in the 1985 Annual Meetings of the IMF and the World Bank. In effect, the only way in which highly-indebted countries can service their external debt is by achieving sustained and satisfactorily high growth rates. Otherwise the present crisis will persist and the problem will not be solved. On the other hand, if external debt service means that alone for interest payments a country should, year after year, assign 7 per cent or 8 per cent of its GDP, nearly half of its domestic savings, and approximately a third of its exports, the possibilities of growth are precarious, and therefore, those of servicing the debt as well.

This is why it is so urgent to find ways and means by heavily-indebted countries can pay less annually in debt service. This, in turn, would allow them to free resources to finance and accelerate their economic development, which would enable them, in the long run, to adequately service their debt. Commercial banks have not been able to give up an exclusively financial point of view that aims at obtaining, in the short term, the maximum possible amount of cash money. The long-term perspective, in which economic growth has primacy, as a means of becoming able to pay their debt in the long term, is strange to them. Understanding this, and incorporating it in the negotiations, is perhaps the main instrument to finding appropriate solutions to the external debt problem.

(b) Another aspect that has represented a serious obstacle to the debt problem, and which has not received enough attention, refers to the fact that a major part of the indebtedness is in the hands of the public sector, and not of the private sector of debtor countries. This means that the only way a country can meet its external obligations is through a surplus in its public finances, generating, in this manner, the necessary foreign exchange. Nevertheless, in general this surplus cannot be obtained through a drastic reduction of public expenditure, but only by increasing revenues, or, in other words, transferring resources from the private sector to the public sector. Thus, debt service implies not only the transfer of a proportion of GDP abroad, but also a domestic transfer from the private to the public sector. The generation of this surplus, however, presents serious difficulties of economic and political orders:

(i) From an economic point of view, the difficulty resides in the fact that the surplus is either the result of a reduction in public expenditure, maintaining the level of revenues, or of an increase in revenues with a constant level of expenditures. In both cases, the risk of damaging the private sector exists. If public expenditures are cut, the quantity and quality of services (justice, national security, education, health) and of the goods produced by the public sector, as well as the state of the infrastructure (energy, transportation), could deteriorate. It would consequently raise the costs of production of the private sector, and harm their competitiveness. On the other hand, it would be equally dangerous to increase public sector revenues by any of the usual means (taxes, public service fares, prices of state-produced goods), as this would decrease the resources available for the normal development of the private sector, with the consequent 'crowding-out'; similarly, it could also affect the costs of production of private firms if, for example, taxes are imposed on public services such as social security and transportation. All these measures entail difficulties in the growth of the private sector, and therefore, of national economic development.

(ii) From a political point of view, the transfer of a significant amount of resources from the private to the public sector always carries serious difficulties, regardless of the nature of the political regime, but particularly in a democracy. In the latter case, the resources allocated to service the external debt are sanctioned by parliament, competing with other demanding national needs.

(c) The governments of the industrialized countries have encountered serious domestic political obstacles to a more active participation in the search of solutions to the external debt problem. These are of a diverse nature:

(i) When the aim is to modify and adapt banking regulations to better fit the circumstances surrounding the external debt problem, the topic of how not to discriminate against troubled domestic sectors or activities inevitably arises. If a preferential treatment or some concession are granted to a foreign country, why not also give it to national banks and firms?

(ii) When the idea is to allocate additional resources, be they for bilateral aid, or for an increase in the resources disposed of by international or regional financial institutions, they face the dilemma of how much in national programmes should be sacrificed in favour of foreign aid.

(iii) When the intention is to help national banks through tax exemptions, or the utilization of a portion of external aid to repurchase debt documents of a debtor country, the political question is why national taxpayers should bail out financially-powerful firms, as commercial banks are supposed to be.

(d) The case of heavily-indebted small countries presents special characteristics that deserve separate comments:

(i) the length of each negotiation (normally several months), and its complexity (cross-conditionality, the meeting of conditions precedent) are particularly burdensome for small debtors, given the extreme scarcity of duly qualified personnel;

(ii) the relatively little importance that small debtors represent for commercial banks frequently induces the latter not to assign the advisory committee duties to key personnel. This means, on the one hand, that they do not possess enough decision-making capacity, and on the other hand, that they must present an inflexible and tough image in order to prove to their bosses that they adequately defend the interests of their bank, and be able to ascend in the bureaucratic scale;

(iii) sometimes small is beautiful. Commercial banks could make certain concessions to small debtors that they cannot make in the case of big debtors. For example, terms and conditions (tenor, grace period, fees, interest rate, capitalization of interest) could be more favourable for small countries, since they do not have a substantial impact on the financial situation of the banks. However, the danger of creating precedents inhibits banks from the possibility of making this kind of concessions;

(iv) small countries, because of their size, have little leverage. In effect, they do not have the capacity of creating a crisis in the international financial markets, although this disadvantage seems to be disappearing, since even big countries have lost a great deal of their capacity of creating crisis. This became evident in the case of Brazil, when it recently suspended interest payments to commercial banks. A few years ago the reaction of the international financial system upon the Brazilian decision would have been of greater dimensions than that which occurred last February.

(v) the little leverage of small debtors means that they hardly expect to clear the way or set the pace. Generally speaking, they walk behind the achievements of the big countries, and try to incorporate advantages and concessions obtained by the big debtors in their negotiations;

(iv) in some cases small countries have to stand in line to carry out their negotiations, as banks prefer to clear the ground first with the big countries, in spite of the good disposition and need of the small debtors to reschedule their obligations.

In summary

In summary, the lesson that has been derived in these past five years is that the external debt problem is much more difficult and complex than it was originally thought to be. Much more time is needed to find the adequate solution. The efforts and the resources required will be considerably higher than the ones devoted to this goal so far. The participation, patience, and willingness of all of the parties involved – debtor countries, commercial banks, governments of industrialized countries, and international financial institutions – will have to be much more significant than they have been up to now. Hence, in order to find the adequate solutions to the external debt problem an approach has to be found in which the medium-term growth of the concerned country should be put in the forefront. Financial gaps and foreign exchange requirements should be estimated on the basis of the attainment of rates of growth high enough to service the external debt in a reasonable way. This is the only manner to overcome the problem.

Possible future steps

The following proposals could be taken into consideration during the search for a solution to the external debt problem. It must be taken into account that a certain degree of repetition is inevitable;

the literature on the topic is so abundant that it is virtually impossible to keep up to date. The suggestions made below have been grouped according to their reference to commercial banks, industrialized countries, or international financial institutions.

Commercial banks

Given the shared responsibility between debtors and creditors, all parties should participate in the search for solutions. Commercial banks are not to be an exception. They made serious mistakes in making sizeable loans to countries with very uncertain financial conditions, to say the least. They made bad financial decisions! Consequently there is no doubt they will have to assume part of the losses. This is one of the main rules of the capitalist system: one cannot make a mistake without paying for it.

Two concrete measures follow – first, commercial banks will have to accept the sale, in the secondary market, of a portion of their loans, which undoubtedly would imply certain losses. Commercial banks already foresee this possibility, and have therefore created important reserves. It is precisely upon the presumption that a part of their credits will not be recovered that loan loss reserves are made. Second, commercial creditors will have to agree to continue granting additional financing. These new loans might take various forms, but the postponement of a portion of the interest payments, that is, a long-term capitalization of interest, is very likely to be one of the most utilized procedures in the near future.

Industrialized countries

The governments of the industrialized countries have already adopted some measures that contribute to the solution of the external debt problem. For instance, tax exemptions are granted to commercial banks that make reserves or assume losses. Much more is to be done, however:

(a) Tax exemptions should not be granted when reserves are increased, but only in those cases in which the commercial bank actually incurs a loss, namely, when the amount of the debtor's obligations is reduced.
(b) Banking regulations should be made more flexible, thus allowing creditors to participate at ease in the rescheduling negotiations with the indebted countries. This is particularly necessary regarding the present regulations within the United

States. In other nations, such as the European countries, regulations are already much more flexible.

(c) Bilateral aid should go through a deep revision. Concretely, it is necessary that the financial support given to debtor countries in the Paris Club ceases to be considered as aid for development rather than commercial aid, as they have been seen up to now. In other words, Paris Club terms and conditions (tenor, grace period, interest rate) should resemble those of official development aid (ODA).

(d) Guidelines for bilateral aid should also consider the possibility of assigning a portion of these funds to the repurchase, by the indebted country, of promissory notes held by the commercial banks of the country that grants the aid. This would constitute a means by which commercial banks would swap sovereign debt for documents of their own government, thus incurring a loss, but reducing their risk. The measure would require that bilateral creditors clearly perceive that, nowadays, the burden of the external debt is the main obstacle to economic development in highly-indebted countries.

(e) Multilateral aid should also undergo substantial changes. Industrialized countries should strengthen their capital contribution to international financial institutions such as the World Bank, and regional banks such as the Inter-American Development Bank, the African Bank, and the Asian Bank. The possibility of opening a new window in these financial entities, this time not for loans, but for buying back debt documents of certain countries at a price close to the one quoted in the secondary markets, should be considered. Commercial banks could receive notes issued by these institutions, supported by a fund created specially for this purpose by means of extraordinary contributions by the industrialized countries.

Multilateral financial institutions

Multilateral financial entities – international, as the World Bank, or regional, as the International Development Bank (IDB), African Bank or Asian Bank – can and should play an active role in the solution of the debt problem of developing countries. Several measures should be accounted for:

(a) To open a new window with the purpose of repurchasing debt, as described above.

(b) To increase the capital of these institutions so as to enlarge their capacity of granting loans to highly-indebted countries. The achievement of an adequate balance between project loans and structural adjustment programme loans is vital. Both are necessary – the former, to increase the quantity and improve the quality of the factors of production; the latter, to enhance the productivity of the factors of production in general.

(c) To re-examine the functions of the IMF. When this institution was created, in the 1940s, its duty was very precisely defined – to support countries with temporary balance-of-payments problems through the concession of credit, provided that the country adopted a set of measures designed to restore equilibrium. A 12 to 18 months programme would suffice to straighten the situation, and the country could repay the IMF within the next few years.

Heavily-indebted countries, however, are currently facing a situation of a very different kind. It is no longer a short-term payments unbalance, but a long-term disequilibrium. The IMF is not prepared, neither legally, that is, institutionally, nor financially, to help the countries meet their financial problems. Some progress has already been achieved through the IMF's extension of some of its programmes, such as the Extended Fund Facility (up to three years) and certain loans to African countries (up to seven years). The IMF, notwithstanding, still suffers serious limitations to support highly-indebted countries. This situation should be modified, but not in the sense frequently proposed. There has been a tendency to enable the IMF to deal with long-term problems. This should not happen. The IMF should continue performing the duties established in its charter and by-rules. It can, however, take a vital role by:

(i) Fully complying with its original objective of supporting member countries in the solution of short-term balance-of-payments problems, and by preventing the countries in difficulties from adopting measures that could jeopardize the normal flow of international trade.

(ii) Monitoring the short-term stabilization policy of the member countries, with a view to promoting the stability of the international monetary system. The World Bank, on its part, would monitor the long-term development policy.

(iii) Fulfilling, jointly with the World Bank, a catalytic function to establish and operate 'consultative groups' for the various countries, as well as participating in the setting up of the 'financial packages' for closing the financial gap of countries with imbalances.

(iv) Continuing the surveillance of the short- and long-term economic policies of the industrialized countries, particularly those of the G-7.

Concluding remarks

It is indispensable that the indebted countries make significant and systematic efforts to re-establish order in their own economy. Two aspects should be emphasized – first, the need to increase the quantity and improve the quality of the factors of production, and second, the adoption of the necessary measures to raise the average productivity of the available factors of production. In the economists' jargon, the first condition consists in implementing an economic growth policy, that is, a shift to the right of the production possibility curve. The second condition refers to the structural adjustment policy, which aims at reaching some point along the production possibility curve, thus avoiding any situation located within the area of the production possibility function. The fulfilment of these two conditions should be the sole responsibility of the indebted countries.

The fulfilment of these two necessary conditions, however is not sufficient for the solution of the problem. It is of utmost importance to set the house in order, but it is equally important also that the external economic environment should be favourable for the development of the heavily-indebted countries. If the external conditions are adverse, economic growth will be very difficult to achieve. The responsibility of creating an internationally favourable economic environment falls on the highly industrialized countries. It is absolutely necessary that the Organization for Economic Co-operation and Development (OECD) countries, and particularly the G-7 countries, adopt a rational economic policy.

First, to safeguard the stability of the international economic milieu is a requirement of the highest importance. Avoiding inflation, recession, and the wide fluctuations of exchange rates is necessary. On this subject, the measures taken by the IMF in order to establish an economic policy surveillance system for the industrialized countries represent an important step, although still insufficient.

Second, the achievement of sustained economic growth should

be another immediate goal of the industrialized countries. The consequence for low-income countries is vital. It is, perhaps, the most important support that indebted nations can receive, in a medium-term perspective. This policy would mean that the industrialized countries would adopt, without hesitation, aggressive internal structural adjustment measures. Third World countries could then expand their exports to industrialized countries, as comparative advantages vary through time, according to changes in income levels, technology, demand availability of natural resources, accumulation of capital, and skilled labour force.

Only if rich countries accept that poor countries can export their flowers and fruits, their shirts and cars, can the latter grow. Otherwise, the growth perspectives of developing countries, in general, and of highly-indebted nations, in particular, will be precarious, and, consequently, the possibilities of solving the debt problem are virtually nil.

Chapter eleven

Exposure management in Latin America – a banker's perspective

Eberhard Weiershäuser

After the speakers before me have looked at aspects of Latin America's indebtedness mainly from a more macroeconomic point of view, I shall deal with some practical microeconomic problems that face banks with commitments in the part of the world.

Basic questions

I would like to begin with some figures which illustrate the dimension of the problems.

Shortly after the beginning of the international debt crisis the total Latin American exposure of nine US money centre banks amounted to more than 50 billion US dollars, that is, 60 per cent of the exposure of all US banks in Latin America. The four major debtor countries (Argentina, Brazil, Mexico, and Venezuela) accounted for more than 44.8 billion US dollars out of the 50 billion US dollar claims of the nine money centre banks. The absolute amount of exposure is even more significant if we relate the exposure to the primary capital of the nine money centre banks: At the end of 1983 claims against the four major Latin American debtor countries amounted to 163 per cent of the primary capital of the nine money centre banks.

Before discussing exposure management itself, I should like to make some general comments related to any effective portfolio management. First of all, any bank has to define its specific goals and objectives which, of course, may differ from institution to institution. It is essential that senior management should focus on a process resulting in specific goals and objectives that suit the respective institution. In order to develop the appropriate set of goals and objectives, the following questions have to be raised and answered:

- What are the medium- and long-term prospects of a continuation business in a specific Latin American country in which the bank has exposure?
- Are there Latin American countries where the exposure of the institution is too high or too low relatively?
- What are the time and manpower requirements for continuation of the service of the portfolio as it is?
- Are there specific situations, such as private sector work-outs or sovereign risk restructurings, in which the institution considers it worthwhile being actively involved?
- Are there Latin American countries that are evaluated on the secondary market in a short-term perspective, and does the institutions' long-term fundamental view differ from the evaluation in the market-place?
- Do attractive alternatives exist for holding the debt as debt?

After having defined a set of objectives and goals in view of the existing portfolio, it is of utmost importance to adjust the once-defined goals and objectives to the realities of the constraints of both the market-place and other factors. Any effective exposure management of Latin American risk will also require that responsible officers for the Latin American risk management are appointed by senior management, for such officers have to act according to the defined objectives and goals when the right opportunity occurs. There is not always the time to involve credit committees or other equivalent bodies of the institution. Therefore, most banks use a limit system for their exposure management as they do in rate risk management and foreign exhcange management.

Defining exposure management

Let me briefly explain why I prefer the term 'management of exposure' to 'portfolio management' or 'loan portfolio management'. In my view the management of Latin American exposure, or risk if you wish, is not confined to the asset side of the balance sheet of a bank but includes a specially-tailored liability management, whereas the term 'loan portfolio management' seems to indicate that the management of risk concentrates on the asset side of the balance sheet. Nevertheless, let me start to explain some of the possibilities of exposure management of the asset side of a bank's balance sheet.

The three main tools of exposure management are:

1. debt-to-debt swaps,
2. debt-equity swaps which can be divided into debt-equity and debt-peso swaps,
3. trading of buying Latin American debt at discounts.

I should mention that the following basic explanations and examples of swap transactions are definitely over-simplifications, and it should be remembered that actual deals are often of a very complex nature and most of the time combine the various types of swaps as well as cash exchange.

Debt-to-debt swaps

Let me start with the debt-to-debt swap. The debt-to-debt swap is simply the change of creditors holding Latin American loans on their portfolio. Typically, the counterparties assign loans or give subparticipations to each other without generally changing the terms of the underlying payments. A debt-to-debt cross-border swap, for example, would include a German bank swapping part of its Mexican against Argentine exposure with a US bank. A debt-to-debt swap may also involve an inside creditor, for example, a Brazilian bank swapping its Mexican debt for Brazilian debt with the US bank. Deals are structured to equalize face values. The motivations for debt-to-debt swaps executed by banks are manifold. Not only risk components play a role, but in many cases transactions are tax-driven, with, for instance, bank A swapping private Mexican debt against a public Mexican debt that can be used by bank A, but not by bank B; for bank A could use tax receipts from the public sector debt to offset income in a country where bank B has no subsidiary. Some debt-to-debt swaps are product-driven, converting, for instance, an existing money market line, which has been frozen in by a rescheduling agreement, into floating rate notes.

Let me give you an example that combines different aspects in a debt-to-debt cross-border swap.

Bank A (a US bank), for instance, swaps 10 million US dollars of restructured long-term Brazilian loans for which no interest is paid at present, against Argentine loans of a swap partner (bank B), which presumably achieve approximately the same price in the secondary market. The advantage for bank A is that it obtains assets which yield regularly; in that case the US banks need not build loan loss reserves.

The interests of bank B are of a different nature; it wants to modify the risk structure of its loan portfolio. Bank B either assumes that the credit standing of the debtor country, that is, its ability to resume normal debt servicing, is in the long term more favourable in the case of Brazil than in the case of Argentina, or it has a long-term strategic interest in Brazil but not in Argentina.

When the opportunity arises, both swap partners may manage the risk and product structure of their loan portfolio even further by exchanging the swapped assets, that is, the Brazilian public sector debt or Argentine public sector debt, in another deal against perpetual floating rate notes of a Canadian or US bank. The difference between the market price of the Brazilian loans and the price of the perpetual floating rate notes is balanced by cash payment or by the additional transfer of relatively good credit risks.

Consequently, the bank would now carry perpetual floating rate notes of a Canadian or US bank on its books, instead of the country risk for Argentina or Brazil.

Surprisingly, in most debt-to-debt swaps the result appears to be a greater concentration rather than diversification of a specific country exposure in bank portfolios. Many banks neglected the argument of diversification and swapped their Latin American loans in an effort to consolidate their exposure into a few countries where they had defined their long-term strategic interests. Or banks decided to eliminate countries from their portfolio which, in their view, offered limited prospects of future improvement. Not all the banks that participate in debt-to-debt swaps, of course, end up with the same few countries, for their long-term strategic interests as well as their risk assessment may differ.

In swaps involving an inside creditor, liquidity is often the motivation, for many Latin American banks were left with liquidity problems after the outbreak of the debt crisis, which in some cases prompted a withdrawal of foreign deposits.

Debt-equity swaps

Let me move on to the debt-equity swap. A debt-equity swap transaction is a deal by which Latin American debt is converted into foreign equity in a domestic corporation. Therefore, the swap serves as a vehicle for foreign direct investment. The equity itself is denominated in the local currency, but in some cases the terms of conversion may grant the potential investor future access to official foreign exchange for the purpose of dividend remittances and capital repatriation. The equity position may be held by the bank that entered into the debt-equity transaction or by a foreign multinational corporation. I believe that soon foreign institutions will start to hold equity exposures through closed-end funds.

When the conversion of Latin American debt involves a resident of the country instead of a foreign investor, the term debt-peso swap is often used, and the term 'peso' simply means domestic currency. Therefore, debt-peso swaps are a kind of *de facto* amnesty of capital flight and are designed to repatriate flight capital. Residents of a Latin American country buy their own country's debt in the secondary market by using their deposits abroad.

The driving force behind the equity swaps has often been the willingness of debtor countries to buy back a debt with local currency, provided it is guaranteed that the proceeds are invested in the country. The multinational corporations' interest in debt-equity swaps is connected with the fact that Latin American debt has been available in a secondary market at discounts to face value. Sometimes the bank that is holding the debt undertakes the investment directly in order to bypass the secondary market and create the possibility of preserving the book value for its assets. In this scenario a creditor could benefit from liquefying an asset with a downside risk and no potential for capital gain and, in return for giving up this asset, from receiving a different asset with some downside risk but at the same time a potential for a gain.

Let me give you a few examples – in the spring of 1987, *American Express* swapped 100 million US dollars of Mexican debt for an equity position in a project to build luxury hotels in Mexico. As I mentioned before, equity positions can also be held through closed-end funds. In this case the fund manager could negotiate the terms of conversion with the government of the respective country and could build up an equity portfolio. Outside Latin America, Shearson Lehman Brothers is putting together a First Philippine Capital Fund with approximately 80 per cent of an envisaged 250 million US dollars issue coming from debt country distributions. The Overseas Private Insurance Corporation (OPIC) has agreed to insure this fund against political and transfer risk. The International Finance Corporation (IFC) is presently exploring the possibility of creating similar funds for Mexico and other countries.

The market for swaps

Let me briefly comment on market structures, price, and development of the secondary market. The market for the two types of swaps has developed rapidly. Sales at a discount and swaps first developed in 1982, when some banks decided to optimize or rebalance their exposure in Latin America and began to trade out and swap some loans into others. One of the initial reasons for this was the following – in the late 1970s some banks had taken Latin American risks on their books even though they had no long-term strategic interests in the region. Another development that greatly facilitated the growth of the secondary market was the fact that the large variety of existing types of debt in a country was bundled into a few types. Since 1982 the number of borrower's types of loans and debt instruments in Latin America has been dramatically reduced because the bulk of any kind of public sector debt has been abolished by rescheduling agreements under the guaranty of the central government or central bank. It should be noted that this development was totally unlike the development in the banking industry in general where within the same period a large variety of innovations of different instruments occurred.

Let me make a few comments on the size of the market. Estimates vary widely, and it should be remembered that very often a chain of transactions is necessary to complete a deal, and therefore, doublecounting is likely. Approximately 12 billion US dollars of asset swaps have been accomplished since 1982, counting only net shifts in portfolios. In 1986, swaps involving about 5 billion US dollars took place after debt-to-debt swaps ultimately linked to debt-equity conversions had been netted out. However, from an economic point of view the impact of debt-equity swaps should not be overestimated. In proportion to the 267 billion US dollars total debt of the eleven LDCs which established some form of a debt-equity conversion scheme, only a modest 2.2 per cent of their bank debt has been converted. On the other hand, Chile alone succeeded in converting about 14 per cent of its debt into equity or local currency. The supply of debt for the above-mentioned swaps seems to come mainly from European banks and regional US banks. Some of the American money centre banks along with investment banks in New York participate in the market mainly as intermediaries. The volume of the typical deal is between 2 and 5 million US dollars of debt that is regularly traded. The deals are very complex, require a customized documentation, and sometimes involve more than ten banks and the debt of more than twelve countries. Some intermediaries also provide price lists for cash sales of various Latin American loans and ratios for debt-to-debt swaps. A consistent pattern of the market has been a substantial narrowing of bid-offer spreads, which could indicate increasing liquidity in the market. But this observation seems to be somewhat misleading. It should be mentioned that the quoted prices and ratios are merely indicative. And no firm quotes do actually exist.

Asset trading

Beside the debt-to-debt and debt-equity swap, the actual selling of a loan at a discount base is the third major tool to manage Latin American exposure on the asset side of a bank's balance sheet. Acting as an intermediary in the secondary market, which some of the US money centre banks frequently do, is also a way of generating fee income to improve the overall yield of existing exposure. Please note that most of the time discounts are deeper than reserves. Therefore, portfolio contamination has kept especially many US banks from using the different tools within the secondary market. The likelihood of portfolio contamination is particularly strong when a loan is sold at a discount.

Currency options

As I mentioned before, the management of Latin American exposure is not limited to the asset side of a bank's balance sheet. Let us briefly examine the currency aspect of the transactions because this will automatically lead to different liability considerations. The existing currency mix of a Latin American exposure is of special importance to any non-US-based bank primarily in Europe and Japan. Before the debt crisis, the typical multi-currency loan facility left the currency option to the borrower, whereas in almost all Latin American rescheduling agreements the currency option is shifted to the banks. The currency option is, of course, connected with the option of the interest base, which, in the rescheduling agreement, is also shifted to the banks. The decision of a bank to choose a special currency and base rate can be difficult. Several points should be taken into account in such a discussion:

- Tax and accounting regulations may be less favourable or more favourable in a country, and therefore, a bank may want to book a loan into a foreign branch or subsidiary, which requires a funding in a currency other than the home currency of the bank.
- Yield improvement might occur in a certain currency because the bank may have a comparative advantage of funding itself in that particular currency.

- Loan provisions already made, which the bank wants to keep stable at a certain percentage, may require the choice of a certain currency.

Managing the exposure management

Let me briefly comment on some of the currency options most frequently included in Latin American restructurings – let us take a deutsche mark-based bank that holds Latin American debt denominated in US dollars. In order to provide for the loans risks in the case of country A, for instance, the bank intends to form a provision, covering, for instance, 50 per cent of its exposure in the corresponding country. As the bank's balance sheet is prepared in deutsche marks, the absolute amount of its exposure, and consequently the amount of the provision to be made, depend on the development of the US dollar exchange rate at the respective balance sheet dates.

If the existing commitment amounts to 100 million US dollars, for example, and if a US dollar exchange rate of DM2 is assumed, the deutsche mark equivalent would be 200 million deutsche marks; consequently, a provision of 100 million deutsche marks is required if a provision of 50 per cent of the respective holdings is intended. If the US dollar exchange rate rises by just 20 pfennigs to 2.20 deutsche marks at the next balance sheet date, the provision amount required will increase by 10 million deutsche marks to 110 million deutsche marks, provided the provision ratio of 50 per cent is to be maintained.

Furthermore, there is an interest rate differential between deutsche mark and US dollar funds, which presently ranges at about 3½ per cent. This means that in case interest payments cease (as, for instance, in the case of Peru, Bolivia, and at present also in the case of Brazil and Ecuador), the bank's expense for refinancing the US-dollar-denominated loans at a LIBOR-rate of presently 7½ per cent would be almost twice as high as in the case of a deutsche mark refinancing.

Thus the situation is complex, but manageable. One of the means to limit such risks is the possibility of a currency option on the part of the creditor bank. If a West German bank converts the loans into its home currency, deutsche marks, the amount of the commitment is more or less fixed and the expense for the corresponding provisions is foreseeable and permits a long-term management.

On the liability side of a bank's balance sheet, exposure management continues, and sometimes becomes even more difficult. Let me enlarge upon this. Any yield calculation on a given portfolio refers to the projected cash flows of such a given portfolio; so does any liability management related to a certain portfolio. Since over the past years the cash flow of Latin American portfolios has been somewhat different from what was laid down in the loan and restructuring agreements, and since in some cases interest has not been paid at all, the adjustment of liability management related to Latin American exposure has become essential to banks.

Conclusions

I started with a couple of figures to show the dimension of the problem for banks exposed to Latin American risk. Let me use those figures again to show a form of exposure management on the liability side of a bank's balance sheet:

> The claims of nine money centre banks on the Baker countries declined from nearly 200 per cent in 1982 to about 120 per cent of their total primary capital, which consisted of loan loss reserves, equity capital, and certain subordinated debt at the end of 1986. While the level of their claims was practically unchanged, the banks' primary capital increased by an average of over 12 per cent p.a. The recent wave of reserving led by Citibank shows that US banks are still not content with their claims-to-capital ratios. Banks can increase their primary capital either by increasing provisions for loan losses out of future retained earnings, or by increasing stockholder's equity.

Management of Latin American exposure has proven to be a challenge for the banks involved, and often it is necessary for the banks to leave the safe harbour of classic and conservative portfolio management to enter unchartered waters. In view of the magnitude of the financial problems faced by many Latin American countries, management of Latin American exposure by banks, and the tools used for such purpose, are only a small step on the long way to the solution of the debt crisis. In conclusion, let me say that the common goal of the debtor countries, the banks, and all the other parties involved, is to re-establish the credit-worthiness of Latin American countries.

Chapter twelve

The Latin American external debt problem, and the International Monetary Fund and World Bank conditionalities[1]

Patricio Meller

Introduction

The debt crisis induced the Latin American countries to carry out a long and expensive adjustment process. In the course of this adjustment process Latin America transferred a considerable amount of real and financial resources abroad; nevertheless, the problem of foreign indebtedness has not been solved yet. The International Monetary Fund (IMF) played an important part as a mediator between the debtor countries and the creditor banks; in this role it served different purposes from the original ones that were laid down in Bretton Woods in 1944. In order to reconcile the problem of foreign indebtedness with the Latin American countries' economic growth, it has been suggested adopting the strategy of 'adjustment plus growth'. Both the IMF and the World Bank will take an important part in this strategy, and therefore the control and co-ordination of the conditionality of both institutions is required.

The purpose of this contribution is to investigate and delimit the problems associated with the issues mentioned above. The next section of this contribution deals in detail with the adjustment costs and the transfer of resources that Latin America had to take on between 1982 and 1986 in order to fulfil its foreign debt services. In the third section, the goals and the roles of the IMF and the World Bank are examined schematically, and the criticism of the IMF's adjustment programmes in the Latin American literature is briefly considered. In the fourth section the role of the various economic participants in the development of the problems of foreign indebtedness are analyzed; special emphasis is put on the new part that the IMF has played. In the fifth and last section, different elements connected with the 'adjustment plus growth' strategy are discussed

Latin America's adjustment process in the 1980s

In the 1970s Latin America had a rate of economic growth of more than 5 per cent annually; between 1981 and 1986 the average annual rate of growth came to only 1 per cent (see Figure 12.1).

Figure 12.1 Growth of GDP in Latin America.

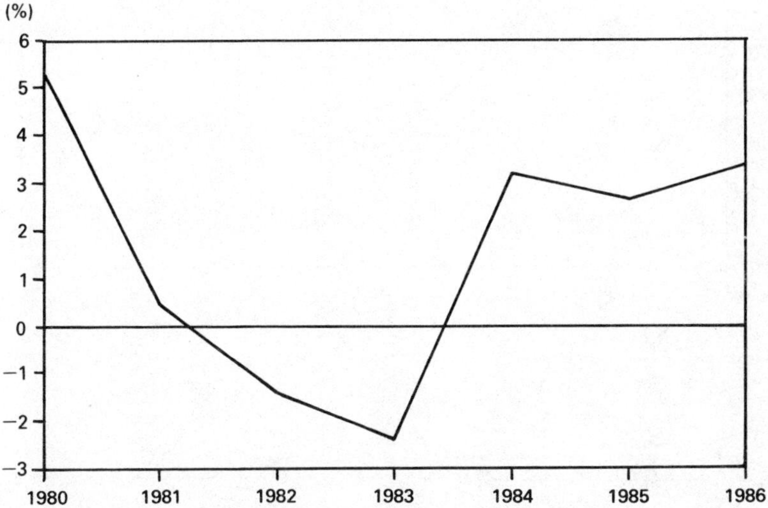

Source: Comision Económica para América Latina (CEPAL).

With a given high relative rate of growth of the population, the worsening of the terms of trade, and the transfer of resources abroad, it can be assumed on the basis of the corresponding figures that the Latin American per capita income in 1986 was by 14.2 per cent lower than in 1980 (see Figure 12.2).

The fact that these figures refer to a local average implies that in 1986 many Latin American countries had a per capita income equivalent to that of ten years ago, while for other countries this figure was equivalent to that of fifteen years ago. Therefore the 1980s have been called 'a lost decade for Latin America'.

If 1980 is taken as the base year, the trade balance shows that Latin America's external adjustment can be put down to a fundamental dwindling of imports. In fact, according to Figure 12.3, the amount of Latin American imports, which came to over 90 billion

Figure 12.2 Income per capita (development in Latin America) (1980 = 100).

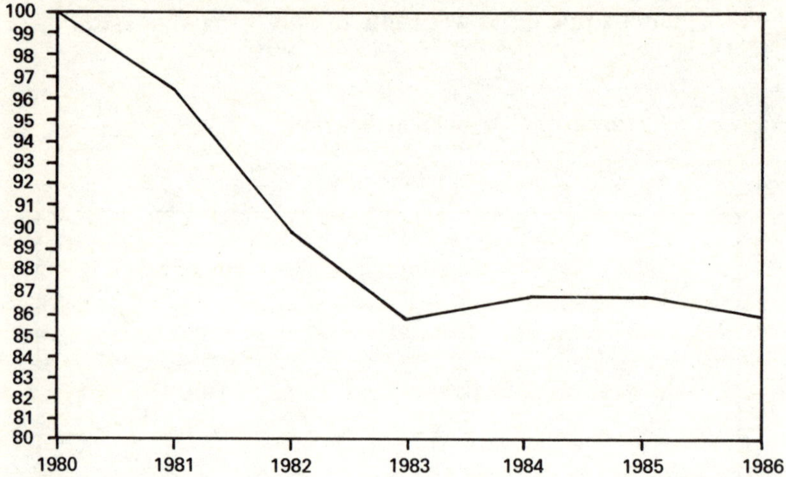

Source: CEPAL.

Figure 12.3 Exports and imports.

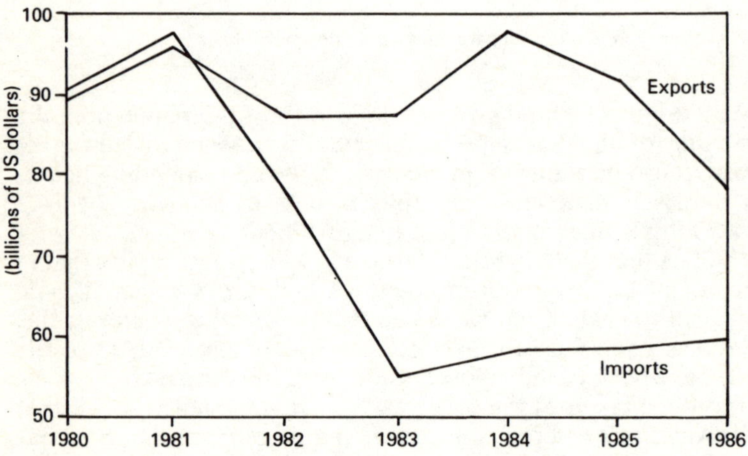

Source: CEPAL.

US dollars in the 1980s, dropped to less than 60 billion US dollars from 1983 to 1986. On the other hand, the amount of Latin American exports was about 90 billion US dollars between 1980 and 1985; however, in 1986 the exports were already dropping[2] (see Figure 12.3).

The fact that the export rates are evaluated in current US dollar creates a distortion in two respects: (a) on the one hand there is a diminution in Latin American imports; a comparison of the amount of imports (in current US dollar) in 1981 and 1986, for instance, would reveal a fall by 38.6 per cent; (b) on the other hand, the Latin American export rate seems to be constant with the exception of 1986; apparently Latin America made no special effort regarding its exports during the period of adjustment. To sum up, one can say that the achieving of a trade surplus can be put down mainly to the diminution of imports.

Nevertheless, the use of a real, quantitative index for the Latin American exports and imports reveals the following (see Figure 12.4):

(a) Although the real import value index went down considerably, this fall came to less than 30 per cent between 1984 and 1986.

Figure 12.4 Real exports and real imports (development in Latin America) (1980 = 100).

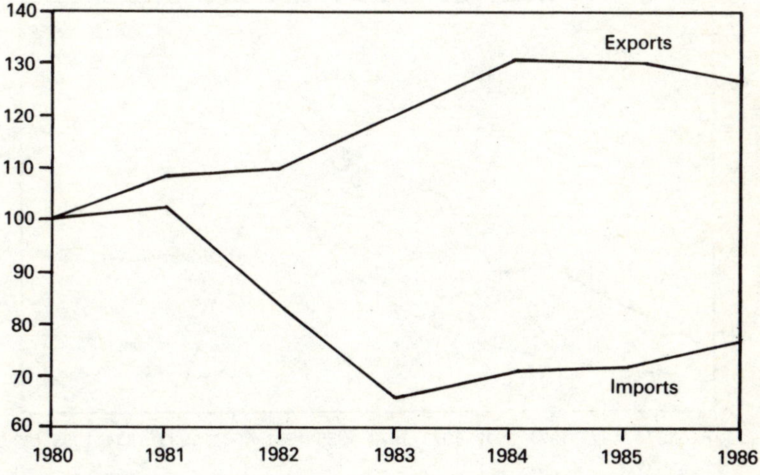

Source: CEPAL.

(b) On the other hand, the real export volume index rose by about 30 per cent between 1980 and 1986; thus the annual rate of growth of Latin America's export indices amounts to about 4.1 per cent. Still one can see that the greatest growth of the export indices was reached by a rate of growth of about 9 per cent in 1983 and 1984, while there was a period of stagnation afterwards.

In sum, if one takes into consideration Latin America's almost even trade balance in 1980, one can say that, in the course of the adjustment process in the 1980s, Latin America made the same quantitative efforts regarding its export indices as regarding the import indices in order to achieve a trade surplus. While the import index went down by 30 per cent, the export index rose by the same figure.

Figure 12.5 shows a synopsis of Latin America's net flows of capital between 1973 and 1986. On the one hand, one can see that from 1973 onwards the flow of external net credits (that is, new credits plus direct investments and minus the redemption of old credits) into Latin America grew steadily up to a peak of 37.5 billion US dollars in 1981; from 1983 onwards this annual flow went down continually to less than ten billion US dollars. On the other hand, Latin America's annual net payments for credits

Figure 12.5 Net capital flows

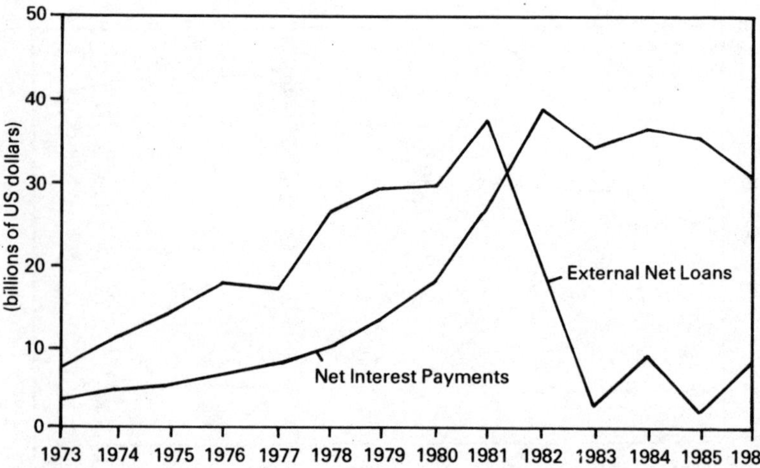

Source: CEPAL.

received (that is, for its foreign debt) and the flow of profit transfers (for factors of production whose owners are foreigners) came to less than 10 billion US dollars in most of the years between 1970 and 1979, whereas in the 1980s the flow of net payments exceeded 30 billion US dollars every year from 1982 onwards.

In the 1980s Latin America suffered two different, serious shocks: the fall in the terms of trade and the rise in the international interest rate. There is a third external shock related to the sudden reduction of external credit which is the one shown in Figures 12.5 and 12.7. Let us examine these shocks separately.

Figure 12.6 shows the deterioration of Latin America's terms of trade, which went down from a base level of 100 in 1980 to 78.1 in 1986. Thus, in the 1980s Latin America's terms of trade fell by more than 20 per cent. However, referring to the year 1980 as a benchmark overstates the deterioration of Latin America's terms of trade.

As regards the second shock, that is, the rise in the international interest rate in the 1980s (see Table 12.1), it is important to distinguish between two different effects:[3]

(a) The first effect is connected with the existence of a higher nominal interest rate, with the real interest rate assumed to be fixed. In this case, that is, in the case of higher (international)

Figure 12.6 Terms of trade (development in Latin America) (1980 = 100).

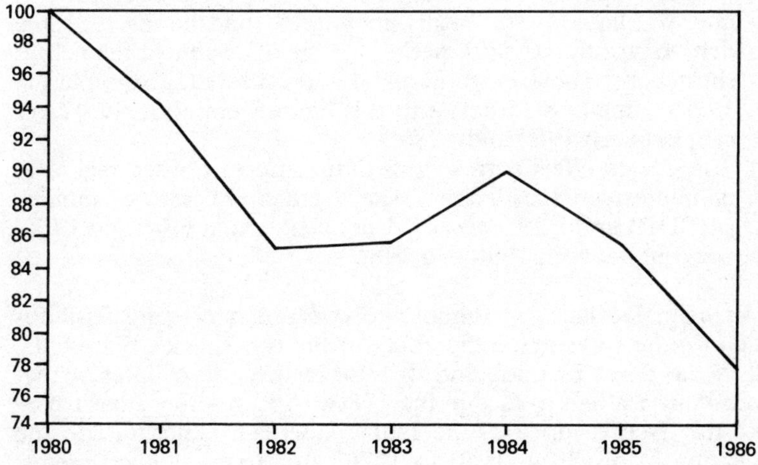

Source: CEPAL.

Table 12.1 International LIBOR interest rates, 1970–86 (in per cent)

	LIBOR interest rates (nominal)[a]	*LIBOR interest rates (real)*[b]
1970	8.47	2.7
1971	6.79	1.5
1972	5.41	0.7
1973	9.31	1.5
1974	11.20	−1.9
1975	7.61	−3.1
1976	6.12	−2.0
1977	6.42	−1.8
1978	8.33	1.1
1979	11.99	2.6
1980	14.15	2.0
1981	16.52	6.0
1982	13.25	5.3
1983	9.79	4.6
1984	11.20	6.1
1985	8.64	4.3
1986	6.71	4.8

Source: Bianchi, Devlin, and Ramos (1987) on the basis of basic information obtained from the Morgan Guaranty Trust; World Financial Markets and IMF, International Financial Statistics.

Notes:

a 180 days.
b Discounted by the weighted price index for the consumer in industrial nations.

nominal interest rates, together with a fixed real rate of interest, liquidity problems may arise on the part of the debtors, for the payback period for the real value of the debt is shortened.[4] The average nominal interest rate (LIBOR) in the 1970s came to 8.15 per cent; this figure went up to 11.42 per cent between 1980 and 1986.

(b) The second effect corresponds to the effect of raised real rates of interest on the debtors. The average real rate of interest (LIBOR) in the 1970s was 0.1 per cent, and it went up to 4.72 per cent between 1980 and 1986.[5]

Bianchi, Devlin, and Ramos[6] go over an interesting fictitious case in order to examine the effect of the two shocks, that is, the fall in the terms of trade and the rise in the rate of interest that Latin America had to face in the 1980s. As a reference basis they take the average price of the Latin American exports (with the exception of oil) from 1960 to 1970[7] and a real rate of interest (LIBOR) of 2 per cent.[8]

Bianchi, Devlin, and Ramos conclude that between 1983 and 1984 Latin America's current account could have produced an important surplus of more than 12 billion US dollars, if Latin America had not suffered the unfavourable shocks caused by the fall in export prices and the rise in the rates of interest (see Table 12.2). The surplus would be even higher if the calculation shown in Table 12.2 had taken into account the nominal shock of the high international interest rates in the 1980s.

It might be interesting to compare the ratio of the gross interest of Latin America's foreign debt to the war compensatory payments of France (1872–5) and Germany (1925–32). Bianchi, Devlin, and Ramos carry out such a comparison; similar comparisons are made by Reisen[9] and Fraga.[10] Table 12.3 gives an updated synopsis of these comparisons, in which two alternative indicators are used: the gross interest payments (or war compensations) in percentage of the gross geographical product (GGP) and in percentage of the export volume. Generally one can say that the gross interest payments of Latin America's foreign debt as a whole is twice as big (in relative numbers) as the war compensations that Germany had to pay after the First World War; the percentage is slightly higher than that which corresponds to the war compensatory payments of France in the nineteenth century. In some Latin American countries, for example in Argentina and in Chile, the corresponding percentage comes to at least three

Table 12.2 The effect of the unfavourable external shocks on Latin America (in billion US dollars)

	Deficit in the account current because of:			
	export price (crude oil excluded) below the real average 1950–70	*real LIBOR above the historic rate of 2%*	*actual situation current account*	*hypothetical situation – current account minus the fall in export prices and the rise in the real LIBOR*
	(1)	*(2)*	*(3)*	*(4)=(3)–(1)–(2)*
1981	4.7	5.4	−40.3	−30.2
1982	9.8	7.5	−41.0	−23.7
1983	12.8	6.8	−7.6	12.0
1984	10.8	8.6	−0.2	19.2
1985	11.7	5.0	−4.0	12.7
1986	8.5	7.0	−14.2	1.3

Source: Bianchi, Devlin, and Ramos (1987).

Table 12.3 Comparison of the gross interest payments of Latin America's foreign debt and war compensatory payments by France and Germany (in percentage)

	Interest or compensatory payments GGP	*Interest or compensatory payments exports*
France 1872–5	5.6	30.0
Germany 1925–32	2.5	13.4
Latin America 1982–6[a]	5.7	35.4
Argentina	8.4	54.5
Brazil	4.7	43.1
Chile	10.6	43.2
Colombia	3.2	—
Costa Rica	10.1	—
Ecuador	6.8	28.6
Mexico	6.6	39.3
Peru	4.8	30.8
Uruguay	6.2	28.6
Venezuela	6.3	23.5

Source: Germany and France: Machlup, F., (1964). Latin America: Bianchi, Devlin, and Ramos (1987); Ramos, J. (1987) 'Lo central de la transferencia de recursos en los procesos de ajuste, estabilización y desarrollo', mimeographed, CEPAL, November.

Note:

a For 1986 preliminary figures were entered in the table.

times the amount of what Germany had to pay as a war compensation.

With regard to the cost of finance that the foreign debt service involves, Latin America's net transfer of financial resources is of special interest. This transfer is illustrated in Figure 12.7.

Between 1973 and 1981 there was a positive net flow of funds into Latin America, a low that in general amounted to nominally over 10 billion US dollars per annum, and in 1978 and 1979 a peak of about 16 billion US dollars per annum was reached. Since 1982 there has been a negative net flow of funds, that is, financial resources flow out of Latin America; on average, these net transfers of financial resources amount to more than 20 billion US dollars per annum, and in 1983 and 1985 they even exceeded the 30 billion US dollars limit. Besides, it is interesting to observe that, valued in terms of the real US dollar of 1986, the net flow of funds that flowed into Latin America between 1973 and 1981 practically corresponds to the net transfer of funds out of Latin America from 1982 to 1986 (in this calculation, the value of the real US dollar of 1986 was ascertained by taking the IPM index of the USA as a

Figure 12.7 Net capital inflows.

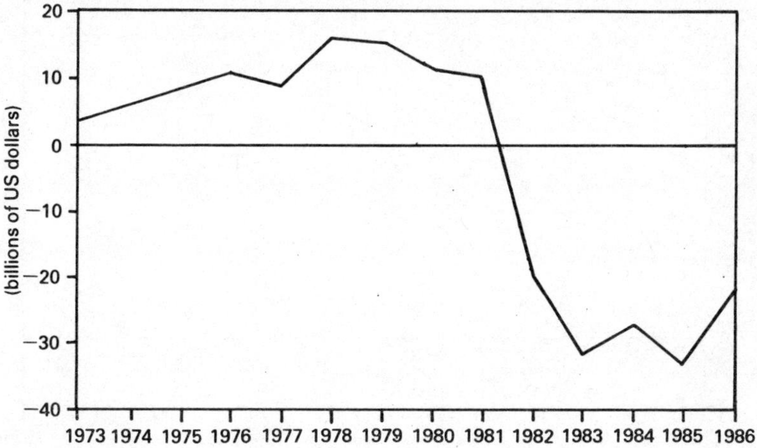

Source: CEPAL.

discount factor). In this context it is worth mentioning that, during a large part of the period of time in which Germany had to make war compensations, that is, from 1925 to 1928, there was a positive flow of financial resources into Germany.[11]

With given finite international reserves, the amount of which is too small in proportion to the annual demand owing to the foreign debt service, Latin America must of necessity achieve a trade surplus in order to carry out the net transfer of funds, and such a trade surplus implies a real transfer of resources. Figure 12.8 shows the respective real transfers of resources that Latin America made between 1982 and 1986. As Figure 12.8 shows, the transfer exceeded 30 billion US dollars from 1983 to 1985. In Table 12.4 the real transfers of resources that Latin America made in order to fulfil its foreign debt service are by means of relative numbers compared with the transfers that France and Germany carried out in order to make their war compensatory payments. If one compares Latin America's real transfer of resources with respect to national income or its export volume as a whole with those of Germany or France, the results for Latin America are at least twice as high as those for Germany and France. For countries such as Mexico and Venezuela, the relative numbers of the real transfers come to more than three times the percentage that corresponds to Germany and France.

Figure 12.8 Net capital transfers

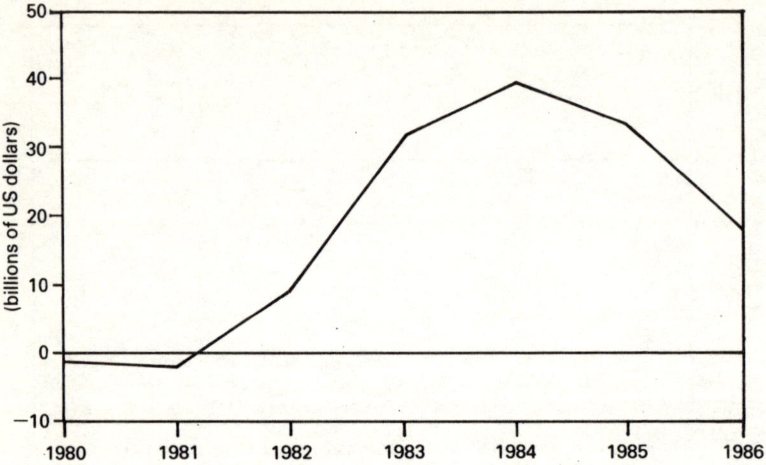

Source: CEPAL.

Table 12.4 Comparison of Latin America's real transfer of resources with that of France and Germany for war compensations (in per cent)

	Trade surplus income	*Trade surplus exports*
France 1872–5	2.3	12.3
Germany 1925–8[a]	—	—
1929–32	2.5	13.8
Latin America 1982–5	4.3	31.1
Argentina	5.9	48.0
Brazil	3.7	34.6
Chile	2.6	14.3
Colombia	−2.8	−25.0
Costa Rica	−0.4	−1.5
Ecuador	6.6	32.2
Mexico	7.0	46.8
Peru	2.3	15.8
Uruguay	4.6	23.7
Venezuela	11.2	43.3

Source: France and Germany: Machlup, F. (1964). Latin America: Bianchi, Devlin, and Ramos, (1987).

Note: In this period of time a trade deficit is observable.

Table 12.5 Latin America's foreign debt (in per cent)

	1980	*1981*	*1982*	*1983*	*1984*	*1985*	*1986*
Interest payment/ exports	20.2	28.0	41.0	36.0	35.3	35.2	35.1
Foreign debt exports	2.14	2.48	3.21	3.43	3.22	3.42	4.01
Gross foreign debt (in billions of US dollars)	230.4	287.8	330.7	350.8	366.9	373.2	382.1

Source: CEPAL.

In sum, Latin America carried out a difficult and painful adjustment process, and in so doing, it made a real and financial transfer of resources that far exceeded the historical experiences regarding war compensatory payments.[12] Nevertheless, the coefficients in connection with the foreign debt indicate no improvement. In fact, as Table 12.5 shows, the coefficient that represents the ratio of interest payments to exports goes up from 20.2 per cent in 1980 to 41 per cent in 1982, and since 1983 it has found its level at slightly more than 35 per cent.

On the other hand, the coefficient representing the ratio foreign debt to exports went up steadily from 2.14 per cent in 1980 to 3.21 per cent in 1982 and in 1986 it exceeded 4.0 per cent.

General aspects regarding the International Monetary Fund and the World Bank

Data about the relation between the IMF and the World Bank on the one hand and Latin America on the other hand

The IMF was repeatedly and over a long period of time present in Latin America. From 1954 to 1980 the Latin American countries signed 231 programmes with the IMF; during this time most of the countries had ten programmes, and some of them, such as Bolivia and Colombia, had up to fifteen programmes, or even nineteen programmes, as was the case with Peru and Haiti (see Table 12.6). Recently, that is, from 1982 to 1986, the Latin American countries signed with the IMF twenty-nine stand-by programmes and six extended-fund facility programmes.[13]

In these recent agreements between the Latin American countries and the IMF the following can be seen.[14]

Table 12.6 Programmes of the IMF in Latin America, 1954–80

Countries	*Number of programmes*	*Credits extended by the IMF (in millions of SDR)*
Argentina	10	1,385
Bolivia	15	220
Brazil	10	765
Chile	12	503
Colombia	15	528
Costa Rica	6	134
Dominican Republic	2	36
Ecuador	9	103
El Salvador	12	134
Granada	3	1
Guatemala	8	103
Guyana	11	108
Haiti	19	109
Honduras	13	159
Jamaica	5	560
Mexico	5	798
Nicaragua	8	93
Panama	12	195
Paraguay	10	51
Peru	19	1,014
Uruguay	11	242
Venezuela	1	100
	216	7,341

Source: SELA (1986).

(a) Despite the marked actual improvement in the trade balance, many of the programmes were interrupted or even discontinued because some of the quantitative targets that had been laid down in these programmes could not be reached. Therefore, in some Latin American countries almost 50 per cent of the credits that were recently extended by the IMF could not be used.

(b) One of the conclusions from this situation is that the diminution of the external disequilibrium and even a trade surplus can be achieved without reaching certain quantitative targets that were previously laid down in the IMF programmes and that refer to internal variables such as government deficit, and the expansion of the internal credit volume.

Before the 1980s the credits extended by the World Bank were insignificant as far as quantity is concerned. Nevertheless, before 1977 the access to loans extended by the World Bank was far easier for Latin America than afterwards. In fact, from 1958 to 1968 and from 1968 to 1977 the credits that the World Bank gave to Latin America increased on average by 11.4 per cent and 9.6 per cent respectively per annum; accordingly the annual rates of growth of the total amount of credits extended by the World Bank came to 1.1 per cent from 1958 to 1968 and to 14.1 per cent from 1968 to 1977. The situation was different between 1981 and 1984 when the total credits of the World Bank increased by 19.8 per cent per annum, whereas the credits for Latin America annually increased by only 3.5 per cent on average.[15]

There are two reasons for this relative fall in the amount of credits that the World Bank extended to Latin America:[16]

(a) The recent adjustment on the part of the Latin American countries caused a fall in the investment level. Many of the projects that had been approved by the World Bank had to be cancelled because the respective country did not have the funds at its disposal in order to make the local financial contribution. In many cases this local financing was cut by the restrictive expansion of internal credits imposed by the quantitative targets of the IMF.
(b) The new credits that the World Bank offers now are very often of the SAL type (structural adjustment loan), and owing to their stipulations they are not very attractive to many Latin American countries.

Schematic characteristics of the IMF and the World Bank

In Bretton Woods (1944) the roles of the IMF and the World Bank were defined as follows – the IMF's main concern is the short-term adjustment of a country with an external disequilibrium; in that case the IMF grants a loan so that the country in question can correct the disequilibrium in its balance of payments; the World Bank endeavours to support growth and economic development, and to this end it extends loans for specific capital investment projects and development projects. The IMF focuses mainly on macroeconomic matters, and its goals are the balance of payments and inflation. It tries to achieve these goals through measures concerning the fiscal policy, the monetary policy, and the foreign exchange policy. The World Bank on the other hand focuses on microeconomic matters and aims at supporting savings and investments, and thereby economic growth. In order to achieve these goals, the World Bank concentrates on relative prices and commercial policy. The IMF's methods are directed towards controlling the aggregate demand. To this end the IMF uses a flow analysis of nominal variables. The methods of the World Bank on the other hand are directed towards influencing the aggregate supply. To this end the World Bank analysis consists of evaluation of projects; this analysis is based on real variables and makes use of the input-output table, the national accounts, and a consistent analytical framework.

The division of labour between the IMF and the World Bank has broken down in the 1980s. Today it is generally known that on the one hand the disequilibria in the balance of payments of the Latin American countries and the developing countries in general are due to structural reasons and therefore require a long-term perspective. On the other hand, the short-term macroeconomic adjustment influences the development of long-term growth, too. In other words, short-term measures have an effect on long-term measures. Besides, the solution of short-term problems requires that these problems are considered from a long-term point of view, too. This insight caused the IMF to adopt a longer-term point of view; the introduction of EFF programmes (extended fund facility) and SAF programmes (structural adjustment facility) aims at influencing the aggregate supply. The World Bank for its part directly introduced the analysis and the macroeconomic variables for the evaluation of the loans that it extends in order to promote savings, investment, and growth.

The sum up one can say that on the one hand it is difficult to distinguish between the IMF's EFF and SAF programmes and the World Bank's SAL programme. On the other hand, owing to the interdependence of short-term and long-term measures, the economic programmes that the IMF and the World Bank suggest must be co-ordinated. This exactly is the new issue that is called double conditionality.

In our opinion, Latin America's future prospects are as follows: on the one hand the Latin American countries short-term and medium-term – that is, relating to the next five years – access to the international capital markets will be limited. Therefore the credits that the IMF and the World Bank will extend will be of great importance. On the other hand, Latin America will be faced with a short-term and a long-term conditionality because of the double conditionality on the part of the IMF and the World Bank. On account of previous experiences, especially with the IMF (as will be explained in the following section), Latin America's internal economic policy will in future be constrained by outside multilateral institutions.[17]

Latin America's criticism of the IMF's conditionality

The Latin American criticism of the IMF's conditionality[18] comprises five different aspects: (a) the IMF uses the same recipe everywhere, (b) there are problems about the control of the IMF's quantitative targets, (c) the programmes of the IMF are unnecessarily recessionary, (d) the programmes of the IMF have a regressive effect on the distribution, (e) there is an international asymmetry in the adjustment costs when there are external disequilibria; the latter aspect will be dealt with later on. In the following, the first four critical arguments will be discussed briefly.

The standard IMF programme

The analytical framework of the IMF includes the following elements:

(a) The external disequilibrium is produced by an internal disequilibrium; a country tries to spend more than it produces (internal disequilibrium), and this gap is filled by a surplus of imports compared with the exports (external disequilibrium).
(b) The internal disequilibrium is caused mainly by the government, that is, in the end the fiscal deficit can be held accountable for the external disequilibrium.
(c) One more factor that causes an external disequilibrium is the domestic credit expansion, for the external disequilibrium can only be financed in this way.
(d) The economic programme of the IMF aims at the reduction of internal expenses (or the control of the aggregate demand) by means of a fiscal policy that is meant to diminish the fiscal deficit, and a monetary policy (credit policy) that is meant to control inflation. Besides, the foreign exchange policy concentrates on changing the composition of expenditure and production.
(e) The IMF presupposes these elements and sets quantitative goals, which are connected with changes of the level of international reserves, with the level of the fiscal deficit, with the rate of growth of domestic credits, and with the level of credits to the public sector.

Moreover, instead of analysing the facts concerning each individual case, the IMF always uses the same analytical approach in order to explain the external disequilibrium. In other words, even before their visit the experts of the IMF know better than the Latin American economists how to tackle the problem of an external disequilibrium. Dialogues with the IMF have always the same results: 'This country spends more than it is able to afford', that is, 'there is an excess in demand that must be reduced'.

Latin America criticises this diagnosis as follows.[19]

(a) How can a country with an unemployment rate of more than 15 per cent and a capacity utilization of less than 75 per cent have an excess in demand?
(b) In one period of time (t_1) a country might have external equilibrium. Then, in the following period of time (t_2), this country might be caught by an unfavourable external shock, such as a dramatic drop in the price of its most important export product, and this shock would cause a diminution of the total export volume and thereby an external disequilibrium. Therefore, external factors are the ones which produce the external disequilibrium, and this has not been produced by a domestic mismanagement of economic policy.

The problem of monitoring the IMF programmes

The control system of the IMF is scheduled to supervise the economy every three months. This means that every three months the country in question must reach certain targets regarding the indicators that were laid down in the IMF programmes, for example, international reserves, domestic credit, and so on. If it fails to reach these targets, it does not receive the IMF's and the international banks' quarterly financial payouts of loans, which enable the country to cover the deficit in its external sector. Therefore, the central worry of the ministers of finance is how to achieve the quarterly targets set by the IMF, and their efforts are only considered to be successful if they achieve these goals. In sum, the economy on the whole has recently begun to work in quarterly periods of time.[20]

The IMF Programmes are very recessionary

It is empirically observable that most of the time the external goals of the IMF are realized at a considerable internal cost. Thus there is a kind of overkill.

Why are the IMF programmes so recessionary? It is generally agreed that the extremely strict and recessionary character of the IMF programmes should be modified. The following elements contribute to the recessionary course of the programme:

(a) It is difficult to have complete control of the economic means by which the programme is implemented; the money supply, for instance, is mainly endogenous. These difficulties produce even more restrictive measures whenever the financing is in danger in order to avoid the risk of not achieving the quantitative targets that were laid down by the IMF.
(b) Instead of lowering the pressure on economy by laying down plausible ranks for the achievement of the respective goals, the IMF fixes the goals in terms of absolute numbers even for the quarterly periods of time; this fixing assumes a degree of exactness and of control that cannot be reached by economics.

The distributive effect of the adjustment costs

From the point of view of redistribution, the internal adjustment costs of the IMF programmes produce regressive results in general, that is, the greatest part of the adjustment costs is born by the groups with the lowest relative income. In fact, the currency devaluation, together with the control of wages, means a real loss of purchasing power for the workers. The diminution of public spending brings about an increase in the rate of unemployment because public investments go down. Moreover, the cut in subsidies for primary consumer goods (food, public transport, and so on), and in the reduction of social expenditure, cause a diminution of the welfare of the groups with the lowest income.

When Chile or Brazil want to devise a cost-cutting programme for instance, the question arises why the IMF interferes in its preparation. The price of bread and milk as well as the whole agricultural policy in general 'are internal matters, concerning only the respective country' . . . 'Why should a cut in the subsidies for wheat solve Brazil's problems regarding its external disequilibrium? Where is the macroeconomic study that proves such an assumption?'[21] Moreover, why should a salary cut for teachers at public schools contribute to a rise in international competitiveness? Why are such steps taken while there is an unemployment rate of more than 15 per cent?

Adjustment and financing

Despite the harsh criticism of the IMF's role, it should be kept in mind that the Fund did not cause the existing economic problems; Latin America's economic disequilibria were already existing before the IMF's intervention. In fact, the Latin American countries resort to the IMF only when there is nothing else left for them to do. Adjustment in the case of an external disequilibrium necessarily entails costs, no matter whether the IMF is involved or not.

If a country is faced with an external disequilibrium, there seem to be two different possibilities: adjustment and financing. However, these alternatives are interdependent. Even though a decision in favour of financing implies a postponement of the adjustment to the future, the creditors who supply the money for financing the external disequilibrium will only do so if they can observe that the respective country takes measures that guarantee the realization of such an adjustment in the future. To this end, the IMF supplies its financial resources for a limited period of time, provided that the country in question accepts its conditions. These conditions in turn aim at overcoming the existing external disequilibrium.

The IMF has different functions. On the one hand this institution was created in order to lend funds to countries with external liquidity problems. On the other hand it could be regarded as a sort of 'credit club', which applies certain rules in order to preserve the welfare of all its members. Thus the IMF has to reconcile the specific national interest in the period of adjustment with the general interest of the other members of the club, especially of those creditor countries that supply the greatest part of the IMF's fund. Among these rules are the free convertibility of currencies, the free access to the money market, and the opening of the borders for imports. In the third place the IMF has a catalytic effect on financings from other sources. Thus the IMF and its programmes are the prerequisite that the international private banking industry and the governments demand, before they extend credits to a country that has difficulties over its trade balance.

To sum up, one can say that the Latin American countries resort to the IMF only at the last moment, that is, only when the economic authorities are desperate and see no other alternative way. In other words, the Fund is a lender of last resort. This has two consequences for Latin America. On the one hand the IMF is a necessary institution, and a less rigorous adjustment requires its credits. On the other hand, the Latin American countries' bargaining power is limited as far as the adjustment policy is concerned.

The central problem in Latin America is not the existence of the IMF; on the contrary, the Latin American countries need the IMF. The central problem is connected with the adjustment policy, which imposes the IMF's conditionality on these countries. The central question, however, is not related to the existence or non-existence of a conditionality. For two reasons a conditionality is indispensable:

(a) The IMF does not make presents, but loans, which have to be paid back.
(b) The credits of the IMF must be used for the express purpose of diminishing the existing external disequilibrium.

Until recently, most of the Latin American countries complied with the two requirements of the IMF's conditionality; however, the incurring internal costs were too high. In sum, Latin America's central problem consists in the type of conditionality that is connected with the adjustment programmes. It is the time for the Latin American countries to devise and propose an alternative type of conditionality that can be implemented in the adjustment programmes which they carry out.

Latin America's foreign debt and the role of the IMF

The new role of the International Monetary Fund

When the quasi-crisis of the international financial system, which had been triggered off in 1982 by the problem of Latin America's foreign debt, was settled, the IMF played an important part as a mediator between the debtor countries and the creditor banks. To this end the Fund organized and co-ordinated complicated financial packages of very different origins, and in so doing it helped many Latin American countries to solve their liquidity problems from 1982 to 1985. Moreover, during this period of time the IMF increased considerably its credit volume regarding its own financial resources.

When taking the part of a mediator, the IMF imposed conditions to both the debtor countries and the creditors. The debtor countries had to accept an adjustment programme that included the complete payment of the external foreign debt service. The creditor banks for their part had to allocate additional financial resources to a financial package, in which the funds of the IMF were only one component.

It should be recalled that the original principal task of the IMF consisted in extending credits to countries with short-term problems about external disequilibria. In other words, the IMF's role is short run and concentrated on the disequilibrium of the balance-of-payments flows. Bacha[22] points to the fact that the IMF takes on a long-term stock problem by taking the part of a mediator regarding Latin America's foreign debt.

This way of looking at the problem is based on the opinion that Latin America's foreign debt and the punctual payment of the debt service are not a temporary liquidity problem, but can be put down to be a problem of unbalanced stocks, as will be explained below.

Owing to its new role as a mediator the IMF is faced with new dilemmas.[23] If a country cannot carry out the adjustment programme that it signed with the IMF, two things might happen:

(a) The IMF might cancel the programme; such a step would cause an economic crisis in the country in question, for no country can obtain external funds without the IMF's consent. Thus an economic programme signed with the IMF gives the required external credibility to the economic programme of a country.[24] When an adjustment programme that was proposed or even imposed by the IMF is discontinued, the economic crisis thereby caused brings up the question why the Fund proposed such an impracticable economic programme, which cannot be implemented.
(b) If, on the other hand, the IMF maintains the credit flow, although the goals of the programme were not reached, it might lose some of its external credibility as an international monitoring agent.[25]

Latin America's point of view

In order to keep up the necessary flows for the foreign debt service, the Latin American countries have agreed to a long and painful adjustment process since 1982. This process entailed a fall in income, in the per capita consumption, and in real wages, and a decrease of investments and economic growth.

Now, after this adjustment policy has been practised for a few years, the question arises whether the problem of foreign indebtedness has been solved or at least alleviated. It was already mentioned that the majority of indicators regarding foreign indebtedness show that the situation is still the same or even worse than before. What then was the use of this long and painful adjustment? What would have happened if all the Latin American countries had simultaneously discontinued their foreign debt service as early as 1982?

Latin America's long and costly adjustment process was useful in so far as it prevented the collapse of the international financial system. With the preservation of the international financial system being a public good of world-wide importance, the question arises why Latin America of all was burdened most heavily with its maintenance.[26] Since 1985 the institutional financing agreements of 1982, which aim at managing the problem of Latin America's foreign debt, have been in a critical phase. The Baker plan or Baker initiative and changes in the top management of the IMF and the World Bank are external indicators of this situation. The long adjustment process has exhausted the debtor countries; the international banking industry is not willing to put fresh funds at their disposal. The IMF's available funds have diminished. Besides, there is a negative flow of funds into Latin America. Thus the following question arises – what kind of pressure can be brought to bear on the Latin American countries in order to make them accept the conditionality of the adjustment programmes, a conditionality which implies among other things the payment of the whole foreign debt service?

The problem of Latin America's debt overhang

At the present moment it is obvious that Latin America's foreign indebtedness is not a temporary liquidity problem. Owing to Latin America's foreign indebtedness the region has a problem of disequilibria of stocks, that is, a long-term problem of growth.

From Latin America's point of view, the IMF's and the World Bank's role should consist in convincing the international creditor banks that the Latin American countries cannot grow and at the same time fulfil their foreign debt service. The Latin American countries have come to a point now where they do not have enough financial resources with which to pay their debts, although they are quite willing to pay. For a debtor country with a growing economy it is easier to pay off its foreign debt than it is for a country whose economy stagnates or even dwindles.

The following example illustrates this 'pay or grow' dilemma. To have an annual rate of growth of 5 per cent a Latin American country needs an average propensity to invest of 20 per cent (in relation to the GGP). Furthermore, it needs a propensity to save of 25 per cent in order to finance this propensity to invest and to meet the interest payments for its foreign debt, which make 5 per cent of the GGP. Thus, a Latin American country needs a savings rate of 25 per cent for a growth of 5 per cent and the simultaneous fulfilment of its foreign debt service.[27] At present the Latin American countries' savings rate varies between 15 per cent and 18 per cent. A Latin American country needs an increase of 30 per cent to 50 per cent in its domestic savings rate, if it wants to pay off its debt and to grow at the same time. However, how can the domestic savings rate increase with a per capita consumption level that has fallen by 15 per cent?

On the other hand, the level of the external debt overhang is a factor of uncertainty both for national and for foreign investors, and thus they arouse negative expectations. Therefore the question is as follows: How can the rate of investments increase and thereby produce the necessary growth?

Adjustment plus growth

The strategy of adjustment plus growth

This strategy corresponds to a long-standing Latin American suggestion. There is a wide consensus that the numerous adjustment programmes that were repeatedly signed by the Latin American countries and the IMF reduce the external disequilibrium. However, they bring about two problems: (a) as was mentioned before, they entail very high internal costs; (b) since they do not produce the required structural change, they cannot lead the economy to a stable, high, and feasible growth path.

Today everybody favours 'adjustment plus growth'. Nevertheless, opinions differ widely regarding the set of economic measures that the implementation of this strategy requires.

The potential conflict between adjustment and growth

A macroeconomic adjustment programme might require a considerable reduction of the fiscal deficit and a fall in the rate of growth of internal credit. A reduction of the fiscal deficit presupposes an increase in the taxation of all the economic participants involved, including among others the exporters, and a decrease in public spending, including public investment. On the other hand, a decrease in internal credits has a negative impact on the financing of investments because it diminishes the available funds for it. Consequently, the previous macroeconomic programmes, which focused on achieving and implementing the adjustment, would not provide positive incentives to growth, that is, there would be a trade-off between adjustment and growth.

Nevertheless, one could argue that the macroeconomic adjustment is a prerequisite condition to long-term and lasting growth. A stable macroeconomic environment without potential disequilibria, no matter whether they are internal or external, and stable economic rules, encourage the economic agents to adopt a long-term planning horizon.

The future, double conditionality of the IMF and the World Bank

The example of the successful experience of economic growth in the Asian exporting countries suggest that the future double conditionality of the IMF and the World Bank will support the development strategy of encouraging exports, that is, the so-called outwards-oriented development. It is worth mentioning that today most of the Latin American economists, CEPAL included, are convinced that this is the development strategy that should be used. The central difference of opinion concerns the set of economic policy measures that the implementation of this strategy requires.

The introduction of this strategy of export promotion, to which the double conditionality of the IMF and the World Bank will amount implicitly or explicitly, includes the following elements.[28]

(a) A liberalization of the external sector, which corresponds to an import liberalization.
(b) A domestic currency devaluation.
(c) The private sector is the engine of economic growth. This expression is a euphemism for the privatization of public enterprises.
(d) Stable and permanent economic rules. A prerequisite condition to such rules is a reduction of the government's interference in the economy. Besides, and this is connected with the point just mentioned, the state's share in the economy must be reduced.

The examination of the Asian experience

In the economic literature opinions seem to differ widely about the successful export growth of the Asian experience. In this context, Sachs's observation[29] seems to be interesting.

From 1950 to 1973 Japan achieved one of the highest average rates of economic growth per annum, and during this period of time it used the following set of economic policy measures:[30]

1. Foreign exchange policy – the government had total control over the foreign exchange; the exporters gave all the acquired foreign exchange to the government. There was no special rule about the distribution of foreign exchange; the government bureaucrats allocated it to the different sectors and enterprises. Between 1950 and 1964 no public foreign exchange was provided for tourism.
2. Capital accounts – the government was the only economic agent entitled to engage in foreign credits. Foreign investments were rigorously controlled, and multinational enterprises with a foreign majority control were not admitted.
3. The rate of interest – the real rate of interest was low and was

not allowed to exceed a maximum limit; credits were allocated arbitrarily.

4. Incentives for exporters – exports were not promoted by a liberalization of imports, but by special tax benefits, such as subsidies and tax exemptions. This kind of incentive was also granted to exports with natural comparative advantages.

According to Sachs,[31] one can conclude in sum that the Japanese export experience was based neither on free trade, nor on the unrestricted development of free-market mechanism, nor on the government's restraint. It is worth mentioning that some Latin American countries used a similar programme; the result was not the same though. What is the reason for this difference in results?

As regards a successful export strategy for countries other than Japan, the following aspects should be taken into account.[32]

(a) Export promotion is the engine of economic growth.
(b) However, export promotion does not correspond to the liberalization of imports, nor is it a prerequisite condition to export promotion.
(c) A similar observation can be made regarding privatization and the government's role. In Korea, the government promotes the formation of business enterprises and marketing organizations for export products. There is nothing like the Japanese MITI, which is famous for the lay-out of its future export column. However, the Korean government has direct connections to the big export firms and thus plays an important and active part in the implementation of the export promotion strategy.

To sum up, one can say that the economic policy package that resulted in the successful Asian export promotion strategy and the strategy of 'liberalization plus deregulation' which the potential future double conditionality of the IMF and the World Bank would entail, are not the same.

The problem of distribution

From the point of view of a country with an external disequilibrium, the achievement of an adjustment is a public good, which is to the advantage of every economic agent in the country in question. Why then do not all the economic agents co-operate to the same extent and make sacrifices to this end? How can the adjustment costs be justly distributed? What kind of economic policy could achieve a fair distribution? The same set of questions applies to the strategy of adjustment plus growth. In this last case one could argue that those who make sacrifices now will gain from a higher rate of growth in the future. Nevertheless, there are some problems involved in this train of thought – (a) what measures can guarantee that those who make the greatest sacrifices now will be compensated for them in the future? Will this future compensation be greater for those who make more sacrifices now?; (b) how can the present loss of affluence be compared to the potential gain that is expected for the future? Those economic agents who have been unemployed for six months, thus facilitating the adjustment, wonder at what price the future gain should be fixed that would balance the present economic, psychological, and social costs.

The financing of the strategy

Doubtlessly the central problem about the strategy of adjustment plus growth consists in the fact that a country needs a greater relative volume of resources for a longer period of time in order to implement it.

In view of the current international economic situation and the above mentioned problems, Latin America's prospects are as follows – (a) the international banking industry will not grant long-term or medium-term loans, (b) the amount of funds from foreign investment and from possible future aid by the governments of the developed countries is relatively small compared with what the implementation of the strategy in question requires.

There are only two possibilities left – (a) a rise in the credit funds available from the IMF and the World Bank. Such a rise could be achieved by means of various mechanisms, such as a greater contribution by the governments that belong to these institutions, a more frequent use of the SDR on the part of the IMF, and a proportional increase in the amount of credits by the World Bank in proportion to its assets.[33] This means that the international organizations, IMF and World Bank, will play a predominant role in the Latin American countries' near future. This is why the discussion about double conditionality is so important; (b) the remaining alternative consists in a reduction of the negative flow of funds out of Latin America or even in the abolition of this flow in extreme circumstances. In other words, the flow of the funds that are destined for the foreign debt service should be reduced considerably.

The problem of asymmetry

The traditional problem of an international asymmetry in the adjustment costs reveals some of the difficulties that the strategy of adjustment plus growth might entail. This section deals with various aspects in connection with the problem of asymmetry:

1. As regards the problem of the external disequilibrium, there is an asymmetry between the already developed and the developing countries. The IMF is unable to convince the developed countries to carry out a coherent and consistent economic programme, which would support the international financial stability and the growth of the world economy.

   Moreover, the external disequilibrium and the fiscal deficit in the North American economy are central factors in the problematic functioning of the world economy, and the IMF can do nothing about these factors. What would the North American government's and the North American people's reaction be if the IMF suggested a reduction of the North American fiscal deficit from 4 per cent (of the GGP) to 2 per cent within a year? Comparable and in some cases much severer conditions are agreed on in most of the stand-by programmes that the Latin American countries sign with the IMF.
2. The economic programmes that the IMF traditionally proposes to each country, and in particular the current strategy of export promotion involve one fundamental difficulty. They are based on the implicit assumption that each country is able to solve the problem of its external disequilibrium in a one-sided way. In reality, however, the reduction of one country's trade deficit entails the reduction of the trade surplus of another country or a group of countries at the same time. Thus the problem cannot be solved as easily as that, and this has been observed now.

However, in the case of Latin America, the situation seems to be even more difficult. In order to obtain the financial resources that it needs for the payments of its foreign debt service, Latin America must produce a trade surplus; this in turn requires that some countries accept trade deficits (which would correspond to those of the Latin American countries). Thus the suggestion that those non-debtor countries that achieve a trade surplus should grant special economic advantages to the debtor countries seems to be plausible. However, the countries of origin of the creditor banks are not exactly identical with the countries that have a trade surplus; and even if they were, this would not necessarily mean that the developed countries would change the structure of their economic policy in order to guarantee the required greater flow of exports from the debtor countries. The same argument is valid for the implementation of the export promotion strategy in the developing countries.[34]

Final suggestions

The purpose of this article was to analyse some aspects of the current problems and interdependences concerning the conditionality of the IMF and the World Bank, aspects of Latin America's foreign indebtedness and its adjustment process, and of the strategy of adjustment plus growth. As this article marks only the initial stage of an investigation of the above-mentioned aspects, it can do no more than suggest a possible direction for the analysis to take, and to mention critically those directions that it should not take. The second stage of the investigation should concentrate in detail on the analysis of the special set of measures for the implementation of the strategy of adjustment plus growth, and on the analysis of the principles that should govern the international organizations' conditionality.

A few suggestions are shortlisted below:

1. The fact that Latin America's transfer of resources into foreign countries amounts to 5 per cent of the GGP is incompatible with the implementation of the strategy of adjustment plus growth. The Latin American countries can no longer stand a negative flow of resources on this scale. Thus, the final solution of the problem of Latin America's foreign indebtedness can no longer be delayed. It is time to implement some of the suggested solutions.[35]
2. The conditionalities of the international organizations, that is, of the IMF and the World Bank, must be reviewed and readjusted, so that the Latin American countries are not forced to agree to excessive adjustment costs, or to accept technical and ideological solutions that conflict with most people's wishes and aspirations. On the other hand it stands to reason that the conditionalities of the IMF and the World Bank should be coherent and consistent with each other, if both institutions are simultaneously present in a certain country. Even so, the host country should have a chance to give its own opinion and to influence the arrangement of the double conditionalities that are imposed on it.
3. Basic principles of the IMF's conditionalities:[36]
   (a) *Inverse conditionality.* Each country should be responsible for its own adjustment programme, which should take into account the existing external restrictions. In this

way the homogeneous and uniform programmes of the IMF would be replaced by 'home-made' adjustment programmes, which could be devised from case to case.

(b) *Conditionality with real variables.* In order to set a maximum limit to the internal adjustment costs, an additional increase in external credits should be agreed on in case of an excessive fall in the rate of growth or in case of an excessive rise in the unemployment rate. In the programme signed with Mexico in 1985 a corresponding clause was added.

(c) *Conditionality on two levels.* In this case a distinction is suggested between the external variables in terms of foreign currency, that is, those that are connected with the balance of payments and the international reserves, and the internal variables in terms of domestic currency, such as the fiscal deficit, internal credits, and inflation. The prior conditionality of the IMF should then correspond to the variables that are expressed in foreign currency. Moreover, the IMF should loosen the internal targets after the external targets have been reached.[37]

4. It is commonly agreed that a strategy of export promotion is necessary. In the interdependent modern world the external sector is very important for small and medium-sized countries – and all the Latin American countries can be categorized as such. Some of the measures that could promote exports are the following:

(a) The maintenance of a stable exchange rate policy, in which the domestic currency is permanently slightly undervalued for a relatively long period of time, that is, for five to ten years.

(b) In addition, for an initial period of at least five years, a direct mechanism for the subsidizing of marginal and/or new exports is required. Afterwards these subsidies should be gradually abolished. Analogous arguments could be used in order to justify these measures as those used regarding the protection of infant industries. The mechanism of export subsidy is doubtlessly preferable to an unrestricted liberalization of imports.

(c) Obviously the private sector reacts positively to appropriate economic incentives; from this reaction it can be concluded that, if the above-mentioned measures are introduced, the private sector will be an indispensable agent in the expansion of exports from the Latin American countries.

(d) Nevertheless, the public sector can play an important part. Success in the competitive world of today requires that no economic agent is excluded; all the economic agents of a country must go together in the same direction. The moral of this situation is obviously that the Latin American countries must necessarily have a mixed economy in which both the private sector and the government play an important part. Polar systems, which attribute a predominant role either to the public sector exclusively or to the private sector exclusively, are doomed to failure. But, every country has to determine appropriate roles for its private and its public sector in its own way.

Notes and references

1. This contribution is part of a research project of CIEPLAN about macroeconomics and international economics, a project that was sponsored by the Centro Internacional de Investigaciones para el Desarrollo (CIID-IDRC) and by the Ford Foundation. A preliminary version of this paper has already been presented at the conference, 'Neostructuralismo y Neoliberalismo', which was organized by the Universidad Catolica de Ecuador (Quito, November 1987).
2. On the basis of preliminary estimates, a figure similar to that for the period from 1980 is to be expected for 1987.
3. Dornbusch, R. (1987) *Debt Problems and the World Macro Economy*, mimeographed, Cambridge/Mass.: MIT.
4. Let us assume that a debtor has liabilities of 400 in period t_0 and that there is a fixed real rate of interest of 2 per cent. For the first period let us assume two different situations, one with an inflation rate of 3 per cent and a resulting nominal interest rate of 5 per cent, and the other with an inflation rate of 10 per cent and thus a nominal interest rate of 12 per cent. In the first case the debtor interest payments are 20 per cent, 8 of which correspond to the real rate of interest and 12 to the devaluation (or redemption) of the total debt owing to the inflation of 3 per cent. In the second case the debtor interest payments are 48 per cent, 8 of which correspond to the real rate of interest and 40 to the redemption of the real part of the total debt with an inflation of 10 per cent.
5. The figures concerning the international real rate of interest were ascertained by discounting the nominal rate of interest by the developed countries' price index. If the discounting is based on the price index of Latin America's export products, the result is the real rate of interest with which the Latin American countries were faced; to compare the resulting figures, see Bianchi, A., Devlin, R., and Ramos, J. (1987) 'El proceso de ajuste en la América Latina, 1981–1986, *El Trimestre Económico* LIV (216): 855–911.

6. Bianchi, A., Devlin, R., and Ramos, J., ibid.
7. If they had taken the period between 1950 and 1980 as a basis for their calculations, the fall actually suffered in Latin America's terms of trade would have been even greater. Consequently, the results of their computations, which are shown in Table 12.2, are conservative.
8. This interest rate would correspond to an estimated average (of its highest value) for a period of fifty years (before 1980). It should be taken into account that the mean interest rate of the real LIBOR-rate of interest in the 1970s was 0.1 per cent.
9. Reisen, H. (1986) 'The Latin American Transfer Problem in Historical Perspective', mimeographed by OECD, Paris.
10. Fraga, A. (1987) 'Las reparaciones de guerra de Alemania y la deuda de Brasil, un estudio comparativo', *Comercio Exterior* 37 (4): 304–18, Mexico.
11. See Machlup, F. (1964) *International Payments, Debt and Gold*, New York. In this context Machlup points to the fact that from 1925 to 1928 Germany had no difficulty in fulfilling its war compensatory obligations because the loans that it obtained came to more than the amount that was needed for the compensatory payments. As a result, there was even a considerable trade deficit.
12. Many Latin Americans wonder why they have to pay amounts that are twice as high as those that Germany had to pay after its defeat in the First World War, and that France had to pay after its defeat by Prussia in the nineteenth century. After all, they have not been at war against anybody.
13. Cardoso, E. (1987) 'Payments Crisis and Inflation: The IMF in Latin America', *Discussion Paper Series*, no. 70, Boston.
14. Bacha, E. (1986) 'El papel futuro del FMI en América Latina: temas y proposiciones', *SELA* (1986) El FMI, Banco Mundial y la Crisis Latinoamericana, XXI: 60–77, Mexico.
15. *SELA*, ibid.
16. Bacha, E. and Feinberg, R.E. (1986) 'El Banco Mundial y el ajuste estructural en América Latina', *SELA*, ibid. pp. 78–104.
17. Why do the Latin American economists not discuss a topic that is of such great importance to Latin America? The book by the *SELA* (1986) op. cit., and the report by the Group of 24 (see Grupo de los 24 (1987) 'Deputies' Report on Fund's Role in Promoting Adjustment with Growth', *IMF Survey*, August) set an outstanding example of the kind of discussion that Latin America needs.
18. Bibliographic references to this subject: Bacha, E. (1983) 'Prologo para a terceira carta', *Forum Gazeta Mercantil* (comp.), 'FMI and Brasil. A armadilha da recessao', Sao Paulo, pp. 113–128; Buira, A. (1983) 'La programación financiera y la condicionalidad del FMI', *El Trimestre Económico* L (1) 197): 117–49; Ground, R.L. (1984) 'Los programas ortodoxos de ajuste en América Latina: un examen critico de las politicas del Fondo Monetario Internacional', *Revista de la CEPAL* 23: 47–84; Killick, T. (ed.) (1984) *The Quest for Economic Stabilization: The IMF and the Third World*, New York: Martin's

Press. David, W.L. (1985) *The IMF Paradigm*, New York: Praeger. About more recent discussion see *SELA*, op. cit., Meller, P. (1987) Revisión de los enfoques teóricos sobre ajuste externo y su relevancia para América Latina', *Revista de la CEPAL*, 32: 177–217, and Pastor, M. (1987) 'The Effects of IMF Programs in the Third World: Debate and Evidence from Latin America', *World Development* 15 (2): 249–62.

19. Bacha, E. (1983) op. cit. and Ground, R.L. (1984) op. cit.
20. A former Latin American critical argument was as follows – the period of time granted by the IMF for the adjustment to the external disequilibrium varied between 12 and 24 months. In general, a country had to carry out a great deal of the adjustment practically within one year. This was a result of the IMF's role which was specified to be of a short run nature. If the existing disequilibria was of a considerable magnitude, the question arose whether it was really necessary to make the adjustments of economy in a short period of time. It was no longer understandable why the period of adjustment and the duration of the IMF programme must concur. After some time the IMF accepted these arguments and created the EFF programmes, which have replaced some of the stand-by programmes.
21. Diaz-Alejandro, E.F. (1983) 'Some Aspects of the 1982–83 Brazilian Payment Crisis', *Brookings Papers on Economic Activity* 2: 515–52.
22. Bacha, E. (1985) 'The Future Role of the International Monetary Fund in Latin America: Issues and Proposals', mimeographed, Rio de Janeiro: Universidad Católica.
23. Bacha, E. (1986) op. cit.
24. Sometimes an economic programme signed with the IMF creates a certain international credibility. However, this type of programme sometimes sets off internal disequilibria.
25. Bacha, E. (1986) op. cit.
26. A possible answer to this question is that Latin America has run into foreign debts and therefore has to pay them back. Still, as Keynes has already pointed out, if an individual owes a bank 100,000 US dollars, this debt causes a problem for the debtor. However, if he owes 100 billion US dollars to the bank, then, it is the bank's problem. Doubtlessly the creditor banks and the Latin American countries share the guilt regarding the level reached by Latin America's foreign debt; about this point see Devlin, R. (1986) 'La estructura y comportamiento de la banca internacional en los años setenta y, su impacto en la crisis de América Latina', *Collección Estudios CIEPLAN* 19: 5–55.
27. This calculation implies that the amount of foreign credits coming from international capital markets equals nil and that the flow of foreign investments will be limited. Up to now, the flow of foreign investments into Latin America has varied between 10 per cent and 15 per cent of the required interest payments for its foreign debt.
28. Guitian, M. (1981) 'Fund Conditionality. Evolution of Principles and Practices', *IMF Pamphlet Series*, no. 38; Guitian, M. (1987) 'Adjustment and Economic Growth. Their Fundamental Complementarity',

in IMF and World Bank, *Symposium on Growth-oriented Adjustment Programs*, Washington, DC; Krueger, A.O. (1978) 'Foreign Trade Regimes and Economic Development: Liberalization Attempts and Consequences', *National Bureau of Economic Research*, New York; Balassa, B., Kuczynski, P.P., and Simonsen, M.H. (1986) 'Hacia una Renovación del Crecimiento Económico en América Latina', Institute for International Economics, Washington, DC; and Michalopoulos, C. (1987) 'World Bank Programs for Adjustment and Growth', in IMF and World Bank, Symposium on Growth-Oriented Adjustment Programs, Washington, DC.

29. Sachs, J. (1987) 'Trade and Exchange Rate Policies in Growth-Oriented Adjustment Programs', in IMF and World Bank, Symposium on Growth-Oriented Adjustment Programs, Washington, DC.
30. Ibid.
31. Ibid.
32. Ibid.
33. SELA (1986) op. cit.; Grupo de los 24 (1987) op. cit.
34. There is one more problem involved in the international asymmetry. The fact that there are countries with a trade deficit means that there must be other countries with a trade surplus. Why must only the countries with a deficit bear the adjustment costs in the case of a disequilibrium? A plausible answer would be that only the countries with trade deficits have liquidity problems, and these problems compel them to turn to the IMF. However, this need not be so. In the 1940s, when the establishment of the IMF and the World Bank was still being discussed, Keynes advocated a symmetrical distribution of the adjustment costs.

    The countries with a trade surplus must grant the countries with trade deficits access to their markets, so that the latter can generate the foreign exchange that they need in order to finance the deficit. This is exactly what the United States recently suggested to Japan. In order to lower the adjustment costs in connection with the North American external deficit, Japan will increase its imports from the United States and 'voluntarily' decrease its exports into the North American market. The IMF should have various mechanisms at its disposal for making the countries with a trade surplus facilitate the access to their markets for exports from countries with a trade deficit.
35. Massad, C. (1985) 'La deuda: un panorama general', *Revista de la Planificación del Desarrollo*, 16: 3–24; and de Carmoy, H. (1987) 'Debt and Growth in Latin America: A European Banker's Proposal', Working Paper of the Instituto de Relaciones Europeo-Latinoamericanas, No. 9.
36. Grupo de los 24, op. cit.; Bacha, E. (1985) op. cit.; and SELA (1986) op. cit.
37. The Grupo de los 24 makes some more suggestions, such as the following:
    (a) Instead of fixing quantitative targets, the IMF should fix only the range of the critical variables.

(b) The EFF programmes should definitely replace the stand-by programmes.
(c) The CFF programme (Compensatory Financing Facility) should take into account fluctuations in the international rates of interest because the shocks that the fluctuation of these rates are very important for the Latin American debtor countries.

Part five

Summary

Chapter thirteen

Conclusions on the present international debt crisis

Manfred Borchert

General remarks

The current international debt crisis is due to a whole range of different reasons, which in turn caused the Latin American countries borrowing from international banks and thereby creating a debt crisis, too. One of these reasons is the low economic activity of the western industrial countries in the 1970s combined with an abundant liquidity of the banks. In international lending both the now-indebted Latin American countries and the international banks made mistakes, which became obvious at the beginning of the 1980s, that is, the time of the sudden slump in the price of oil.

When discussing international indebtedness one should distinguish between private and public loan financing in the Latin American countries. The crucial point is that it was the private sector which imported the so to speak cheap money of the international commercial banks into the Latin American countries. On account of the national and international economic development, credit security arrangements in the form of guarantees by the governments of the debtor countries gained increasing importance. Today the external indebtedness weighs mostly on the public sector, which, unlike the private sector, has hardly any external claims. The asymmetrical situation is called ‘capital flight’. It is among other things due to the way in which the financial infrastructure of the debtor countries was built up. A lack of trust in the governments of today encourages the financial intermediation of foreign banks which have their headquarters in the debtor countries, and at the same time, this intermediation results in external indebtedness.

It is commonly agreed that up to now plans for repairing the debt crisis have not promised a proper solution yet. The Baker plan, the political initiative of the former US Minister of Finance can at best be taken as a new impulse to rethink the situation. The

Baker initiative fails mainly because of its contradictoriness. On the one hand the debtor countries are advised to act according to free-market principles, whereas the industrial countries are by no means reminded of their duties. On the other hand the Baker plan considers certain countries to be in need of help and thus discriminates against them, although they carry out a very sound debt-management policy. Besides, the intended extent of the injection of new funds is by no means wide enough.

Besides, the capitalization of interest rates as well as an increasing securitization or the substitutability of the debts for local currency by means of debt-equity swaps could lower the pressure produced by the present debt crisis. No great importance was attached to debt-equity swaps as a means of debt management. As soon as the way they work becomes obvious, debt-equity swaps will hardly give rise to any new investments; nor will they cause a recovery of the flight capital because they do not change any of the economic components. Apart from the fact that their transaction costs are hardly lower than those of orthodox credits, debt-equity swaps do not encourage a free-market approach, for the profit prospects which would make them more attractive can prosper only on a regulated market. Thus, they create misleading investment signals and obstruct an optimal allocation of resources.

Lastly, long-term investments in the form of special drawing rights of the International Monetary Fund (IMF) should be taken into consideration as a way of participating to a larger extent in funding international debts. This suggestion, which stresses the central importance of the IMF, aims at including it in every debt-management strategy.

In the course of the discussion the Latin American participants demanded emphatically for the future that the industrial countries' economic growth should be supported and that their protectionist measures should be reduced at the same time in order to improve the exports of the Latin American countries.

A comparison between the economic development of Japan and the economic policy claimed for Latin America shows that Japan by no means gained its present economic importance through open markets, but primarily through an export strategy combined with an extensive protection of its home markets. This example illustrates how difficult it is to convince the debtor countries of the export-orientated policy of the IMF. Therefore, so to speak, a home-made adjustment programme is demanded by the IMF, or a kind of South-South-co-operation[1] as demanded – *inter alia* – by the World Bank.

Development of the international debt crisis

Ludwig Trippen

Ludwig Trippen, in his article, points out that the debt management of the banks in the 1980s prevented the international financial system from collapsing; still, there is no financial solution of the debt problem in sight yet.

The observed capital flight from Latin American countries is a symptom of seriously economic, social and political problems in consequence of the debt crisis. The national economic difficulties of the debtor countries were aggravated by overvalued currencies and negative real interest rates. Debt reschedulings did reduce the debt burden as expected by equity swaps but there is no other way out of the crisis than by stimulating economic growth; thereby foreign direct investments ought to be attracted, which in turn would intensify the impulse of economic growth. In addition, undisturbed growth in the debtor countries requires a gradual abolition of protectionism in the highly-developed industrialized nations.

Eduardo de Sousa Ferreira

Eduardo de Sousa Ferreira, in his contribution, claims a relief programme which would give the debtor countries the opportunity to develop their economies first, and to repay their international debts afterwards.

Above all, he pleads for a political solution of the international indebtedness problem. Of course, the traditional instruments of debt repayments and debt prolongations should be used further on, but beyond that the debtor countries must be enabled to repay their debts by economic growth while keeping up a reasonable standard of living.

It seems to be crucial that the solution is both a political and an economic one. Ferreira calls attention to the fact that a historical shift in power from the Mediterranean to the Atlantic has taken place, and nowadays the power is shifting from the Atlantic to the Pacific. Such strategic developments could be turned into an undisturbed equilibrium by political harmonizing with the present debtor countries in Latin America.

Causes, consequences and debt management

Leonardo Auernheimer

Leonardo Auernheimer analyses theoretically and empirically

some fundamentals of the causes of the international indebtedness and of its repayment, referring especially to Argentina. Therefore he assumes a simple framework of alternative forms of repayment of government debt.

Assuming a theoretical model of a small open economy with one tradable and one non-tradable commodity, he concentrates on the budget problem as the basis for the monetary transfer and the following real transfer.

On the basis of this model it is demonstrated that, (a) a rise in the exchange rate has no influence on the real exchange rate; (b) an increase in the tax rates will be matched by the rate of debt accumulation; (c) a reduction in government expenditure would increase the consumption of tradable goods as well as the real exchange rate and the real volume of money.

To solve the debt problem the following propositions emerge from the model:

- The current problem of debt is a problem of the government budget more than a 'balance-of-payments' problem. Of course, in any macroeconomic set-up all variables interact, and policy changes in the components of the government budget do have balance of payments implications, but as can be shown, there are cases in which any effective changes do not necessarily imply or result in either an improvement of the balance of trade or of the current account, if the country balance of payments is correctly defined.
- In particular, policies aimed at only 'improving' the balance of payments do not necessarily imply an improvement in the debt situation, unless they affect one or more of the three variables that would allow government to solve its debt situation: conventional taxes, the 'inflation tax', or the level of expenditures.
- There seems to be a distinctive advantage of stabilizing the governments' debt situation by a reduction in government expenditures. Not only is such reduction a gain in itself and seems to be increasingly supported by public opinion, but it seems to have a stronger effect on the debt situation than equal increases in the level of taxation.

Rolf Schinke

Rolf Schinke examines the importance of debt-equity swaps to improve the creditworthiness of the present debtor countries, and thereby to create a more favourable climate for investments particularly in the case of Chile.

It has been demonstrated that additional investment occurs only if there are substantial illusions about the true nature of debt-equity swaps. But even if there are illusions it is not altogether clear whether a country which engages in debt-equity swaps activities can reap appreciable gains from them. It may happen that costs exceed the benefits of a system with debt-equity swaps. Most likely a different evaluation of such a system stems from the fact that usually a wrong comparison is executed.

Compared with traditional means of financing foreign investment, there is no reason to expect additional investments from debt-equity swaps if the present value of the subsidy is the same in both. The same idea applies to the argument that debt-equity swaps might facilitate the repatriation of flight capital.

It has been demonstrated that although debt-equity swaps can improve creditworthiness, subsidy induced direct investments with their accompanying increase in reserves will most likely increase creditworthiness even more.

The argument that debt-equity swaps represent a market approach to the solution of the debt problem is misleading. When there are certain yields, as in the Chilean debt-equity swaps system, that are lasting for some time, there must be something wrong in the state of the markets. As a matter of fact such profits are only possible if these markets are regulated. Under such circumstances the market will possibly give the wrong signals for investment.

Hans-Rimbert Hemmer

Hans-Rimbert Hemmer compiles the most significant arguments regarding the causes and the solvability of international indebtedness for Peru and other countries. During the last twenty years international loans have been used by Latin American countries especially:

- for more or less effective consumption purposes;
- for long-term infrastructural projects whose growth effects lag behind quite considerably;
- for capital intensification of production;
- in order to postpone necessary corrections of internal economic policy.

The international banks were pushed in the 1970s to recycle the petrodollars earned by the Organization of Petroleum-Exporting Countries (OPEC). The international banks:

- overestimated the development potential of the credit-seeking country, especially if it was richly endowed with oil or other raw materials.
- assumed an economically productive utilization of the credits without taking notice of the setting-free effect.
- misjudged economic misdevelopments in the country, either generally or to their extent.

But partly the behaviour of the banks was fully rational from their point of view and with respect to the given framework:

- credits had been given to governments or had been guaranteed by them; therefore the risk for the banks of a loss of credits seemed to be reduced;
- public political declarations could lead to the impression that the central banks in the creditors' countries, or the IMF, or the World Bank, would compensate in case of credit losses (in some cases the creditworthiness of a country was even identified with its relationships with the IMF or with the World Bank).
- credits had to be granted in order to get the licence for bank activities in that country; if the expected profits out of these new activities had been higher than the loss out of the credit to the country, such a policy was nevertheless rational.

But all agreements up to now about a restruction of debts, however, cannot help to get over the fact that a solution of the debt crisis is only possible if world trade expands even stronger than in the last year, and if the indebted countries participate in that expansion. This will only be the outcome if three conditions are fulfilled:

- economic growth in industrialized countries has to accelerate;
- protectionism of industrialized countries has to be reduced in order to (re)open their markets for the exports from Latin American countries;
- export orientation of Latin American countries has to be strengthened on the basis of competitive products which generate macroeconomic profits for these countries.

Latin American debt problems

Miguel S. Wionczek

Miguel S. Wionczek describes three phases of international indebtedness from the point of view of the debtor countries – (a) the burst of the 'debt bubble' all over the region between the time of the Mexican announcement and the fall of 1983; (b) the merry-go-round of the increased number of reschedulings between the 1983 IMF/World Bank meeting and the early 1986 meeting; and (c) the relentless crisis presently affecting practically all Latin American countries.

The foreign private creditors have worked out a new line of defence against possible risks involving their operations in Latin America. It consists of a brief list of measures which Latin American debtor countries should adopt to get out of their present financial, economic and social misery, which is accompanied by another list of what would not be acceptable for the creditors.

Their recipe for Latin America's salvation can be resumed in a few points which coincide with the philosophy underlying the Baker plan:

- privatize the respective debt-ridden economies top-heavy with the presence of public enterprises in the sectors of strategic importance for development;
- create a better climate for foreign private investment by eliminating all controls and restrictions upon profit remittances, foreign capital participation in economic activities, and technology transfers;
- swap debt for equity investment; and
- do away with all existing limitations on the activities of foreign enterprises in the sector services (bank, insurance companies, communications, transport, and tourist facilities).

All liberalization and privatization measures should be supported – the private international banking community insists – by the reactivation of lending at commercial terms by governments, governmental export agencies, and international development financing bodies like the World Bank and Inter-American Development Bank.

While not necessarily resulting in a world-wide financial débâcle, a possibly disorderly Latin America's debt default would not only destroy the region's development prospects, but would affect seriously, albeit indirectly, the industrial countries themselves. It would deprive them, and particularly the United States, of sizeable export markets at the time when the global international trade has practically stopped expanding. Thus, instead of thinking of the Latin American debt default apocalypsis, it would be better perhaps to start thinking about the instrumentation of a Latin American default agreed upon on the initiative of the creditors by the region's debtors and creditors.

Carlos Massad

Carlos Massad starts with examining the recent developments of the indebtedness problem and the burden of the debt service. He compares the present situation, both with the period of the great depression during the 1930s, and with the German reparation payments after the First World War, as well as the observed recessions of the last century.

Thereafter he develops a simulation model of a growing economy in order to assess the necessary extent of efforts to be made by the debtor countries in the form of savings and exports assuming variant interest rates and variant external financing.

Subsequently he proposes several alternatives to reduce the debt burden in such a way that the debt repayments and the adjustment programmes are harmonized with the conditions for economic growth.

In Latin America the crisis in the 1980s shows some characteristics which equal those of the crisis in the 1930s, or are even worse. During the crisis in the 1930s a general agreement between the creditors and the debtors had been reached which reduced the amount of debt and lowered the interest rates under the market level. In addition, the time limit was extended. Similar agreements have not been reached during the crisis in the 1980s. On the contrary, the transfer of real resources made by the debtor countries to foreign countries, which were due to the interest payments on the debts, exceed – measured by the importexport-ration – many times the payments which were made by Germany after the Versaille Treaty as reparation payments and interest payments for foreign debts and for dividend transfer to foreign investors.

To evaluate the necessary scope of efforts by the debtor countries to fulfil their debt duties, a model has been developed which sets into relation the growth rate of indebtedness and the external interest rate, as well as the debt-gross national product (GNP) ratio and the external imbalance (or the difference between saving and investments). Estimations for seven Latin American countries were made – Argentina, Brazil, Colombia, Chile, Mexico, Peru, and Venezuela.

The solutions aiming at a relief of the debt burden imply that:

- the creditors as well as the debtors are responsible for the fast increase in indebtedness;
- the evolution of the debt problem is a consequence of determinants (a combination of policies in the industrialized countries, international recession, the procyclical behaviour of the international financing) which can be controlled neither by the debtor countries nor by domestic policies;
- the lasting recessive economic adjustment is no longer acceptable;
- it is in the interest of creditor and debtor countries to find an immediate solution for the actual crisis.

Alberto Valdés

Alberto Valdés begins by describing some fundamentals of the traditionally-emerging issues which are of interest to the less-developed countries and relate to negotiations in agriculture in the General Agreement on Tariffs and Trades (GATT) framework. This is followed by a presentation of the results of models simulating trade liberalization and its effects on developed and developing countries. This Third World is made up of many countries – with imports and exports of both tropical and temperate zone products, and the complex pattern of the incidence of agricultural protection in The Organization for Economic and Co-operative Development (OECD) countries on less-developed countries is one central theme of this contribution.

Futhermore, a brief overview of the trends and structure of agricultural trade between Latin America and the European Economic Community during 1962–84 is described. Finally, some thoughts on approaches to negotiations by less-developed countries in the Uruguay Round of the multilateral trade negotiations are presented.

The launching of the Uruguay Rounds in 1986 is an encouraging sign that many governments intend to strengthen GATT's authority on agricultural trade. During the last few decades agricultural trade has been drifting towards bilateral agreements and market-sharing arrangements, with the tacit acceptance of generous 'safeguards' against so-called 'unfair practices'. It is common belief that the international agricultural trade environment is worsening.

There has been a dramatic increase in subsidies to agriculture in industrial countries compared to the levels prevailing ten years ago. In terms of levels of protection, world agriculture has become more restrictive than at the beginning of the Tokyo Rounds in 1973, and there has been no clear stand against the prevailing system of managed trade in agricultural products. In the past the major actors in trade have not shown a commitment to freer multilateral trade, nor to a stronger GATT with power to establish rules and to enforce them. The relative ineffectiveness of GATT in dealing with temperate and subtropical agricultural products in the past has been recognized by most analysts.

But because, in terms of market power, less-developed countries are individually fairly weak in bilateral bargaining, it is in the interest of the weaker countries that the binding of the strong on international rules will be accepted. In this sense, the GATT could serve as a safeguard for the weaker powers. It would appear that less-developed countries have no real alternative to the GATT system.

Low and middle-income countries have different bargaining powers in international trade negotiations. But this differentiation between low- and middle-income countries does not imply that low-income countries have no incentives to support middle-income countries in their new (hypothetical) stance in the negotiations. On the one hand, if the same level of implicit income transfer from non-reciprocity and preferential treatment is now reserved exclusively for low-income countries, this would presumably be considered a benefit for them. Furthermore, the product mix of their exports is changing, and the pressure of middle-income countries for more access to OECD markets and to other middle-income countries' products such as sugar and derivatives, vegetable oils, beverages, tobacco, fruits, and others, is also of great potential interest to low-income countries as exporters. But in the end, formation of coalitions involves many variables, of which interest on agricultural negotiations is only one.

International monetary fundamentals

Eduardo Lizano

Eduardo Lizano raises four questions – first, what is the origin of the problem?; second, what has been done to encounter it?; third, which are the main lessons that can be derived from this effort?; and fourth, in what direction should further action take place?

Through the years, it has become evident that the debt problem for heavily-indebted countries could not have been the responsibility of only one of the concerned parties – neither of commercial banks, governments of industrialized countries, nor of international financial institutions. The active participation and concurrence of all of them, in a simultaneous and co-ordinated way, is required.

From the point of view of indebted countries it is indispensable that the indebted countries make significant and systematic efforts to re-establish order in their own economy. Two aspects should be emphasized. First, the need to increase the quantity and improve the quality of the factors of production, and second, the adoption of the necessary measures to raise the average productivity of the available factors of production. In the economists' jargon, the first condition consists in implementing an economic growth policy, that is, a shift to the right of the production possibility curve. The second condition refers to the structural adjustment policy, which aims at reaching some point along the production possibility curve, thus avoiding any situation located within the area of the production possibility function. The fulfilment of these two conditions should be the sole responsibility of the indebted countries.

The fulfilment of these two necessary conditions, however, is not sufficient for the solution of the problem. It is of utmost importance to put the house in order, but it is equally important also that the external economic environment be favourable for the development of the heavily-indebted countries. If the external conditions are adverse, economic growth will be very difficult to achieve. The responsibility of creating an international favourable economic environment falls on the highly industrialized countries. It is absolutely necessary that the OECD countries, and particularly the G-7 countries, adopt a rational economic policy.

Eberhard Weiershäuser

Eberhard Weiershäuser sketches the exposure management in Latin America from the point of view of a banker. Basically there are three main tools of exposure management:

- debt-to-debt swaps;
- debt-equity swaps which can be divided into debt-equity and debt-peso swaps;
- selling or buying Latin American debt at discounts.

Surprisingly, in most debt-to-debt swaps the result appears to be a greater concentration of a specific country exposure in bank portfolios rather than greater diversification. Many banks have neglected the argument of diversification and have been swapping their Latin American loans in an effort to consolidate their exposure into a few countries where they have defined their long-term strategic interests. Or banks have decided to eliminate countries from their portfolio which, in their view, offer limited prospects of future improvement. All the banks that participate in debt-to-debt swaps, of course, do not end up with the same few countries, since their long-term strategic interests may differ as well as their risk assessment. Therefore, debt-to-debt swaps tend to lead banks to Latin American countries where they perceive to have a competitive and comparative advantage.

The driving force behind the equity swaps has often been the willingness of debtor countries to buy back a debt using local currency, if it is assured that the proceeds are invested in the country. Interest by multinational corporations in the area of debt-equity swaps relates to the fact that Latin American debt has been available in a secondary market at discounts to face value. Sometimes the bank that is holding the debt will undertake the investment directly in order to bypass the secondary market and achieve the possibility to preserve the book value for its assets. In this scenario a creditor could benefit from liquifying, and in return for giving up the asset receiving a different asset with some downside risk, but at the same time a potential for a gain.

Beside the debt-to-debt and debt-equity swap, the actual selling of a loan at a discount base is the third major tool to manage Latin American exposure on the asset side of the balance sheet of a bank. Acting as an intermediary in the secondary market, which some of the US money centre banks frequently do, is also a way to generate fee income to improve the overall yield of existing exposure.

Patricio Meller

Patricio Meller examines the role of the IMF and the World Bank in the present international debt crisis. He considers particularly the adjustment costs and the transfer of resources that Latin America had to take on between 1982 and 1986 in order to fulfil its foreign debt services.

As a result he shows that Latin America carried out a difficult and expensive adjustment process, and in so doing, it made a real and financial transfer of resources that far exceeded the historical experiences regarding war compensatory payments. Nevertheless, the empirical data regarding foreign debt indicate no improvement. In fact, all coefficients that represent the ratio of interest payments to exports went up from 20.2 per cent in 1980 to 41 per cent in 1982, and since 1983 it has found its level at slightly more than 35 per cent. On the other hand, the coefficient representing the ratio foreign debt to exports went up steadily from 2.14 per cent in 1980 to 3.21 per cent in 1982 and in 1986 it exceeded 4 per cent.

Originally, the roles of the IMF and the World Bank were defined as follows – the IMF's main concern is the short-term adjustment of a country with an external disequilibrium; in that case the IMF grants a loan so that the country in question can correct the disequilibrium in its balance of payments. The World Bank endeavours to support growth and economic development; to this end it extends loans for specific capital investment projects and development projects. The IMF focuses mainly on macroeconomic matters, and its goals are the balance of payments and inflation. It tries to achieve these goals through measures concerning the tax policy, the monetary policy, and the foreign exchange policy.

The World Bank, on the other hand, focuses on microeconomic matters and aims at supporting savings and investments, and thereby economic growth. In order to achieve these goals, the World Bank concentrates on relative prices and economic policy.

The IMF's methods are directed towards controlling the aggregate demand. To this end the Fund analyses the flows and the nominal variables. The methods of the World Bank on the other hand are directed towards influencing the aggregate supply. To this end the World Bank analyses the evaluation of projects; this analysis is based on real variables and makes use of the input-output table, the overall economic accounting, and a consistent analytical framework.

Therefore one can say that it is difficult to distinguish between the IMF's extended fund facility and structural adjustment programmes on the one hand, and the World Bank's structural adjustment loans programme on the other hand. This exactly is the new aspect that is called double conditionality.

On the one hand the Latin American countries' short-term and medium-term – that is, relating to the next five years – access to the international capital markets will be limited. Therefore the credits that the IMF and the World Bank will extend will be of great importance. On the other hand, Latin America will be faced with a short-term and a long-term conditionality because of the double conditionality on the part of the IMF and the World Bank.

The central problem in Latin America is not the existence of the

IMF; on the contrary, the Latin American countries need the Fund. The central problem is connected with the adjustment policy, which imposes the Fund's conditionality on these countries. The central question, however, is not related to the existence or non-existence of a conditionality. For two reasons a conditionality is indispensable: (a) the IMF does not make presents, but loans, which must probably be paid back; (b) the credits of the IMF must be used for the express purpose of diminishing the existing external disequilibrium. Until recently, most of the Latin American countries complied with the two requirements of the Fund's conditionality; however, the incurring internal costs were too high.

The conditionalities of the IMF and the World Bank must be reviewed and readjusted, so that the Latin American countries are not forced to agree to excessive adjustment costs, or to accept technical and ideological solutions that conflict with most people's wishes and aspirations. On the other hand, it stands to reason that the conditionalities of the International Monetary Fund and the World Bank should be coherent and consistent with each other, if both institutions are simultaneously present in a certain country.

Reference

Borchert, M. (1988) *Basic Issues in International Monetary Economics*, Berlin, pp. 109.

Sponsors

Public sponsors

Staatskanzlei des Landes Nordrhein-Westfalen, Düsseldorf
Ministerium für Wissenschaft und Forschung des Landes Nordrhein-Westfalen, Düsseldorf
Deutsche Forschungsgemeinschaft, Bonn-Bad Godesberg
Bundesministerium für wirtschaftliche Zusammenarbeit, Bonn

Private sponsors

BASF, Muenster
Deutsche Bundesbank, Frankfurt
Deutsche Bank AG, Frankfurt
Deutscher Ibero-Amerika-Verein, Hamburg
Westdeutsche Landesbank, Münster and Düsseldorf

Author Index

Subject Index